THE CASABLANCA MAN

The cinema of Michael Curtiz

James C. Robertson

London and New York

First published 1993
by Routledge
11 New Fetter Lane, London EC4P 4EE

Simultaneously published in the USA and Canada
by Routledge
29 West 35th Street, New York, NY 10001

© 1993 James C. Robertson

Set in 10/12 pt Times by Intype Ltd, London
Printed and bound in Great Britain by TJ Press (Padstow) Ltd, Cornwall

British Library Cataloguing in Publication Data
Robertson, James C.
The Casablanca Man: The cinema of Michael Curtiz
I. Title
791.43092

Library of Congress Cataloging in Publication Data
Robertson, James C. (James Crighton)
The Casablanca Man: the cinema of Michael Curtiz/James
C. Robertson.
p. cm.
Includes bibliographical references (p. 169–73) and
indexes.
Filmography: p. 174–91
1. Curtiz, Michael, 1888–1962 – Criticism and
interpretation.
I. Title.
PN1998.3.C87R63 1993
791.43'0233'092–dc20 92–33281

ISBN 0–415–06804–5

CONTENTS

ILLUSTRATIONS

ACKNOWLEDGEMENTS

Like all authors, I am indebted to many people, not least to Michael Curtiz himself for my enjoyment of his films over the past half century. This book owed much to a very generous award from the British Academy which enabled me to conduct research at the University of Southern California (USC) in Los Angeles and at the Margaret Herrick Library of the Academy of Motion Picture Arts and Sciences in Beverly Hills. At USC Leith Adams and Stuart Ng, the Warner Brothers archivists, and Ned Comstock in the Department of Special Collections were unsparing in their efforts to assist me and drew my attention to vital material I should otherwise have missed. I am truly grateful to them not only for their professional expertise, without which this work would be the poorer, but also for their personal kindnesses which made my visit to Los Angeles so memorable and informative beyond the subject research concerned. Samuel Gill at the Margaret Herrick Library also placed useful material in my path. My gratitude is also due to The Scarecrow Press and to Warner Brothers for permission to quote from material to which they own the copyright. The film stills are reproduced by courtesy of the National Film Archive Stills Division and of the film companies involved. The staffs of the British Film Institute Library, the USC Cinema-Television School Library, the Margaret Herrick Library, and the National Film Archive Stills Division never failed to meet my many requests for research material with unfailing cheerfulness. Finally, my editors, Rebecca Barden and her predecessor Helena Reckitt, were encouraging and provided me with much moral support.

ABBREVIATIONS

HUAC	House Un-American Activities Committee
IRA	Irish Republican Army
MGM	Metro-Goldwyn-Mayer
OWI	Office of War Information
TCF	Twentieth Century-Fox
USC	University of Southern California

INTRODUCTION

For just over half a century the author has been an incurable but inexpert film fan whom *Yankee Doodle Dandy, Casablanca*, and *Mildred Pierce* much impressed when as a boy in his early teens he first saw them in the 1940s. As an adult he has seen each of them again many times, initial wonderment being gradually transformed into a fascination extending to other post–1945 films of Hungarian-born director Michael Curtiz as well as to some of Curtiz's earlier works which he had been too young to see upon their original release. Puzzled in later life as to why a director who could turn out such outstanding films remained comparatively unrecognized relative to other eminent contemporary Hollywood directors, he at length set out to discover as much about Curtiz and his films as possible.

Nowadays Curtiz is best known for the superb *Casablanca*, for a handful of other 1930s and 1940s features, for his genre versatility, for his fractured English, and for his verbal abuse of players. However, there was clearly much more to his career than all this, for his overall output from 1912 to 1961 remains one of the highest in cinema history. More than two-thirds of his approximately 160 films were made outside his own country, while about half of them were sound movies not in his native tongue. This of itself ranks as a considerable achievement even if all his films had been mediocre, but in fact some like *Captain Blood* (1935), *The Charge of the Light Brigade* (1936), and *Angels With Dirty Faces* (1938) as well as the three 1940s films already mentioned are acknowledged classics of their various genres and many others are of well above average quality. Yet at Curtiz's death in 1962, when the cinema was in manifest decline, he was accorded little more than token recognition.

At that time an academic debate was in full swing between writers who saw the director as the main element, or the auteur, of a film, purveying an identifiable attitude or message, and critics who denied that the director's function was all-important. As early as 1917 in Hungary Curtiz expressed the view that the director acted as the supreme

1

co-ordinator,[1] but by virtue of his position as the recently appointed head of the Phoenix company he was then both director and producer, and it is unclear how he regarded the function of a separate producer as the representative of studio administration and policy, the later American pattern within which he worked after joining Warner Brothers in 1926. Although, like all Hollywood directors, Curtiz from then onwards operated within a studio assembly-line system, the Warner Brothers records at the University of Southern California reveal conclusively that his basic 1917 film-making philosophy never changed. It might have lain largely subdued prior to the mid–1930s success of *Captain Blood*, but when he had become Warners' top director, he once compared a film scene with characters and background to an artist's unfinished canvas and saw himself as mixing the paints to finish the canvas properly.[2]

Thus Curtiz might have been an example for the auteurists to cite in support of their theory. However, because his individualism was hidden from public view and he could not be associated with any one genre, they implicitly regarded him as merely a studio workhorse. This was an interpretation to which his long service for Warners lent surface plausibility. Those who challenged the validity of auteurism, the disciples in varying degrees of distinguished American film critic Robert Warshow who had died in 1955, viewed Curtiz in much the same way since the course of his Hollywood career seemed to confirm the accuracy of their general approach.

The disagreement over auteurism persists to this day. In Curtiz's case neither faction was ready to claim him directly in his immediate *post mortem* years, but whereas the auteurists simply ignored him, some film writers tending towards anti-auterism applied the theory to his work. The most influential was Andrew Sarris who within a year of Curtiz's death declared,

> Perhaps more than any other director, Curtiz reflected the strengths and weaknesses of the studio system in Hollywood. This most amiable of Warners' technicians faithfully served the studio's contract players. . . . If many of the early Curtiz films are hardly worth remembering, none of the later ones are even worth seeing. . . . The director's one enduring masterpiece is, of course, *Casablanca*, the happiest of happy accidents, and the most decisive exception to the auteur theory.[3]

In the same vein an article soon afterwards attributed the quality of *Casablanca* more to its players than to Curtiz without taking into account the possibility that Curtiz had chosen the players in the first place.[4] This 1960s trend went so far that one retrospective *Casablanca* reviewer commented that nobody had yet erected Curtiz into a cult figure, and that it was hard to imagine anyone ever would do so.[5]

However, by the late 1960s the Sarris vision of Curtiz was called into question by John Baxter,[6] a Curtiz admirer prepared to judge him by what he saw on the screen. During the 1970s Baxter was supported by a number of other authors,[7] but by the later part of the decade the Sarris interpretation was still much prevalent and no consensus had emerged. This can be seen in contrasting, near-simultaneous late 1970s observations by two eminent film historians. In his discussion of the individual contributions to *Captain Blood* Jeffrey Richards remarked that Curtiz was a master technician and supreme visual stylist who had been consistently undervalued because his work lacked a programmatic auteurism.[8] On the other hand William K. Everson regarded him as a loyal studio director who accepted whatever films were assigned to him and delivered them to studio specification rather than personal preference. He used stylistic innovations, but he did not rebel artistically. Surprisingly he became a tasteful and personal director towards the end of his career, and *The Breaking Point* was arguably his one masterpiece which, however, came too late in his career and was too commercially unsuccessful for it to open up new career opportunities.[9]

This dichotomy has scarcely altered to the present day. One article and one book during the 1980s were favourable to Curtiz, but their coverage of his work lacked depth despite the availability of the massive Warners production records since 1978. Consequently Curtiz has remained suspended in a half-way house situation, although the 'studio hack' view still exerts a powerful sway, as demonstrated recently by Joel Finler. In his view Curtiz was an extremely skilled and efficient filmmaker, whose visual style was owed to his art directors and cameramen. Even though his budgets increased and his output decreased in later years, he retained a contract director's mentality to the very end of his career.[10]

Responsibility for the divisions of opinion lies partly with Curtiz himself. Too busy making films to write an autobiography, he also made only rare contributions to film journals, while his press interviews, although more frequent, were none the less few and far between. What little exists in these respects is unreliable owing to Curtiz's poor memory regarding his own past. There were discrepancies in his various Hollywood statements concerning his life in Europe,[11] but this was not an isolated phenomenon. In 1948 he recalled that his Austrian film career had begun twenty-five years earlier whereas in fact it was twenty-nine.[12] In the mid–1950s he stated that Harry Warner had signed him when he was 26 years old in Paris while he was filming *Sodom and Gomorrah*,[13] but he was actually 36 years of age (in 1925), the film had been completed two years previously, and none of it had been shot in Paris. He once imagined that he had directed Humphrey Bogart in *Santa Fe Trail*, which he had probably confused with *Virginia City*.[14] He took little interest in his own films after their release and was surprised when reminded about sequences from them.[15] Although he seems to have left no private correspondence or other papers, this gap is partly filled by the Warners production material, particularly for the important years of 1935–51, when the studio documentation is at its most detailed. This plum source is supplemented by other papers, most notably those of Jack Warner. Impressions of Curtiz at work on the set appear in the daily reports of the unit managers to the Warners top hierarchy, while the daily time sheets and records of footage and sequences filmed, together with locations, help to establish his film priorities. He rarely committed himself to paper while actually directing a film, but on other occasions he did do so, sometimes at length, usually over scripts or casting. In addition the contemporary, largely unpublished memoranda of the unit managers have from time to time been retroactively supplemented by memoirs of some others who worked with him, mostly players.

While the Warners material is indispensable to an overall evaluation of Curtiz, it sheds almost no light on his European career because there are no extant records of his early Warners years regarding film production in action, while such material from 1931 to mid–1935 is also very sparse. English-language writers on Curtiz have tended to treat his European work as a mere prelude to a Hollywood career pinnacle and to assume that the American influence upon him was greater than vice versa. This is certainly possible, even probable, but it cannot be assumed, for when he arrived in the United States, he was already 37 years old with some sixty films behind him. It is thus unlikely that the influencing process lay purely in one direction, if only because he was the one Warners director in the late 1920s and 1930s who had also been the head of a film company, however small by comparison. The Curtiz propensity in his first Warners years to exercise his own initiative has been recorded by two of his few Hollywood close friends, Jack Warner and Hal Wallis, although their memoirs, both published after Curtiz's death, contain only brief references to him. Other reminiscences mainly reflect Hollywood gossip about his pre–1926 life rather than authenticated fact, for he was known there as a very private man, while no Curtiz family member has expanded our knowledge of his European life.

All these factors, always coupled with Curtiz's exceptionally heavy film output, go far to explain why no comprehensive study of his work has previously been undertaken and therefore why diametrically opposed views of him as a director still obtain so long after his death. In particular his European career has been almost totally neglected, although it was in Europe where his formative, possibly the most crucial, professional years of his life were spent, and where any panoramic survey of Curtiz's work must begin.

1

EUROPE, 1888 to 1926

Nothing definite is known about Michael Curtiz's early life except that he was born as Mihaly Kertesz in Hungary during the late nineteenth century. All other supposed data ultimately derive, in one form or another, from Curtiz himself who is unreliable since he gave out different versions at different times. For example, in 1929 his father was an architect,[1] whereas in 1947 he had become an impoverished carpenter.[2] In other respects Curtiz's 1929 biography, as issued by Warner Brothers publicity department, contains several now demonstrable glaring inaccuracies, while two 1947 press interviews he gave are inconsistent in that one claimed his family was in Vienna when he was 10 years old,[3] and the other that he attended high school and university in Hungary before going to Vienna.[4] The totality of the evidence is complex and the whole truth will probably never emerge beyond all doubt, but the greatest likelihood is that he was born in Budapest on or about 24 December 1888 to upper middle-class Jewish parents, and that he attended high school, university and drama academy before making his Budapest acting début in 1910. He might also have left home for a short time in 1906 or thereabouts to become a travelling circus member.[5]

From 1910 to 1912 Curtiz, whose mother was perhaps a concert singer, acted in and possibly directed plays before he turned his attention to filmmaking. At that time Hungary possessed no established film industry, but Budapest's newly emerged thriving cultural life was centred upon cafés where many Jews, comprising one-quarter of the city population, were deeply involved in creative activity. Actors and theatre critics frequented such cafés which showed films, and Curtiz probably first came into contact with film in this way and naturally gravitated towards films, as many actors did, either to earn extra money or to compensate for an inability to obtain good stage parts.[6] In 1910 the only Hungarian film company was Projectograph, founded in 1898, but it had merely distributed foreign fiction films and produced short education films and newsreels for showing in Hungary until 1912 when the threat of competition appeared from new Hungarian film companies preparing to make feature films. This prompted Projectograph to film *Today and Tomorrow*,[7] the first Hungarian feature, in which Curtiz starred. He possibly directed it as well, for thirty-five years later he plausibly maintained that when he arrived for the film, he found that Projectograph had not been able to afford a director and he himself took over as director from the cameraman on the basis of his stage experience.[8] After directing two or three more feature films he went to Copenhagen in 1913 to learn as much as possible about film-making at the Nordisk company, then the most important in Europe, with which Projectograph had close links.[9]

During his six-month stay at Nordisk, Curtiz changed his name to Michael Courtice, was taught the latest directing and editing techniques, starred in August Blom's *Atlantis*, and possibly directed another film, now unknown. Early in 1914 he returned to Budapest and directed several more films in a freelance capacity – alternating between the Projectograph, Uher and Kinoriport companies – before the First World War broke out. One of his pre-war Kinoriport films, *Bank ban* (a proper name), was Curtiz's first major commercial success and the first Hungarian film to be shot on location. When war erupted, Curtiz evidently joined the Austro-Hungarian army as an officer, but his military service ended in 1915 when he was apparently wounded seriously enough to be unable to fight again and was released to make documentary films to bolster Red Cross funds (another 1929 unsubstantiated Curtiz claim). However, before 1915 was out he was directing in Budapest once more and by the end of 1916 he had directed many more features and become a major figure in the Hungarian film world. Most of his films had been financially successful, with the result that when a new company, Phoenix, was formed from Projectograph at the beginning of 1917, he became its head and in this producer–director position considerably increased his output over the next two years. In this period he registered several large box-office draws.

During 1919 political events halted his thus far spectacular career progress. In November 1918 the Austro-Hungarian Empire and its German ally had lost the war, and in the process Hungarian internal stability had given way to turmoil. In March 1919 there came to power a Communist government which lasted barely five months, but this was long enough for the Hungarian film industry to be nationalized in April. Undoubtedly Curtiz fled from the country during 1919 when he was filming what would have been the first version of Ferenc Molnar's play, *Liliom*, but it is uncertain whether he left to escape Communist domination of his studio or collaborated with the Communists, perhaps unwillingly, and then feared anti-Communist retribution after the Communist government fell.

Whatever the reason for his flight from Hungary, Vienna was his natural destination because it was the pre-war Austro-Hungarian

Empire's acknowledged cultural centre and was still exerting a powerful hold upon the central European creative mind. Moreover, Austria was more politically stable than Hungary and had no major film industry. Although the first Austrian feature film had been made in 1912, fewer than a hundred features had appeared by the end of the war and almost half of these had been made during 1918 itself. In 1919 a dramatic rise in Austrian feature-film output was taking place, and in Vienna Curtiz contacted Count Alexander Kolowrat, a most remarkable wealthy nobleman nicknamed Sascha, to whose pioneering endeavours the burgeoning Austrian film industry had owed much. Between 1914 and 1916 Kolowrat had had built a large film studio in Vienna which had produced more than twenty films by the end of the war. Under his leadership the Sascha company had become dominant within the Austrian film industry which he intended to make the most important in Europe. Accordingly he hired Curtiz, a decision which led to a fruitful collaboration between them until mid–1926 when Kolowrat was dying of the cancer which eventually killed him in December 1927. Reverting in Vienna to the name of Michael Courtice, Curtiz by the end of 1920 had established himself as the Sascha studio's leading director despite his then rudimentary knowledge of German.[10]

From 1921 until his move to Hollywood Curtiz directed close to a score of films for Sascha, and in 1922–3 he broke new ground for the Austrian film industry with *Sodom and Gomorrah*. This two-part Biblical epic was the first Austrian film to be shot on location, with spectacular sets influenced by the Babylonian sequences in D. W. Griffith's *Intolerance*. In 1924 Curtiz directed his best Austrian feature, *The Slave Queen*, known as *Moon of Israel* in Britain and the United States, the first film that the Sascha studio co-produced with a foreign company, Stoll-Phoebus Picture Productions of London. A virtual remake of Cecil B. de Mille's 1923 *The Ten Commandments*, its epic nature rendered it ideal for a repeat performance of the location shooting which had characterized *Sodom and Gomorrah*. Based upon the novel by Sir H. Rider Haggard who wrote the sub-titles for the British version, *The Slave Queen* traces the romance between heir to the ancient Egyptian throne Adelqui Millar and Jewish slave girl Maria Corda. However, the screenplay of Ladislaus (Laszlo) Vadja, with whom Curtiz had worked in Hungary, and Curtiz's own direction subordinated the plot to magnificent spectacle. The highlight is the Jews' flight across the Red Sea, a sequence involving 5,000 extras and splendid special effects created by Kolowrat personally. The film opened in Vienna on 24 October 1924 and a shortened version in London less than a month later.[11] One British review concluded that the film's high quality was due mainly to Curtiz.[12]

Initially *The Slave Queen* did not win its director recognition, still less acclaim, in the English-speaking world because it was not released in the United States where Paramount bought the American rights and then kept it out of circulation in case it outshone *The Ten Commandments*. But *The Slave Queen*'s success in London gave rise to further Sascha international productions which for Curtiz meant trips to Paris, Copenhagen and Berlin for scenes in his last three Austrian films. However, the president of Warner Brothers, Harry M. Warner, had travelled to Europe in November 1925 in search of new talent, and he met Curtiz in Paris when the latter was directing *The Plaything of Paris* (*Red Heels* in the United States). Agreement in principle for Curtiz to join Warners was apparently reached on the spot, but as a follow-up Warner instructed brother Jack L. Warner to find a print of *The Slave Queen* for viewing. Jack unearthed the Paramount print, and when the two brothers saw it after Harry's return to the United States, they were sufficiently impressed in March 1926 to offer Curtiz a contract by cable, which he accepted immediately.[13]

The contract was finalized on 10 May in Berlin where Curtiz was filming *The Golden Butterfly*. He was to be ready to begin work in Hollywood by 1 June, and Warners would pay his travelling expenses from Berlin. His yearly salary was 15,600 dollars, Warners receiving annual options on his services until June 1930. If these were exercised, the salary would rise to 21,600 dollars in June 1927, 28,800 dollars in June 1928, and 36,000 dollars in June 1929. In return Curtiz was obliged to accept whatever films he was assigned to, with no annual maximum limit, and to enter the United States in a legal form enabling him to remain there permanently.

Curtiz seems to have taken this contract none too seriously at the time, for he had also just entered into other contractual commitments which in February 1927 cost Warners 3,100 dollars to eliminate.[14] He also entered the United States on a temporary, six-month visa which caused Warners headaches with the American immigration authorities of progressively increasing difficulty until 1930. He arrived in New York on 6 June 1926 (not 4 July, as has often been stated on the basis of Jack Warner's 1964 autobiography), having possibly first paid a visit to Budapest before sailing from Cherbourg, perhaps an indication that he had not worked for the Communists in 1919. Much to Jack Warner's annoyance, Curtiz then remained in New York to meet Harry Warner again (according to Curtiz, at the behest of Albert 'Abe' Warner) to go over story material before Curtiz proceeded to Hollywood, reaching there on 21 June.[15] He had committed himself to the studio for the time being. He apparently possessed only a sketchy command of spoken English, but it speaks volumes for a self-confidence bordering on arrogance that he signed a contract for work in a distant nation which he had never even visited, although his poor spoken German in 1919 had not prevented his swift success in Vienna. As matters were to develop, he had arrived in the country which was to be his home for the remainder of his life.

2

HOLLYWOOD BAPTISM,
1926 to 1929

Warner Brothers, the only family concern in Hollywood, was founded in and made its first feature film as recently as 1918, but the four brothers, the sons of Polish Jews who had emigrated to the United States in the 1890s, possessed unlimited ambition. The eldest was Harry (1881–1957), an extreme financial conservative who had become company president in 1924 and directed all aspects of the studio's operations from the New York office. Abe (1884–1967) was the second son who acted as treasurer and controlled film distribution, while Sam (1888–1927), who was to die before the studio took a place among the motion picture giants, and Jack (1892–1981) were responsible for actual film production in California. By 1924 annual production had reached only seventeen films, but, with Harry as the driving force, Warners had become hell-bent on expansion at a time of general American prosperity by the end of that year. The financial basis for this was to be the credit supplied by Wall Street bankers Goldman Sachs. During 1925 this was extended to three million dollars, with the likelihood of more to come if required, the company having raised production to thirty-one features and in April announced its intention to go over to sound films. Increased production went hand in hand with investment in distribution centres at home and abroad, in cinemas, in a radio station, and in experiments with sound for films. As a result the financial statement of March 1926 had shown a loss of more than 1,300,000 dollars, but there was no danger of imminent bankruptcy owing to Goldman Sachs' continued willingness to lend Warners money and the 1925 acquisitions of assets which could be sold if necessary. Moreover, the recent film-making expansion had already begun to pay off in that of the twenty-nine features released in the fiscal year ending in March 1926 only one had registered a loss, and that a small one. The year's film profit turned out to be almost four million dollars, but this was not fully reflected in the March 1926 statement because the box-office receipts had yet to be finalized and the available figures were submerged in the large property investments.

By mid–1926, just as Curtiz joined Warners, the studio had produced its first sound film, Alan Crosland's *Don Juan* (no spoken dialogue, but a musical score and sound effects), with a highly publicized prestige release and the charismatic presence of star John Barrymore in the title role. The film made a handsome profit of over one million dollars,[1] but it nevertheless failed to do as well as Warners had hoped.

If bankruptcy was not an immediate danger, the studio was all the same too committed to sound films to consider a retreat if the 1925 investments were to fulfil their maximum profit potential and the studio debts to be paid off. The 1926 film output had been only marginally increased to thirty-three films, but the rapid 1925–6 expansion had been undertaken without full regard to its company structure side-effects. In particular Jack Warner had become much more involved in administration and had often been drawn away from actual filming supervision. This vacuum was mostly and at first unofficially filled by chief scriptwriter Darryl F. Zanuck, signed by the studio in 1924, who had abundant creativity and wrote under three pseudonyms to conceal Warners' reliance upon his talent. By 1926 his supervisory duties covered most of the routine action adventures, comedies, and melodramas, while Jack Warner took charge of the few prestige pictures like *Don Juan*.

The remaining studio scriptwriters were nondescript except for Bess Meredyth, the future second Mrs Michael Curtiz. Born in Buffalo, New York, in 1890, she had joined the Biograph film company as a teenager and moved to Hollywood in 1911. Her subsequent career with Universal had included acting, directing, and writing, but in the mid–1920s she seemingly turned exclusively to freelance screenplay work. While her writing for Warners was spasmodic, she was entrusted with studio prestige enterprises such as Millard Webb's *The Sea Beast*, a 1925 loose adaptation of Herman Melville's novel *Moby Dick*. As a Barrymore star vehicle it was Warners' largest 1926 money spinner, and she was also commissioned to write the *Don Juan* script. Since signing for Warners in 1924 Barrymore had towered head and shoulders above all the other studio contract players but, because he was costly, his permanent contract was terminated at the end of 1926. Only the Alsatian dog Rin Tin Tin had rivalled Barrymore as a studio star box-office attraction, the other chief contract players being competent but either relatively unknown or lacking in star quality.

Warners' foremost director in 1926 was Ernst Lubitsch, whose first four films for the studio since 1924 had all been stylish critical successes, although none had produced a large profit. His last Warners film in 1926, *So This is Paris*, had done much better financially, but even so his contract was not renewed. This decision, like that ending Barrymore's contract, arose from Harry Warner's policy of cutting the number of prestige productions within a limited overall film-making budget and instead concentrating almost exclusively upon routine fare, with intended

11

small but consistent profits in every case, until Warners had recovered much more of its investment outlay. By comparison with Lubitsch the other main studio directors were merely efficient journeymen – the ever-reliable Lloyd Bacon, veteran Hollywood Briton J. Stuart Blackton, James Flood, Erle C. Kenton, Herman Raymaker and, second only to Lubitsch, Roy Del Ruth. In this context the acquisition of Curtiz was only one element of a wider 1925–6 search to improve Warners' directorial quality, for other new directors of the time included Alan Crosland, Ray Enright, Henry Lehrman, and Archie Mayo, while studio ace cameraman Byron 'Bun' Haskin was allowed to direct as well in 1927. Haskin, who had beautifully photographed both *The Sea Beast* and *Don Juan*, was challenged as chief cinematographer only by Hal Mohr until the 1927 arrival of veteran Barney McGill.

Thus far the studio had yet to arrive as a major Hollywood movie-making force. It still needed to attract and retain exceptional talent in sufficient depth to be able to compete with, particularly, Metro-Goldwyn-Mayer (MGM) and Paramount. Furthermore, Warners had failed to develop any clear trademark which would distinguish the content and style of its films from those of other studios. Consequently, by mid–1926 its deep financial commitment to expansion had become a policy in which prestige features were to be kept to a bare minimum for the indefinite future.

This was the studio background into which Curtiz stepped. According to his own 1947 testimony, which in this case there is no reason to doubt, he expected to direct *Noah's Ark* immediately upon his arrival in Hollywood in line with Harry Warner's promise to him at their Paris meeting. Instead Jack Warner personally assigned him, without any explanation, to *The Third Degree*.[2] This event is consistent with Harry Warner's recent policy change against costly prestige films, and Curtiz feared that his Hollywood career might be at risk if he did not acquit himself well. As a result he speedily acquainted himself with American legal procedure and spent ten days with the Los Angeles sheriff accompanying him on his official duties. He actually lived in prison, ate with policemen, studied fingerprinting methods, and attended prisoner roll calls in the morning.[3]

Based upon Charles Klein's 1908 play and a subsequent novel, *The Third Degree* had already been filmed twice, in 1913 and 1919. Its lengthy popularity was founded upon the notion that the police use of the stringent 'third degree' interrogation method might lead to false confessions. Additionally the leading female part carried a strong sentimental appeal, and Warners' revival of such material was probably motivated by a wish for another vehicle for its newest rising star Dolores Costello, John Barrymore's mistress and later second wife. However, it was also arguably an early manifestation of the Warners 1930s style, a concern with contemporary social issues from the viewpoint of the underdog.

The story centres upon circus artist Louise Dresser, who deserts her husband to run off with upper-class cad Rockliffe Fellowes and in the process leaves behind her small daughter Annie. Fifteen years later Annie (Dolores Costello), a trapeze performer in a Coney Island side show, falls in love with unemployed Jason Robards Senior. She marries him in spite of the disapproval of his wealthy father who, however, hires Fellowes to break up the couple. When Dresser discovers this, she decides to leave Fellowes but instead shoots him after a quarrel. Robards falls under suspicion and confesses to the murder while under the police 'third degree'. Costello comes to realize that her mother is the real culprit. Costello herself also confesses to save both Dresser and Robards, but at length Dresser comes forward to admit to her crime.

Even in 1926 this was outmoded material, and Curtiz, who now took the name by which he was known for the rest of his life, collaborated with scriptwriter C. Graham Baker to make numerous changes, both to the original play and to Baker's screenplay. These were mostly concerned with the circus, Robards's job-hunting and the interrogation sequences, all of which involved unorthodox camera placements. The circus shots include two of the most exciting moments in silent film history – a motor cycle accident during a Wall of Death act and a 40-ft human dive into a tiny pool of water filmed from a camera at the transparent pool bottom. Robards's fruitless attempt to gain employment is presented as a series of constantly moving, skilfully superimposed images, culminating in a long tracking shot that follows his feet through a rubbish-strewn slum area until a passing car splashes mud over him. In the 'third degree' scene, tension is built up by a progression of speedy forceful shots which end with the words 'Confess, confess' flying out of the screen until an explosion signifies Robards's confession. At one point the camera assumes the part of a speeding bullet in mid-air. Cameraman Hal Mohr recalled many years later that he had never had to work so hard on a film, and that Curtiz was incessantly prowling around the set seeking new camera angles. Curtiz rounded off the film by having the circus ringmaster hang his hat on the camera, thereby indicating to the audience its crucial role in the film's atmosphere and narrative.[4]

Critical reaction to *The Third Degree* was mixed upon its release early in 1927. The unprecedented camera angles were criticized, while Curtiz did not forge the clumsily structured script into a balanced, coherent drama. Nevertheless he had achieved enough with routine material to convince Jack Warner that he was no run-of-the-mill director, as quite apart from his camera imagination he had shown a capacity, albeit sporadically, for tension-laden, economical narrative and had guided Dolores Costello to a competent performance consolidating her position as

13

Warners' latest rising star. For his efforts Curtiz's salary was increased in January 1927.[5]

During 1927 Harry Warner raised the company's film-making budget for a record output of forty-three films, only one of which was for prestige. Consequently Curtiz found himself assigned to three cheaply produced, now largely forgotten programme fillers. The first, released in May 1927, was *A Million Bid*, in which Dolores Costello, falsely believing husband Warner Oland to be dead, marries again only to discover that he is alive after all. Released three months later, by which time Warners had picked up its first option on Curtiz's services, was *The Desired Woman*, standard fare dealing with the havoc wrought by British officer's wife Irene Rich among his fellow officers in an isolated desert fortress. *Good Time Charley*, released towards the end of the year, is a sentimental tale of veteran actor Warner Oland's sacrifices to further the stage career of daughter Helene Costello.

In each case Curtiz strove valiantly but unsuccessfully to revitalize unconvincing scripts through spectacular camera work and strong central performances, the most noteworthy features of all three. However, these films, all just over one hour long, contributed to Curtiz's Hollywood career in that they familiarized him with Warners' methods and brought him into contact with technicians like cameramen Hal Mohr and Barney McGill. They also involved collaboration with Henry Blanke, Lubitsch's former assistant who had remained at Warners when Lubitsch had left and who acted as Curtiz's assistant in the first two films. Zanuck also scripted the last two and, as Warners' newly appointed production chief under Jack Warner, supervised the same two. Both Blanke and Zanuck at once recognized Curtiz's potential, which was to have an important bearing on the latter's progress at the studio. So far all four of his American films had, like most Warners films of the time, registered only moderate profits. Costly location shooting at Warners was rare at this time, yet *The Desired Woman* was shot partly in Yuma, Arizona, and one of its strongest assets was the striking desert background. This might indicate that, in spite of his recent arrival at Warners, Curtiz could already influence the filming conditions of routine material. However, it did not fare as well at the box-office as *A Million Bid* and was more expensive to produce.

Warners' financial position received a spectacular boost during 1928. The tremendous impact of Alan Crosland's part-talkie *The Jazz Singer* after its December 1927 general release had transformed the studio's economic position to the point where in just under a year many of the outstanding debts had been paid off. The success of *The Jazz Singer* had also given the company a head start in sound film production, which had to be maintained for as long as possible if Warners was to reap the maximum economic harvest. However, *The Jazz Singer*'s huge profit of

14

over two million dollars had taken Warners by surprise, with the result that planned silent films and some already in production had to be converted hastily into part-sound movies. Three of these appeared early in 1928 before the studio completed its first all-talkie film. The first of the three was the Curtiz-directed *Tenderloin*, and his assignment to such an economically important production was a sign of how highly he was already regarded. *Tenderloin* is an underworld saga in which café dancer Dolores Costello walks home one night and sees someone throw a bag over a fence. Retrieving it, she finds it contains money stolen in a bank raid, after which she attracts the attention of both the bank raid gang and the police before a detective posing as a gang member (Conrad Nagel) establishes her innocence. Only approximately fifteen minutes of *Tenderloin*'s eighty-eight minutes' running time, Curtiz's longest Warners film to date, is devoted to the spoken dialogue, which is so stilted that at its prestige opening the film brought about derisive laughter. None the less it made almost 800,000 dollars because of its novelty and cheap production costs, but now its main interest lies not so much in its primitive talking sequences as in its depiction of underworld life, another early portent of the Warners 1930s trademark. Under Curtiz's direction Mohr's haunting photography lingers on cold, wet streets and cheap, sordid rooms. The gang members – Mitchell Lewis, Dan Wohlheim, and Pat Hartigan – bring criminal characters vividly to life, while Curtiz once more showed Dolores Costello, with whom he evidently established an excellent working relationship, to very good effect. Warners rewarded Curtiz by taking up its second option on his services with a salary increase which took him above the salary laid down in his 1926 contract.

By the end of 1928 Warners was expanding still further and bought a controlling interest in First National Pictures. As film profits soared, the rising studio film budget at last enabled Harry Warner to allow Curtiz to direct *Noah's Ark*, which under Zanuck's supervision was Warners' most ambitious and longest project thus far. For prestige reasons all the production stops were pulled out. Zanuck himself co-wrote the script, newly signed ace art director Anton Grot designed the sets, and Mohr was the cinematographer. The main players were Dolores Costello, Noah Beery Senior, Louise Fazenda, Guinn 'Big Boy' Williams, and George O'Brien, all in dual roles. The film cost slightly more than one million dollars to produce, an enormous outlay by Warners' standards of the time.

Dominated by an anti-war theme, *Noah's Ark* connects the famous Biblical story with one set in the First World War. The first 35 minutes of the film's original 135 minutes were silent, but the later dialogue sequences compare very favourably with most other contemporary sound or part-sound movies and even with many early 1930s productions. The highlight of the Biblical section is the great flood sequence, in which

Curtiz bettered even his own excellence in *The Slave Queen*. For this scene he had assembled a huge tank containing 500,000 tons of water which were to be released on to a massive Babylonian set. This was intended to collapse, while several hundred extras and stuntmen were to be left to thrash about in the deluge as fifteen cameramen filmed the scene. As a child who had experienced the 1906 San Francisco earthquake, Mohr was apprehensive about the physical perils to the players involved, protested to Curtiz before filming of the scene began, lost his Warners post in consequence, and was replaced by Barney McGill. In the event Curtiz badly underestimated the technical problems of releasing so much water in one scene, the water went out of control, and many player injuries occurred.[6] However, the outcome is one of the most spectacular incidents in film history. Although today this scene is that for which *Noah's Ark* is most remembered, the entire Biblical section is little more than an excuse for the then more topical anti-war modern story and for Curtiz to exercise his gift for epic presentation. The modern story contains a very impressive train crash as a prelude to the outbreak of the First World War. Then an American accidentally kills his friend in a German machine gun emplacement and an innocent woman accused of espionage is saved from imminent execution by an artillery bombardment which kills the entire firing squad. At the end a priest parallels the war with Noah's story, while a long flashback links God's purge of the ancient world with the carnage of the modern war. At the time Curtiz attached more importance to the spiritual theme than to the epic scenes.[7]

Noah's Ark's cinematic merit remains incontestable, and contrary to general belief it was Curtiz's first Warners large box-office hit. In the United States it made only a small profit, but in Europe takings were more than 900,000 dollars, moving the total profit to more than 1,250,000 dollars. However, its post-preview history now makes a complete evaluation impossible. In 1928 the full 135-minute version was premiered, but this was reduced to 105 minutes for its March 1929 general release. It then languished in obscurity until the late 1950s, when American anti-war pressure groups sought a reissue. The outcome was a 1957 75-minute version with considerable restructuring by Warners which included a change of scene order and the elimination of many of the sub-titles and some of the 1928 spoken dialogue in favour of a superimposed spoken commentary. Contemporary American restoration efforts are unlikely to reach more than 100 minutes as the nearest to the 1929 released version that can be achieved.[8] The full version will probably never see the light of day again, but it says much for the film that the 75-minute version shown in London in 1960 was described by critic Dee Wells as 'the best film of the week' and the Biblical part as 'rather wonderful'.[9]

Warners' substantial profit position in 1928 was an excellent basis for further progress. In 1929 First National was totally taken over, a profit of over fourteen million dollars emerged, and film output was all but doubled. Over eighty features were produced, slightly more than half under the First National label, while the personnel quality rose. Among the players acquired from First National were Richard Barthelmess, Douglas Fairbanks Junior, Harry Langdon, Basil Rathbone, and Loretta Young. On the production side new men included directors Alexander Korda and Mervyn LeRoy as well as excellent cinematographers Lee Garmes, Ernest Haller and Sol Polito.

Despite the increased output and vastly improved economic situation, Warners' 1929 productions remained largely routine, many of the part-talkies containing superfluous songs. Curtiz's contribution was a mere four dramas, but one of these, *The Gamblers*, received a prestige build-up and première. Moreover, some Warners films were being distributed abroad more widely than earlier, and among these were not only *Noah's Ark* but also two of Curtiz's 1929 films, *Glad Rag Doll* and *The Gamblers*. The former concerns the infatuation of rich man Ralph Graves with showgirl and suspected gold digger Dolores Costello. Its insubstantial plot was worsened by inept dialogue and a poor sound-track. Curtiz did his utmost to overcome these handicaps by showing the stars to good advantage, but cinematically his endeavours were to no avail. The novelty of sound, 'Bun' Haskin's photography, and cheap production costs, however, produced a profit of more than 800,000 dollars. Hard on the heels of *Glad Rag Doll* came *The Madonna of Avenue A*. In this Dolores Costello plays a girl who has been brought up to believe that mother Louise Dresser is wealthy, whereas in reality she is a hostess in a sleazy night club. When Costello discovers the truth, she marries a crook, whom Dresser, unaware of the marriage, has framed for murder. When Dresser realizes that she has in effect sentenced her own son-in-law to death, she remorsefully commits suicide. Like *Glad Rag Doll*, its chief redeeming characteristics are Costello's performance and Haskin's camera work. However, *The Madonna of Avenue A* is of more than passing interest because Curtiz probably wrote it himself, as he claimed almost thirty years later,[10] and certainly it exhibits some of the traits in his later work. In particular it derides the American preoccupation with the acquisition of wealth and ends on a gloomy note for all the characters concerned. Released in the same month, *The Gamblers* was based upon a play by Charles Klein, the author of *The Third Degree*. Father and son Emerson (George Fawcett and Jason Robards Senior respectively) are company directors about to embezzle five million dollars of clients' money in order to gamble on the stock market to rescue their company from bankruptcy. This unusual drama, of some historical interest on the eve of the Wall Street crash, is intermingled with a triangular romance involving the son, the company lawyer (H. B. Warner), and the latter's wife (Lois Wilson). An unconvincing plot is almost transcended by strong performances and very solid production values. Despite the bleak philosophy underlying both *The Madonna of Avenue A* and *The Gamblers*, each was very successful financially.

The Gamblers finally demonstrated that Curtiz had mastered the use of sound. So, too, did *Hearts in Exile*, his last-released 1929 film starring Dolores Costello as a Moscow fishmonger's daughter who, in frustration at student lover Grant Withers's refusal to wed, marries nobleman James Kirkwood instead. Years later all three meet in exile in Siberia, the noble having been sentenced to twenty years and the student, now a doctor, to two years. As Withers has remained in love with Costello, he arranges to exchange places with Kirkwood who agrees to obtain Withers's release once he is free. The scheme succeeds, but Kirkwood realizes that Costello still loves Withers and obligingly commits suicide so that the young couple can marry. Both a happy and an enigmatic ending were filmed and shown, the one with the couple remaining at liberty happily married and the other with their recapture and return to Siberia. Once again star performances and production values, especially the photography of Bill Reese, who also filmed *The Gamblers*, partly overcame a shaky story. Although a very smooth production, *Hearts in Exile* cost too much to make to register more than a moderate profit.

Curtiz's last 1929 film, unreleased until 1930, was also his first Warners excursion outside melodrama and the beginning of his genre versatility. This was the part-colour Al Jolson musical *Mammy*. Since the success of *The Jazz Singer* and then of Lloyd Bacon's *The Singing Fool*, Jolson's career at Warners had been fading and he was interested only in completing his two remaining contract films as soon as possible so that he could then sign for United Artists.[11] Jolson acts badly in the backstage murder scenes in which he emerges as the prime suspect, but his comedy pieces are good and his minstrel Irving Berlin numbers are engaging even if they do not figure among his finest. At times *Mammy* is tedious, possibly indicating that Jolson had contractual production influence which Curtiz could not nullify, but it springs to life when establishing the showbiz atmosphere as the troupe moves from town to town. Furthermore, the musical numbers are integrated into the story rather than, as so often happened in Warners' early sound musicals, being allowed to disjoint it. At the time Jolson maintained that *Mammy* was his best film, but in retrospect he came to value *The Jazz Singer* and *The Singing Fool* more highly.[12] Today, aside from the songs, *Mammy* looks better than the other two. Reportedly it was Curtiz's first Warners smash hit, but in fact Jolson's popularity was waning, and although the film eventually delivered a small profit, this was merely because of its foreign income, for American box-office receipts failed even to match the high production cost.

Since 1926 Curtiz had shown that he could turn out good, profitable films to broad studio specifications and simultaneously adapt to new technical conditions. It was therefore not surprising that Warners had picked up its third annual option on him in May 1929. However, he had yet to demonstrate that he might rise to the top at Warners, for his record among the studio directors was by no means exceptional. The 1929 output had been spread over more than thirty directors. Among these William A. Seiter had directed six films and Del Ruth was equal with Curtiz at five, while Bacon, William Beaudine, Howard Bretherton, John Francis Dillon, Enright, LeRoy, Frank Lloyd, and Mayo had all managed four. All Curtiz's films since 1926 had made a profit, but at this time only a few Warners films actually lost money and only *Noah's Ark, Tenderloin*, and *Glad Rag Doll* had enjoyed spectacular financial success. But their profits were small fry compared with Bacon's 5,500,000 dollars for *The Singing Fool* and almost 1,800,000 dollars for another Jolson vehicle, *Say It With Songs*, in 1929. Del Ruth had also registered more than three million dollars profit with *Gold Diggers of Broadway* in 1929, more than two million with *The Terror* in 1928, and more than one million with *The Desert Song*, again in 1929. Moreover, Crosland's *On With the Show* had made close to two million dollars, while Mayo's *My Man* and *On Trial* had each grossed more than one million dollars and his Jolson vehicle *Sonny Boy* some 970,000 dollars. Thus Curtiz had held his own among the Warners directors, but he had still to prove himself better than several of these in both financial impact and film quantity, although nowadays it can be seen that the cinematic quality of his films was well above studio average for those years.

3

AN EXPANDING REPERTOIRE,
1930 to 1935

When the October 1929 Wall Street crash ushered in the great depression of the 1930s, Warners was initially unscathed. However, a substantial 1930 profit was followed by hefty losses during the next four years which almost wiped out the company's prosperity of 1927–30. The crisis was especially acute from 1931 to mid–1933 as American unemployment mounted and cinema attendances fell away alarmingly. Studio economies, including redundancies and salary cuts, began in 1931 as approximately one film in six lost money, the profits from most of the remainder were small, and even the most successful gathered in for Warners only half of what could have been expected in the late 1920s. These unwelcome developments convinced the Warner brothers and Zanuck that Warners should break new ground with contemporary, realistic films that made few concessions to traditional entertainment values. Almost every film until 1935, when the studio turned the tide with a very small profit, was allocated a low budget, which lent itself to gloomy, sleazy sets. None the less films focusing upon real-life social problems were the exception rather than the rule, and the studio mix continued much as in the late 1920s until 1935, with the addition of a few horror films and some lavish musicals in the wake of Bacon's *42nd Street* in 1933. These latter films were the main ones making more than one million dollars in 1933–5 as cinema attendances were rising again, the studio being dangerously dependent upon this one genre and three or four star names for its tenuous recovery.

During 1932, the worst year, Warners had resorted to further staff lay-offs and salary cuts as output was reduced to between fifty and sixty films. In March 1933 came the climax of a power struggle between Harry Warner and Zanuck over production control. The company cut the salaries of most employees by 50 per cent for two months, a step which Zanuck opposed contrary to all three Warner brothers. He resigned, to be replaced by his assistant Hal B. Wallis, who had been in charge of publicity from 1922 to 1929 but had then controlled production at the First National Burbank studio when Warners assumed full powers before his appointment as Zanuck's second-in-command in 1930. While Zanuck had sometimes given Curtiz and other Warners staff a tough time off the set,[1] on set he had allowed him close to a free hand. Wallis, however, was less flexible, more authority-conscious, and apt to resent criticism, while he also demanded that directors adhere rigidly to approved scripts.

In addition personnel changes occurred among the directors and players from 1930 to 1935, but although Curtiz's position was by no means secure during 1931, Warners regularly exercised its annual options under his new contract. All Warners directors in these economy-conscious years had to be fast and versatile to survive – LeRoy, for example, directed two Joe E. Brown comedies in 1931 – but Curtiz was faster than everyone except LeRoy at about two minutes, thirty seconds per day running time.[2] Furthermore, unlike other Warners directors of the time, his versatility developed into a film-making philosophy which permitted him to exploit studio policy changes and strengthen his position in the studio's directorial hierarchy.

During 1930 Curtiz directed six films, more than any other Warners director, although Bacon, Del Ruth, Dillon, and Seiter each directed five. The year opened for Curtiz with *River's End*, a melodrama starring Charles Bickford as both a mountie who dies and a fugitive who impersonates him and then falls for the dead man's girl. Previously filmed in 1922 and one of many silent remakes during Warners early sound period, the new version is notable for Robert Kurrle's double exposure photography, superbly handled by Curtiz to enable the two men played by Bickford to be seen in convincing conversation with each other. Although it only broke even financially, the film was well above average entertainment, as even Bickford, who more than thirty years later recalled his distaste for Curtiz and his methods of obtaining screen realism in *River's End*, admitted. Bickford also noted with surprise that Zanuck visited the set only once during eight weeks of filming.[3]

Warners did not wait for the April release of *Mammy* to put Curtiz in charge of another part-colour musical, *Under a Texas Moon*, and the two films were premiered almost simultaneously. However, aided by Reese's impressive outdoors photography, *Under a Texas Moon* enjoyed the greater box-office success. Frank Fay, a vaudeville favourite then married to Barbara Stanwyck, plays a Casanova-type rancher who takes time out between romantic episodes to round up cattle rustlers, but he and Curtiz took an instant dislike to each other to the point where relations soon broke down and Myrna Loy, high in the supporting cast, acted as an intermediary between them.[4] Possibly as a result Fay does not come across well, whereas Curtiz shows Loy to advantage by sometimes allowing the camera to linger upon her, particularly in a scene where she is surrounded by colourful Indian draperies.

His next assignment and also his first Hollywood comedy was *The*

Matrimonial Bed (*A Matrimonial Problem* in Britain), a French farce involving amnesia and bigamy set in contemporary Paris. Despite Fay's uninspiring presence, the film contains amusing moments and shows that Curtiz could handle comedy competently. However, its financial profit was very modest and well below average for the year. Simultaneously Warners remade *The Sea Beast* as *Moby Dick*, retaining Barrymore as Captain Ahab. Bacon directed what proved to be a critical but (contrary to legend) not a huge box-office success. This prompted Warners to produce a German-language equivalent, to which Curtiz was assigned, while the part of Ahab was played by William Diertele, an efficient German actor who was also a very able director and a new Warners recruit. The film was made during long daily hours over two weeks, as Diertele remembered more than forty years later.[5] Entitled *The Sea Demon*, it was filmed in October–November 1930, but since its German release it appears to have been lost, rendering an evaluation impossible.

The reasonable success of *Under a Texas Moon* probably influenced the choice of Curtiz as director for his third colour musical, *Bright Lights*, despite the persistent tension between him and Fay. *Mammy*'s showbiz-crime formula was duplicated, but neither Curtiz nor Lee Garmes's camera work could redeem a leaden script, humdrum songs and an indifferent cast, apart from Dorothy Mackaill as an actress who forsakes stardom for marriage. *Bright Lights* barely broke even financially and lacked a sure hand at the helm, perhaps because it was probably filmed at least partly simultaneously with the Harry Langdon vehicle, *A Soldier's Plaything*, shooting for which began in May 1930 but was not completed until late in the year. Langdon had been a great silent comedian during the first half of the 1920s, but since then his career had declined and he badly needed a hit for personal as well as professional reasons.[6] He thus agreed to star in *A Soldier's Plaything* as his first sound film, with which Warners was seeking to establish a formula to match the successful Edmund Lowe–Victor McLaglen comedies for Fox. A melodramatic opening sees Langdon enlist at Coney Island out of patriotism and pal Ben Lyon act in the same way to avoid gangland revenge. Later the film turns into a series of comic episodes centring upon Langdon, his visual humour, and some amorous escapades. Curtiz integrated Langdon's insipid lines with facial contortions to suit the latter's comedy style, but for some reason the film's release was delayed and meanwhile Langdon completed his second sound film, W. J. Craft's *See America Thirst*, for Universal. On this occasion Langdon was feebly directed and failed to adapt his humour to sound. *See America Thirst* was a commercial disaster, which led Warners to cut fourteen minutes from the original seventy-one minutes of *A Soldier's Plaything*. In consequence the film's flow was badly interrupted and attention was distracted from the carefully designed sets and impressive crowd scenes at the beginning. Released in April

1931 as a mere programmer, it flopped both in the United States and overseas, descended into obscurity, and to date has not been fully restored.[7] It was Curtiz's largest loss-maker until the 1950s.

In 1931 the studio's only striking successes were LeRoy's *Little Caesar* and *Five Star Final*, which brought Edward G. Robinson to stardom, Bacon's *Sit Tight*, John Adolfi's George Arliss vehicle *The Millionaire*, and Dillon's *The Girl of the Golden West*, a varied diet which supplied little clue as to how Warners might halt its losses. Fifteen 1931 films actually lost money, while even the most successful were registering profits well below those of their 1930 counterparts. Curtiz directed only three films during the year, whereas William Wellman directed five, including the powerful James Cagney gangster vehicle *The Public Enemy*, and LeRoy four, including the Oscar best film nomination press melodrama *Five Star Final*. The first of Curtiz's 1931 movies was *God's Gift to Women*, a romantic farce with Fay as a Parisian womanizer. From the film it seems either that their previous disputes had worn Curtiz down or that he decided to let Fay have his head to prove to him that he had no acting ability. Whatever the reason, Fay was allowed to dominate the proceedings, but in the process he killed off his potential stardom, for the film lost 58,000 dollars. The plot unfolds tediously and is enlivened only by the presence of one of the studio's recent signings, gregarious Joan Blondell, as the American girl for whom the philandering Fay genuinely falls.

Much more agreeable to Curtiz was *The Mad Genius*, a follow-up to Barrymore's barnstorming title role performance in *Svengali*. The story concerns a crippled dance teacher who adopts a boy and then raises him to become the same great dancer that he himself once was. On the surface *The Mad Genius* follows the melodramatic atmosphere and substance of *Svengali*, but in Curtiz's hands it was turned into a different kind of film outside any acknowledged genre. Late in 1930 Universal had made Tod Browning's *Dracula* – a commercial success which had commenced the 1930s horror cycle. Curtiz had worked in Hungary with *Dracula*'s star, Bela Lugosi, and could scarcely have been unaware of the film and its potential for other movies. Moreover, none of his films since *Noah's Ark* had given him a chance to show his full talents. Although the setting of *The Mad Genius* is near-contemporary, the film is a semi-horror story juxtaposed with cynical humour and a moral dilemma for adopted son Donald Cook who has to choose between his artistic career, through Barrymore's domination of him, and his love for Marian Marsh. In addition there are unorthodox camera angles, expressionistic lighting, a broody ambience, and much suspense. Above all, although the undisciplined Barrymore loathed Curtiz's strict direction and later reportedly compared it to participation in a marathon dance contest, in fact he turned in one of his best sound performances amidst

Grot's fabulous, revolutionary theatre sets. These were similar to those in *Svengali* – tilted ceilings and floors, out of proportion doors and windows, and unusual staircases.[8]

The Mad Genius lost 49,000 dollars largely due to Barrymore's high salary. Since his last few Warners films had also all either failed or been only moderately successful for the same reason, *The Mad Genius* ended his career at the studio. Its failure might have been held against Curtiz as well, for although the film had been his most polished sound effort to date, he had distorted the studio's intention. This probably explains why his next three assignments amounted to a return to routine material without the participation of any established stars or recently signed talents like Cagney, Paul Muni, William Powell, Robinson, and Barbara Stanwyck. *The Woman from Monte Carlo* towards the end of 1931 was a vehicle for Lil Dagover, a distinguished German stage actress who had appeared in a few early 1920s films and now formed a part of Warners' plans for more star personalities. Presumably it was believed that Curtiz, as a European with Austrian experience, would bring out the best in Dagover. But in the event the film, a remake of Alexander Korda's 1928 *The Night Watch*, was too greatly handicapped by a turgid screenplay dwelling upon the adultery of naval captain Walter Huston's wife with one of his fellow officers. Although the central performance was competent despite contemporary press reports of clashes between Curtiz and Dagover, not even this, the efficient direction, and Haller's effective photography could save the film which only just recovered its production cost.

At the end of 1931 Curtiz directed *Alias the Doctor*, in which surgeon Richard Barthelmess nearly destroys his career in taking the blame for stepbrother Norman Foster's professional malpractices. This half-hearted Warners attempt to latch on to the early 1930s horror craze was not ideal for a Barthelmess vehicle and today has little to recommend it. However, Curtiz made a major effort with his next assignment, the more modestly budgeted *The Strange Love of Molly Louvain*. Ann Dvorak plays a husband-abandoned woman with a young baby who falls for ruthless murderer Leslie Fenton, takes up with washed-up reporter Lee Tracy, and is courted by decent young man Richard Cromwell before winding up in jail when her baby comes back into her life. The bleak story is relentlessly depicted, while the chilling portrayal of gangsterism carries Curtiz's previous work in *The Third Degree* and *Tenderloin* one stage further. Drab slum streets and sleazy hotel rooms are again presented in stark detail via Kurrle's photography. The film is arguably a minor masterpiece, the first strong blend of Curtiz's talent with the studio's new policy of social realism. Although neither a clear-cut success nor an outright failure, *The Strange Love of Molly Louvain*, together with *Alias the Doctor*, which fared significantly better at the box-office, raised Curtiz's standing again at Warners after the four successive disappointments of *A Soldier's Plaything*, *God's Gift to Women*, *The Mad Genius*, and *The Woman from Monte Carlo*.

After Universal had followed up *Dracula* with the very successful James Whale's *Frankenstein* late in 1931, all the Hollywood studios pursued the horror bandwagon. As both Curtiz and Grot had already indirectly shown in projects like *Svengali*, *The Mad Genius* and *Alias the Doctor*, staff with experience of 1920s German expressionist techniques were the logical choices for this genre. However, due to the 1931 losses, all Warners directors except LeRoy were coming under closer supervision, while Jack Warner himself decided upon a colour production clearly distinguishable from the Universal horror style. The chosen devices to this end were a contemporary American urban setting and the provision of studio supporting players with stereotyped character images. To this extent Curtiz had to work within greater studio policy guidelines than usual, under Wallis's supervision, on *Dr X*. The plot deals with reporter Lee Tracy's investigations into a series of murders by moonlight of, among others, a drug addict and a prostitute. He narrows his search to several medical research doctors under Dr Xavier (Lionel Atwill), one of whom, Dr Wells (Preston Foster), is the one-armed culprit growing limbs from synthetic flesh. Curtiz's direction is exaggerated, but the film is genuinely frightening and very lively, while its narrative flows in Curtiz's best manner even if the studio comedy interludes are an annoyance. Grot's sinister sets, coupled with the photography of Warners newcomers Ray Rennahan and Richard Tower, and the Max Factor special effects, create Gothic images that few horror films have equalled. A sequence where Tracy plunges a lighted oil lamp full into Foster's face is especially horrific, and arguably the whole film is as good in the black and white prints seen on television as in colour. Not without reason did one contemporary review describe *Dr X* as a 'production that almost makes *Frankenstein* seem tame and friendly'.[9] Although the horror novelty was rapidly wearing off, *Dr X* none the less gained Warners a respectable profit and improved Curtiz's prestige at the studio.[10]

Wallis next allocated Curtiz to *Cabin in the Cotton*, filmed in May and June 1932 as the great slump was nearing its worst. Its theme was the exploitation of white labour in the Deep South cotton plantations, but mingled with this was the infatuation of sharecropper's son Barthelmess with spoiled planter's daughter Bette Davis. Nowadays the film is best remembered for Davis's first step to stardom, but her role is mere background to the economic struggle between corrupt planter Berton Churchill and his tenants. Fearing adverse Southern reaction, Warners steered a neutral course between the conflicting interests, and an ending whereby they agree henceforth to co-operate with each other lacks credibility. Despite the diluted attack upon the planters, there is much to admire. A hunt which leads to the planters lynching a tenant is excitingly directed, while lively contributions from Churchill, Davis, and veteran Russell Simpson compensate for a tame Barthelmess central performance. The squalor of the tenants' living conditions is contrasted with the luxury of Churchill's mansion, and the occasional superfluous scenes involving negroes are meant to engage the audience's sympathy for the underdogs. The film registered an above average profit in a very poor year.

Derived from the career of Warden Lewis E. Lawes, *20,000 Years in Sing Sing* is an extremely hard-hitting prison drama. In 1904 Lawes had become a prison guard at 19 years of age and risen through the system to be appointed governor of Sing Sing for the twenty years before his death in 1947. Lawes's reforming ideas on convict treatment were based upon those of his Sing Sing predecessor, Thomas M. Osborne, during the 1920s. When Osborne had tried to put reform into practice, however, he had fallen foul of the press and eventually been compelled to resign. As a result, Lawes cultivated the media in a fashion unparalleled in American penal history when he succeeded Osborne and resumed the drive towards reform. One part of his public relations tactic was a book to which Warners bought the rights in January 1932, although Lawes retained the power to amend the script and approve the final film. He also gave Warners access to Sing Sing itself where some scenes were shot, possibly due to Curtiz, who was before his time in his eternal enthusiasm for location filming. The film had been planned as a James Cagney vehicle, but when he was suspended, Warners borrowed Spencer Tracy from MGM to play a hardened criminal who is gradually won over to Warden Arthur Byron's reformist schemes when he becomes a convict. Tracy is temporarily released under the reform system to visit injured girlfriend Bette Davis, but at their meeting with Tracy's corrupt lawyer Louis Calhern, she shoots him to protect Tracy during a vicious fight. He voluntarily returns to prison, admits to the crime to shield Davis, and is executed in the electric chair. This scenario was tough enough, but under Curtiz the film rose to greater heights than a mundane jail melodrama and a plea for a more enlightened treatment of convicts. By mid–1932, when *20,000 Years in Sing Sing* was made, the prison movie was already an established genre as an offshoot of screen gangsterism, but usually the prison was depicted as a stifling arena, providing an excuse for successive action sequences. However, in *20,000 Years in Sing Sing* action is kept to one unsuccessful breakout scene, admittedly spectacular, as a mere antidote to normal prison routine. The mandatory studio humour all stems from the prison environment, which reinforces the film's persistent if sometimes low-key attack upon the American penal system. This is extended to the principle of capital punishment, for in the scene where retarded jailbird Warren Hymer, unquestionably guilty of a pointless murder during the breakout, takes the walk to the electric chair, he does so amid much gallows humour from his fellow convicts awaiting execution. Moreover, it is hinted that the responsibility for converting social misfits into useful citizens does not lie solely with prison reformers but with society in general – when Tracy enters Death Row after his sentence, he is greeted by the other condemned already in their cells with the caustic refrain of *Happy Days Are Here Again*. Curtiz permitted Tracy full rein to reveal that fast-talking tough guys were not a Cagney monopoly, while Davis is superbly surface-tough and laconic as a cover for her own real vulnerability. It was their only film together and whets one's appetite for more, especially under the taut control of a director like Curtiz at his best. Even some sixty years later, after countless prison movies, *20,000 Years in Sing Sing* still packs a powerful punch, impressively conveyed by Grot's coldly realistic cell sets and McGill's excellent photography, with many scenes viewed through prison bars and sometimes bar shadows as well.[11] The film brought in the best American box-office takings for a Curtiz project since *Under a Texas Moon*, but its message was seen as relevant outside the United States where it also did well and ultimately reached an overall profit of nearly 700,000 dollars, an exceptionally good showing in 1932.

Released in February 1933, *The Mystery of the Wax Museum* was another two-processed colour horror feature which carries the ideas embodied in *The Mad Genius* and *Dr X* to a climax rarely surpassed in cinema horror history. Drug addiction, press cynicism, and mental and visual disfigurement were brought together in the story of contemporary New York museum-owner Lionel Atwill who uses corpses for his museum figures until he is uncovered by wisecracking reporter Glenda Farrell. In attempting to transform her friend Fay Wray into a wax Marie Antoinette, Atwill confronts the police, is shot and plunges into a vat of his own molten wax. Particularly terrifying are the London museum fire scene early in the film, when slowly melting wax figures distort into grotesque forms, and Atwill's crumbling face in the climax sequence. Under the supervision of Blanke, with whom Curtiz had by now struck up a very harmonious working relationship, the production ingredients were much the same as for *Dr X*, with Grot's sets and Rennahan's camera work delivering telling contributions to what can now be seen, even in its black and white television prints, as a minor classic. Although the horror fad was on the wane in a fallen American market and, as was pointed out at the time, the film is 'too ghastly for comfort',[12] *The Mystery of the Wax Museum* did more than twice as well in Europe as in the United States and made an eventual profit of more than 800,000 dollars.

After *The Mystery of the Wax Museum* came *The Keyhole*, a sordid drama of private investigator George Brent whom husband Henry Kolker hires to trail wife Kay Francis to obtain evidence for a divorce. Complications ensue when Brent falls for Francis. This was the first of six Brent–Francis romantic teamings, but despite Grot's lavish sets, McGill's good photography, Curtiz's energetic handling of grubby situations, and the sprightly comedy of Glenda Farrell and Allen Jenkins, the film does not overcome a leaden script and an all too predictable outcome. All the same, its success at the box-office was above average. *The Keyhole*'s plot was similar to that of Curtiz's next film, *Private Detective 62*, namely an ex-cop turned private detective, who had slipped from respectability, investigates a lady gambler. However, the screenplay offers more scope for characterization which Curtiz and his stars, William Powell and Margaret Lindsay, exploited fully. The result is a very slick production, admirably photographed by an able addition to the already strong Warners' cinematographic ranks, Tony Gaudio. At the time it was perhaps too close to *The Keyhole*, for it reaped only a moderate profit.

Curtiz then directed additional footage for Archie Mayo's Cagney vehicle, *The Mayor of Hell*, before going on to an amiable comedy, the modestly successful *Goodbye Again* starring Warren William as an author who falls in love again with old flame Genevieve Tobin and suffers the jealous intervention of secretary Joan Blondell. Curtiz was in danger of drifting back into mundane programmers when he was assigned to a film which gave him a much more satisfying task. This was the recasting of William Powell as sleuth Philo Vance in *The Kennel Murder Case*, filmed in July and August 1933. Powell had already played Vance three times for Paramount, but these early sound films had suffered from stiltedness. Responding to Curtiz's stringent direction, Powell was seldom better as the smug but likeable detective who with the aid of two dogs unravels a murder made to appear as suicide. His screen image of effortless debonair charm displaces Vance's superciliousness in the S. S. Van Dine novels, while Curtiz's frequent use of dissolves, wipes and the moving camera keeps the action going at a cracking pace. Competent performances from Mary Astor as the murdered man's niece and Eugene Pallette as a dull-witted copper, in effect Powell's sidekick, and Reese's photography all contribute to making *The Kennel Murder Case* a gem of its genre which earned Warners a profit of close to 400,000 dollars.

Shortly afterwards, early in September 1933 Curtiz was called upon to rescue *Female*, in which the real-life husband-and-wife team of Brent and Ruth Chatterton star as, respectively, an engineer and a daytime high-powered businesswoman and night-time amorous flirt who eventually fall for each other. Diertele began the film with cameraman Sid Hickox, but the former fell ill half-way through and Wellman completed the job. With cameraman Haller, Curtiz reshot more than half the released footage, much but not all of it Wellman's, because fourth billed actor George Blackwood was not convincing enough for Jack Warner and Wallis and was replaced by Johnny Mack Brown. Curtiz insisted upon a screen credit,[13] and his footage contributed substantially to rendering *Female* a lively movie, better than the script warranted, with a profit of 155,000 dollars.

Zanuck's departure had meant the loss of George Arliss, whose Adolfi-directed vehicles had been the nearest thing to Warners prestige films since Barrymore had left in 1931. Among the directors, Warners had lost the sturdy Wellman and been unable to sign Howard Hawks permanently, but had gained Frank Borzage, Diertele, Robert Florey, H. Bruce Humberstone, William Keighley, and William H. McGann. LeRoy continued to be the chief studio director, with Bacon, Crosland, Curtiz, Enright, Alfred E. Green, and Mayo all rendering strong support but Del Ruth fading. After the shaky year of 1931 Curtiz had recovered a solid position within the directorial team, as evidenced by the fact that he had been entrusted with established leading players like Kay Francis, Powell, and Spencer Tracy. The great depression was past its worst, but Warners was still losing money and putting its faith in low-budget routine offerings and the occasional well-staged musical.

Late in 1933 Curtiz filmed *Mandalay*, a steamy tropical drama centring upon Kay Francis whose cad lover Ricardo Cortez leaves her to the mercies of dubious night club proprietor Warner Oland. She saves sufficient money to escape to Mandalay via a riverboat trip during which she reforms and falls for alcoholic doctor Lyle Talbot before her former lover reappears. She poisons the latter, and in a Grand Guignol ending he falls overboard through a porthole. Pedestrianly scripted, the film was given an unexpected panache by Curtiz who emphasizes Francis's immoral conduct in the sleazy night club by adding potentially censorable scenes against Wallis's wishes.[14] Nor did Wallis succeed in preventing the night club being portrayed as a brothel,[15] for when Francis appears wearing a striking dress, a customer at the bar observes 'They call her Spot White', whereupon his companion retorts 'It ought to be Spot Cash'. Moreover, the film includes some lively Rangoon harbour and river location scenes. *Mandalay* is an excellent example of Curtiz's ability to rise above humdrum material and, against studio resistance, bestow upon it a distinction it would not otherwise possess. His judgement was endorsed by its popular success in the shape of a 325,000 dollars profit.

At last Curtiz was given a studio top performer when he was slotted into *Jimmy the Gent* starring Cagney as a property confidence trickster. Bette Davis, now on the way to her emergence as Warners' leading female player, is Cagney's former assistant who has gone to work for an ostensibly honest rival because Cagney will not reform. For Cagney this movie represented a return to the racket business, but Curtiz chose to bring out the comedy aspects. However, the con game background was depicted more seriously with much cynical wisecracking from Davis and Allen Jenkins, while supporting player Alice White shows up well as a dumb blonde. Once more a Curtiz film netted more than 300,000 dollars profit.

Curtiz's 1934 releases ended with two directly political movies. The first, *The Key*, had been shot late in 1933, but Jack Warner had delayed its release until star Powell's first film after he had left the studio had been released. The film is set in Ireland in 1920 and Powell plays a dissolute Black and Tans officer who conducts an affair with Edna Best, the wife of British intelligence captain Colin Clive. When the latter is held as an Irish Republican Army (IRA) hostage, Powell engineers his release at the expense of a three-year jail sentence for himself. Although at the time it was sometimes criticized, especially in Britain, for misleading history, a wooden plot, and an unconvincing central character, *The Key* impresses today as an atmospheric drama with excellent Robert Haas sets and Haller camera work. Powell's amiable bounder characterization lies in his early 1930s screen stereotype, while Curtiz's direction does not flinch from unsavoury Black and Tan efforts to suppress the IRA.

This anti-British tone was repeated in *British Agent*, a spy drama based upon the real-life exploits of R. H. Bruce Lockhart in Russia from 1912 to 1918. The original 1933 screenplay had encountered pre-production British censorship problems,[16] with the result that the eventual scenario had largely been revamped into a romantic melodrama with incidental political trimmings. Leslie Howard in 1917 is sent to Russia ostensibly as an official observer at the British embassy but actually to prevent the new Bolshevik government from signing a peace treaty with Germany. He falls for Kay Francis as a young Russian noblewoman acting as Lenin's secretary who opposes Howard's endeavours to supply British finance to the White counter-revolutionary army. When he hides owing to his suspected complicity in a Lenin assassination attempt, she betrays him but then goes to his hiding place so that they might die together. They are saved by the news that Lenin is not dead after all, and that he has granted an amnesty to all political prisoners. Here Curtiz's direction is sluggish for once, perhaps on account of the political constraints on the script, but J. Carroll Naish and Irving Pichel deliver effective cameos as Trotsky and Stalin respectively. However, Curtiz, again via Haller's camera, brings the film to life in the Bolshevik revolution sequences, particularly when an ambassadorial ball is interrupted by a hail of machine gun bullets splattering across the salon mirrors, soldiers rampage through the streets in old army trucks, and a firing squad carries out an execution. Nevertheless Howard, who had some script influence, was pleased with the film and experienced a harmonious collaboration with Curtiz and, more especially, producer Blanke.[17] *The Key* had delivered only a modest profit, whereas *British Agent* made 447,000 dollars. This was above studio average at the time, but well below the largest 1934 money spinners like Bacon's *Footlight Parade, Wonder Bar*, and *Here Comes the Navy*, all of which had exceeded one million dollars profit.

In 1935 Warners weathered its economic crisis. The studio personnel remained much the same, although Del Ruth had left and Borzage was making his mark, while among the players Pat O'Brien was growing in importance. The scriptwriting team was considerably strengthened by the addition of Julius Epstein, Casey Robinson, and Jerry Wald, while Harry Joe Brown was an extra supervisor. Moreover, the company's first outright prestige production for many years, Max Reinhardt's *A Midsummer Night's Dream*, received an Oscar best film nomination. The studio was plainly on the way up again.

Curtiz's contribution to this recovery was *Black Fury*, another pro-working man social drama shot late in 1934 but not released until the following April. The only 1930s Warners film to be set in an industrial relations context, it was derived, like most of the best social conscience movies of the time, from an actual incident – the 1929 murder of miner John Barkowski at Imperial, Pennsylvania by three coal company policemen. When Judge M. A. Mussmano wrote a book about the case, Warners bought the screen rights and Muni, the chosen lead who had contractual director and script approval, sought additional plot material. He bought the rights to Harry R. Irving's play *Bohunk* before transferring these to Warners. The film is an amalgam of the two works within an Abem Finkel/Carl Erickson screenplay *Black Hell* which Jack Warner renamed *Black Fury*. Anticipating political controversy, Warners kept Mussmano's name out of the pre-publicity because a violent coal strike was in prospect in Pennsylvania when Curtiz and his cinematographer Haskin went there before filming commenced to meet Mussmano, to study the miners' living and working conditions at first hand, and to film a real mining background, a similar technique having already been carried out for plantation conditions over *Cabin in the Cotton*.[18] Furthermore, the John J. Hughes mining sets complete with drills, shafts, tunnels and real coal were built at the Warners ranch at Calabasas and mining company streets at the Burbank and Hollywood studios.

The plot focuses upon Muni as a 'hail fellow well met' miner of Polish origin who, jilted by fiancée Karen Morley just before their planned wedding, becomes involuntarily embroiled in a so-called detective agency's attempt to break the power of the mineworkers' union. Muni sees the light and in the process gets back his girl when friend John Qualen is brutally clubbed to death by the detective agency's thug blacklegs. The company capitulates to the miners' demands after Muni barricades himself in a mine and threatens to blow it up with himself and a policeman inside. This action leads to a Congressional investigation and a finding that detective agency boss Purnell Pratt provoked the strike. Although now dated with a highly predictable ending, *Black Fury* remains powerful cinema. However, despite placing the blame for the miners' grievances upon the detective agency rather than the coal company, the film was too close to the mark for comfort. It aroused political and social opposition in coal mining areas and was banned in several American states. Muni's performance was strong, but although his contractual influence at Warners was powerful, he did not awe Curtiz. When a dispute arose between them over a minor piece of casting, it was Curtiz who had his way.[19] Possibly owing to such firmness, many years later Muni considered Curtiz a delight to work with,[20] although contemporary clashes were rumoured. Nevertheless *Black Fury* is a credit to them both and to supervisor Robert Lord. Later Curtiz considered it to be too socialist in outlook for it to have been successful financially,[21] but in fact it did well enough outside the United States to make a medium-sized profit.

Curtiz opened 1935 proper as a brief substitute for Mayo on *Go Into Your Dance*, before moving on to *The Case of the Curious Bride*. This was the second of four Warners thrillers featuring lawyer Perry Mason, in this instance played by Warren William after the part had first been offered to top star Edward G. Robinson.[22] In July 1934 Wallis had wanted Mason portrayed much as William Powell had played Nick Charles in MGM's *The Thin Man*,[23] but in fact Mason is seen more as an unscrupulous professional who would accept any case for the money regardless of his client's guilt or innocence. The mystery is economically unfolded through frequent out-of-focus shots and swift cuts, although the plot is at times confusing.[24] It was on this film that Curtiz first met Errol Flynn via Wald who had promised to obtain Flynn a small part, but it was ultimately Jack Warner who insisted that Flynn appear in the film against the dual resistance of producer Harry Joe Brown and Curtiz.[25] One British review remarked that the film was not bad as mysteries go and this particular one went 'all the way to the morgue with obvious relish'.[26] However, at the box-office it went only to the tune of a moderate 132,000 dollars profit.

There followed in April and May 1935 *Front Page Woman*, a fast-moving story of rival press reporters engaged to each other (George Brent in another role first offered to Edward G. Robinson,[27] and Bette Davis), in which the lady proves she can scoop a story as well as any man. Curtiz's slick direction and Gaudio's photography figure strongly in this low-budget but entertaining, satisfying and financially successful movie. Interestingly, Errol Flynn was originally cast in a part played by Gordon Westcott, but the Warners documentation on the film does not clarify why the change occurred. Curtiz was then entrusted with Warners' attempt to outshine Shirley Temple, *Little Big Shot*. This starred Sybil Jason as the daughter of a racketeer who, just before his murder, hands her welfare over to confidence tricksters Robert Armstrong and Edward Everett Horton. After a series of adventures all ends happily for her, but Sybil Jason was no Shirley Temple, and her South African accent made it difficult for American audiences to understand her. She did not last, but this was hardly Curtiz's fault, for *Little Big Shot* shows her to much advantage – Curtiz always handled child players well, although his methods at this stage of his career were sometimes dubious – and is a breezy vehicle, with the usual wry glimpse at 1930s gangsterland. It fared moderately well at the box-office.

Thus far Curtiz had adapted himself very well to the changing 1930s Warners studio style, although he had taken opportunities to stamp his personal trademark on those films where he had judged he could get away with it through good box-office returns. What he had lacked to place him indisputably near the peak of the directorial hierarchy was suitable material for his strongest talents which could be turned into a huge hit. This vacuum was at last filled by a fortuitous policy change. Since the 1920s, Warners had steered clear of costume dramas because they were considered box-office suicide, but during 1933 Korda's *The Private Life of Henry VIII* and the Greta Garbo vehicle *Queen Christina*, directed by Rouben Mamoulian for MGM, had revealed that costume films were acceptable to cinema audiences after all. This had been confirmed in 1934 when MGM had followed up *Queen Christina* with Victor Fleming's *Treasure Island*, while Rowland V. Lee's *The Count of Monte Cristo* for Reliance was a major box-office triumph. Additionally, mounting American Roman Catholic church pressure for a stricter film censorship had culminated in the formation of the Legion of Decency during 1934. Historical dramas avoided any contemporary social controversy which might offend the Legion, while Warners had a ready-made instrument to hand in its possession of the screen rights to Rafael Sabatini's popular 1922 novel *Captain Blood*. Vitagraph had made an unsuccessful version of this in 1924, and when Warners had gained control of Vitagraph, these rights had automatically passed over. In 1930 Warners had renegotiated them with Sabatini, presumably intending to produce a sound film. However, this had not materialized, probably because it would have been too costly in the light of Warners' rising 1931 losses. The project had then lain dormant until early 1935 when it was revived with the prospect of Robert Donat, the star of *The Count of Monte Cristo*, and Marion Davies, the mistress of presslord William Randolph Hearst, in the lead roles.[28]

In March 1935 Warners declared that *Captain Blood* would be produced with a 750,000 dollars budget, a figure that rose to one million dollars in early April. But even before these public announcements Casey

Robinson had written an excellent scenario, and Brown had been chosen to produce and Curtiz to direct. By the time the budget had been increased early in April, Grot's sailing vessel sets had been built, but it had been decided that real ships would not be used, and only Donat and Flynn in a very minor part had been cast. When the Donat deal fell through, various replacements were considered,[29] but the choice eventually fell upon the unknown Flynn and the almost equally unknown Olivia de Havilland, then only 19 years of age, for the female lead. How this risky development occurred for such an expensive picture is far from clear. In late March, Flynn had been successfully tested for the Blood crew member part ultimately played by Guy Kibbee, while Bette Davis was in the running for the female lead, with competition from Anita Louise, de Havilland and Jean Muir. Jack Warner had been impressed with Flynn's test,[30] but there remained casting differences between him, Wallis, Brown and possibly Curtiz as well which were resolved only in late July.[31] Unfortunately, the Warners records on *Captain Blood* do not show clearly who took the crucial decisions. However, it was likely to have been Jack Warner, possibly to reduce the production cost after Donat's withdrawal when the budget dropped to 700,000 dollars at the end of July, although this of course was not made public. But this point is academic in that it was unquestionably Curtiz's direction that made stars out of both the young leads despite his initial misgivings about Flynn.[32] At close to two hours running time, *Captain Blood* was Curtiz's longest film since *Noah's Ark*, and he was determined to stamp his personality all over it, evading most of Wallis's efforts at close supervision as the film fell well behind schedule, particularly when Curtiz was filming the battle sequences.[33] 'I don't understand why we are still shooting close shots of the guns firing, and broadsides. There was nothing wrong with the ones we have', Wallis complained at one point.[34] Eventually, in exasperation he closed the unit down towards the end of October after more than two months' shooting by which time Curtiz's extra filming had increased the cost to 995,000 dollars.

The story is concerned with English surgeon Peter Blood (Flynn) who is unjustly sentenced to servitude in the West Indies in 1685 for treating a wounded rebel against King James II. Blood escapes from the West Indies plantation, turns pirate, and then returns to the English patriotic fold to defeat the French. As James II has been deposed and succeeded by William III, Blood is then appointed the new governor of Jamaica. Curtiz keeps the narrative moving briskly, interspersed with bouts of humour and several magnificent action scenes. The highlights of the latter are the fencing clash between Flynn and fellow buccaneer Basil Rathbone at the sea edge, filmed by Mohr in fading light at Laguna Beach,[35] and Blood's battle with the French at Port Royal. In this, a French ship is seen blasted to pieces and blown clear out of the water when a cannonball strikes the powder room. When Blood's men board another enemy ship, they swing on to the French deck with grappling irons. In the ensuing fight there is a vicious struggle in the crow's nest, while groups of men are seen crushed under collapsing decks as the camera sweeps along the swirling mass of combatants. This battle sequence, with inserts filmed by Haskin under Jean Negulesco's direction and Curtiz's arrangement, involved as large a technical crew as had ever been assembled for one film, Curtiz personally interviewing all 2,500 applicants to serve as extras. From the film it seems that Curtiz decided to camouflage Flynn's lack of acting ability and experience by relying upon his real-life debonair youthful exuberance and physical agility, although Flynn gained in confidence as shooting progressed and his early scenes were subsequently refilmed. Olivia de Havilland's beauty was emphasized in several close-ups, and she was given opportunities for character development despite having to play second fiddle to Flynn in most of their scenes together. By such devices Curtiz overcame the handicap of having to use footage from the silent version and from the 1924 David Smith's *The Sea Hawk*. The final element of the film is the rousing first screen score by famous composer Erich Wolfgang Korngold.

Curtiz's artistic judgement in his defiance of Wallis was vindicated, for upon its general release in January 1936 *Captain Blood* proved to be very popular and was nominated for the best film Oscar, although like *A Midsummer Night's Dream*, it lost to Frank Lloyd's *Mutiny on the Bounty* for MGM. American box-office receipts recorded a slight profit of some 90,000 dollars, but foreign takings were substantially higher and the overall profit veered towards 1,500,000 dollars. This exceeded Curtiz's previously most successful American film, *Noah's Ark*, and only William Keighley's topical *G Men*, a Cagney vehicle, made more money from the 1935 output. This triumph did not immediately establish Curtiz as second only to LeRoy at Warners, but his career at the studio never looked back and he had laid the foundation for his elevation to the top director position. Almost sixty years later, *Captain Blood* still carries a strong appeal and ranks as one of Curtiz's finest achievements.[36]

4

NEAR AND AT THE SUMMIT, 1935 to 1941

From the end of 1935 to the Japanese attack on the American Pacific fleet at Pearl Harbor on 7 December 1941, American unemployment steadily lessened, and by degrees cinema attendances boomed to their late 1920s level. This easing of the great depression enabled Warners to recoup its earlier 1930s losses and take a place among the Hollywood studio giants. Increasing international tension, generated by German, Italian and Japanese aggressive nationalism, added a new dimension to Warners' contemporary screen realism, particularly after 3 September 1939 when Anglo-French opposition to Hitler over Poland triggered off a European war. Until then studio output had levelled off at between fifty and sixty films per annum. About half of these were low-budget B features, made under Bryan Foy's management, which normally ran for roughly one hour and afforded A feature supporting players the chance of star parts. Among the contract players Humphrey Bogart, John Garfield, Pat O'Brien, Claude Rains and Ann Sheridan emerged into major prominence, while Muni left the studio in 1941. Of the major directors, Crosland died in 1936, Borzage and LeRoy left for MGM in 1938, and Diertele's contract was not renewed in 1940. In their place came Edmund Goulding, Anatole Litvak, and latterly Raoul Walsh. There were also occasional one-film deals for Frank Capra, Howard Hawks, and William Wyler.

Owing to the war, Hitler's conquest of much of Europe by mid–1940, and the subsequent loss of most European film markets, output was reduced to between forty and fifty films annually and Foy's B feature unit was shut down. But the previous clear division between A and B features through the size of allocated budgets meant that A features emphasized quality more than hitherto. They also became longer – usually from 100 to 120 minutes – and A budget directors like Curtiz were called upon to direct fewer films a year. As the studio profits soared, more scriptwriters were acquired and the services of first-rate composers like Korngold and Max Steiner were secured on a contract basis. For the first time in its history, Warners struck a balance between quality and quantity, and Curtiz propelled himself to the top director position with a succession of huge money-spinners. Nine of his twenty-one full-length films in this period registered a seven-figure profit, while four of the others made more than 800,000 dollars. Now well into middle age, he obtained a softer style with more depth and subtlety, his full talent range functioning with greater freedom as his triumphs mounted.

Late in 1935, prior to the release of *Captain Blood*, Curtiz had directed *The Walking Dead*. This starred Boris Karloff, borrowed from Universal, as a framed man who is executed and then brought back to life to take revenge upon all those responsible for his death. The early 1930s horror cycle had waned by now, partly because of censorship problems with the Hays Office, and post–1933 horror films did not rate A budgets at any Hollywood studio. Despite Karloff's star presence, *The Walking Dead* reflected this diminished stature with an initial budget of under 200,000 dollars. Yet it is lifted well above the normal horror rut by Curtiz's broody use of Mohr's photography and by Karloff's low-key perform-ance. The latter never kills his victims directly but frightens them into suicidal actions, with emotional close-ups of his face being shown after the death of each victim. In addition, early in the film there is a highly dramatic approach of a prison procession towards the electric chair. This moves slowly and regularly, as seen through tilted camera angles, the solemnity being stressed by a mournful musical accompaniment. The scene in which scientist Edmund Gwenn revives Karloff is as good as that in *Frankenstein*, while the finale is as riveting as in any post–1933 horror movie. When Karloff's task nears completion, he wanders around tombstones in a rain-drenched cemetery. However, as the remaining gangsters who have helped to frame him shoot him when he is advancing upon them through the tombstones, they flee and are killed in a car crash. As he dies again, his revenge finished, the camera tracks past him to stop at one of the tombstones.

Curtiz himself was responsible for Peter Milne's screenplay cont-ribution. The former fell badly behind schedule while filming the cem-etery sequence in the closing stages during mid–December 1935 when it seemed likely that *Captain Blood* would be a smash hit. Curtiz's care here took the cost of *The Walking Dead* up to 217,000 dollars, as Wallis wryly pointed out to Curtiz and producer Louis F. Edelman on 20 December. In fact Wallis had underestimated the increased cost, which had risen to 247,000 dollars, but the film none the less prospered to the tune of more than 300,000 dollars. This left the studio with little ground for complaint, and rarely has such an effective movie been crammed into a mere sixty-six minutes.[1]

Early in February 1936, while awaiting his next assignment, Curtiz was called in to film additional location footage for the opening of LeRoy's *Anthony Adverse*.[2] The film begins with a close-up of the faces of galloping horses pulling a coach. An immediate long shot switches to a field where toiling peasants have to jump swiftly out of the way to avoid the rapidly moving coach. It is one of the few lively scenes in a worthy but dull film.

Shortly afterwards Curtiz asked Wallis if he could direct the high-budget, Flynn–de Havilland vehicle *The Charge of the Light Brigade*.[3] The Michael Jacoby/Rowland Leigh story of historical hokum, which Curtiz altered only marginally, deals with the efforts of Flynn as a 27th Lancer captain to thwart the anti-British intrigues of Indian prince Surat Khan (C. Henry Gordon), aided by Russian arms and money. After Khan orders the massacre of the surrendered 27th Lancer garrison at Chukoti, Flynn becomes bent on revenge. He is transferred to the Light Brigade to fight against Russia in the Crimea and learns that Khan is present with the Russian army at Balaclava. Flynn vainly proposes a frontal cavalry charge on the Russian cannons, but he forges orders and himself joins the resulting assault. Against intensely destructive cannon-fire, the Light Brigade incurs heavy casualties but smashes through the Russian defences. In the process Flynn kills Khan but himself dies in the battle.

A distracting sub-plot, involving a romance between Olivia de Havilland as Flynn's fiancée and Patric Knowles as his brother, leads to an unevenly paced film with too many lengthy dialogue sequences, as Curtiz realized while actually filming,[4] but the action represents visual magnificence. In a hunt scene early in the film, shot at Lake Sherwood, native beaters are seen hacking their way through the jungle to drive the scared leopard in the hunter's direction before it is shot as it is about to leap upon Khan. The Chukoti siege shots are exciting, punctuated with David Niven's unsuccessful escape attempt and the visible tension among men who know their chances of survival are slim. For these sequences a British fort was built in the windswept Lasky Mesa, west of the San Fernando Valley, while many of the other exteriors were shot at Lone Pine, California, a frequent Hollywood substitute for India. However, good though the hunt and siege sequences are, they fade into insignificance compared to the climactic charge, filmed mostly at Chatsworth in the San Fernando Valley but partly at Sonora in northern California. The charge footage which ultimately appeared in the film is still one of the most spectacular sequences in cinema history. Hundreds of men and horses move forward with the famous lines of Alfred, Lord Tennyson's poem superimposed on the screen. Wave upon wave advances, but the line remains unbroken as men and horses fall and explosions toss dirt into the air. The advance escalates into a full-scale attack which breaks through by sheer will-power. The success of this scene lies also with editor George Amy, who received some 77,000 ft of film as shot by Curtiz, and second unit director B. Reeves 'Breezy' Eason, whose contribution was sufficiently important for him to be offered a screen credit which he refused in deference to Curtiz's feelings.[5] Amy managed to condense this mass of material to coherence and to instil a sense of accelerating pace without guidance from Jack Warner, Wallis or Curtiz, although the last was sufficiently in control of the overall tenor of the charge, actually directing its climax himself, to question Amy as to when some of the edited version was filmed.[6] Sol Polito and Fred Jackman's photography is excellent, while Steiner supplied an appropriately rousing score.

Despite the filming problems, which had included location climatic conditions and Flynn's erratic behaviour, *The Charge of the Light Brigade* proved to be another smash hit and was in fact the studio's most success-ful 1936 film with a profit in excess of 1,500,000 dollars. It not only confirmed Flynn and de Havilland as stars, but it also thrust Curtiz, whom at one point Wallis had threatened to replace after slow location filming progress,[7] into the top flight of Hollywood directors. The film was especially popular outside the United States, and even the reviews in Britain were euphoric despite the nonsensical history surrounding a British national battle legend. However, over the weeks occupied in filming the charge, one man was killed and many horses had to be destroyed following injuries caused by the use of the 'running W' trip wire. Flynn vainly protested to Curtiz about the trip wires, while the Californian Society for the Prevention of Cruelty to Animals visited Sonora during filming and then sued Warners which, to appease the society, levied small fines on some of the film crew, but not on Curtiz. Even before the film had received its British release in December 1936, the Women's Guild of Empire in London had exerted pressure upon the British Board of Film Censors to ban it altogether in Britain because of the cruelty to the horses and did not desist until October 1936 when Warners took out a libel action against the guild.

From *The Charge of the Light Brigade* Curtiz moved on to *Stolen Holiday*, filmed from July to September 1936 as a medium-budget Kay Francis vehicle. It was loosely based upon the life of Parisian fashion designer Gabrielle Chanel, her affair with a British nobleman, and the 1934 Alexander Stavisky scandal in France. But since Madame Stavisky was a former mannequin, Warners sought to avoid possible legal and political complications by name changes for the principal characters and script amendments playing down the social drama and instead concentrat-ing upon an artificial love interest. Curtiz was unenthusiastic about the project, with good reason, as evidenced by the completed film. Ambitious dress-maker Francis teams up with unscrupulous fortune-hunter Claude Rains. When trouble overtakes them, she stands by him until he commits suicide so that she can marry her newly found true love, staid British diplomat Ian Hunter. The first half, based upon Casey Robinson's imaginative script, is excellent economical narrative until the romantic theme submerges it and effectively converts the film into mundane, passable fare. As one British reviewer noted, it might have been a top-notch movie if the scandal story had been left to run its natural course.[8] This was what both Casey Robinson and Curtiz seemingly wanted before Wallis and producer Brown, necessarily mindful of the legal and political pitfalls, commissioned uncredited script alterations by Warren Duff and other writers. Wallis consistently brought pressure to bear upon Curtiz and even threatened at one point to assign him to B features in future.[9]

Although it was not the film that Curtiz had sought to make, *Stolen Holiday* none the less retains interest for his handling of the scandal drama element – it was significant that he fell well behind schedule while he was filming these early sequences – and for his first contact with Rains. The latter produces a noteworthy performance in only his third film for Warners, which presaged a fruitful collaboration between the two men over the next eleven years. Francis also turned in her best performance since *British Agent*, which enabled her to prop up a declining career for several more years, although *Stolen Holiday* made only a token profit for its time and was one of Curtiz's least successful later 1930s movies.

Curtiz's next film, unreleased however until well into 1937, was *Mountain Justice*. Based upon a real 1935 controversial case in Virginia, it is concerned with backwoods girl Josephine Hutchinson whose ambition to become a nurse is repeatedly frustrated by domineering, religiously fanatical father Robert Barrat. She accidentally kills him, is persecuted by the townsfolk, and is eventually saved from a mob and later from the law by enterprising local attorney George Brent, friendly doctor Guy Kibbee, and a collection of sympathizing women. Curtiz's least successful effort during these years with a profit of less than 70,000 dollars, *Mountain Justice* is now obscure and seldom seen. Nevertheless it is not without significance, particularly for Barrat's performance. He had been a Hollywood character actor since the early silent days. Curtiz had previously directed him in *Captain Blood* and *The Charge of the Light Brigade*, but he had never had as much opportunity to show fully what he was capable of as in *Mountain Justice*. His thoroughly obnoxious fanaticism, masking a homicidal tendency, is portrayed with a chilling intensity, Curtiz allowing him to steal the film. Moreover, this was Curtiz's first feature displaying a concern, aided by Haller's workman-like outdoors photography, with community pressure directed against an individual social nonconformist.

Even before he had finished *Stolen Holiday*, Curtiz had been assigned to *Kid Galahad*, a cynical and hard-boiled boxing drama which gave him his first collaboration with Edward G. Robinson. Although Curtiz had first tested the then virtually unknown Jane Wyman on 4 January 1937,

Bette Davis became the female lead in her second film after she had lost a British court case against Warners over the legal validity of her contract. Davis and Robinson had not worked together before, while Curtiz plumped for the inexperienced Wayne Morris in a key part that probably would have gone to Ross Alexander had he not committed suicide on 2 January.[10] Curtiz also selected Bogart, long a minor Warners player who had recently made a sharp impact as gangster Duke Mantee in Mayo's *The Petrified Forest*. This was an untried combination, with the complicating factor that the two leads were sceptical about each other's talent.[11] On the undoubted credit side of the balance sheet were a crisp Seton I. Miller scenario, Gaudio's suitably harsh photography, and strong support from Jane Bryan and Harry Carey.

Robinson, who accepted the role without first seeing a script,[12] plays a tough boxing manager who converts talented but timid bellhop Morris into a potential champion dubbed 'Kid Galahad' by Davis, Robinson's established mistress. She herself falls for Morris, but his eye alights upon Robinson's sister, Bryan, whom Robinson is determined to distance from boxing. When the latter discovers this liaison, his anger and jealousy are such that he arranges with his arch rival, crooked promoter Bogart, a fight for Morris which he cannot win because of his inexperience. During the early rounds Morris is badly battered owing to Robinson's deliberately false tactical advice, but while the bout remains in progress Bryan and Davis (the latter has left Robinson) convince him that Morris had always been loyal. Robinson changes his advice, Morris wins the title fight, and Bogart loses a fortune through his large bets on Morris's opponent. In the ensuing Robinson–Bogart shoot-out both men are killed, leaving Morris and Bryan free to marry and Davis without either Morris or Robinson.

In the event off-screen problems did not occur, production went smoothly to schedule, and Curtiz directed a fine film on several levels, an excellent example of Warners late 1930s style. It represented the cinema's most biting exposé of the link between American boxing and gangsterism to date, while the fight scenes are among the most brutal and realistic ever screened.[13] Although the fight game's inhumanity and ruthlessness are never avoided or diluted, Curtiz allowed more scope for characterization than usual and in the process adopted a gentle, almost sentimental approach to the main protagonists. Robinson comes across as almost schizophrenic, alternately angry and lovable while simultaneously practising professional trickery as an ingrained habit. Davis is shown as long-suffering in her relationship with Robinson, and it takes the appearance of the chivalrous, naive Morris to alert her to her true shabby situation. Her insight and inherent goodness are such that the audience is wrongly led to anticipate happiness for her, along with Morris and Bryan. Bogart plays a standard 'heavy' but does so strikingly, and Curtiz was probably impressed by their first film together. Robinson gives his habitual formidable performance, but for once he does not quite dominate the film. Instead Davis plays with an unaccustomed warmth for her at this stage of her career, which enables her to rival Robinson in a smaller part. This was perhaps Curtiz's way of helping to enhance her Warners career again after her legal setback in Britain. If so, she seems never to have appreciated it, although in later life she admitted that she had enjoyed making *Kid Galahad*, and that it had consolidated her standing with the public.[14] It also cemented Curtiz's position at Warners, for it made over one million dollars profit on a medium budget and gave further proof, if any was still needed, that he could combine cinematic excellence with studio money-making.

Curtiz was next selected to direct *The Perfect Specimen*, filmed from May to July 1937 as a Flynn comedy vehicle based upon a script worked over by many writers since Warners had bought the story in mid–1936 for Robert Montgomery and Marion Davies.[15] An unconvincing plot has the wealthy Flynn raised by aunt May Robson to be the embodiment of a sound mind in a healthy body by shutting him away from all worldly contact. Consequently keen of intellect but socially gauche, he is ill-equipped to deal with lively presswoman Joan Blondell who shows him the real, imperfect world while they fall in love. At this time comedy was Curtiz's least impressive genre, while Flynn's acting limitations remained considerable. These included an inability to deliver verbal comedy, and it is no accident that he scarcely has a comic line while the comedy relies almost wholly upon other players. Only in a boxing scene does he hold centre stage, but here the comedy is physical, close to slapstick, rather than verbal. When Curtiz entertained doubts about a leading player, he habitually surrounded him or her with strong character players. This explains why the film is heavily dependent upon a sharp Blondell performance and lively support from Edward Everett Horton, May Robson, Allen Jenkins, Dennie Moore, Harry Davenport (as Blondell's absent-minded professor father), and Hugh Herbert. With their assistance Curtiz strove to conceal the overstretched, unlikely basic plot, which develops into a series of Flynn–Blondell adventures after his family thinks he has been kidnapped. Curtiz also gave Flynn sufficient scope to project his debonair appeal. All of this does not hide the film's defects, but it does make them less obvious than in many later 1930s comedies. One scene displays a remarkable Curtiz capacity to use a heavy melodramatic situation for comedy effect when Herbert as a suspected kidnapper undergoes the police third-degree interrogation. It begins with an overhead shot from a staircase of the entire group around a table. Then the camera descends to Herbert in close-up as he watches a policeman open a pen knife, another reload his revolver and a third crack nuts in his hands accompanied by a loud crunching sound – all three images are presented in a close-up in swift succession before the camera reverts to Herbert's startled face, again in close-up. *The Perfect Specimen* now ranks as something of a curiosity, but at the time it was favourably reviewed and made Warners 771,000 dollars.

It was significant that Curtiz rather than LeRoy was selected to direct Warners' first technicolor showpiece, *Gold is Where You Find It*, filmed late in 1937 and released early in 1938. A routine story of an 1870s conflict between Californian ranchers and incoming gold rushers, it represented the studio's initial attempt at a lavish western at a time when that particular genre had lain in the doldrums since the early 1930s. The screenplay was adequate, the photography was impeccable, and Curtiz pepped things up with a forceful role for Rains as the ranchers' leader and with intermittent action, especially a short, low-key bar-room brawl and a spectacular flood climax when a dam is dynamited. Other notable Curtiz touches are a joyous crowd scene outside a telegraph office when a favourable message arrives, and much close-up work of the technical side of gold-mining involving water and the resulting mud residue which pollutes the rivers from which animals drink. However, Polito's strong location filming is partly marred by some obviously painted backgrounds in long shots, female leads Olivia de Havilland and Margaret Lindsay are mainly decorative, and George Brent's performance lacks sparkle. The overall impact is agreeable but uninspired. Its profit was only 240,000 dollars, but as a portent towards the better-known and superior *Dodge City* it deserves more attention than it has received. Even before the film was completed, Jack Warner was impressed enough with Curtiz's handling of technicolor to substitute him for Keighley on *The Adventures of Robin Hood*.

The story of this change and of the film in general is well known, and the Warners documents add nothing important. Curtiz took over at short notice on 1 December 1937, when filming was already two weeks behind schedule, and replaced Gaudio with Polito as cameraman. The delays under Keighley had pushed the budget up to almost two million dollars, the studio's most expensive film to date. But in the light of Curtiz's work on *Captain Blood* and *The Charge of the Light Brigade*, Wallis in particular realized the risk of going even further behind schedule and over budget, for most of the interiors, including a sword fight in the castle, had yet to be shot. Under the take-over circumstances, at first Curtiz was allowed much latitude,[16] but by mid-January 1938 Wallis had become very impatient at more delays.[17] Eventually filming closed on 22 January when the cost had risen to 2,033,000 dollars. The interiors are mostly directed by Curtiz who also refilmed some of the Sherwood Forest action material at Lake Sherwood, previously shot by Keighley at Chico, California, as well as some of the archery tournament sequence at Busch Gardens, Pasadena. Korngold's score was composed in February–March

1938 and superimposed on the edited version, while Miller had brushed up Norman Reilly Raine's script. Carl Jules Weyl's castle sets and Milo Anderson's costumes provide highly impressive finishing touches. The total footage had run to 193 minutes, and Ralph Dawson's superb editing to reduce this to two hours made a substantial contribution to the production before its release in May 1938.

Rebel high-born Robin of Locksley's outwitting of rascally Sir Guy of Gisbourne (Rathbone), the inept Sheriff of Nottingham (Melville Cooper), and the wily Prince John (Rains) to save England from tyranny has become ingrained in film folklore. *The Adventures of Robin Hood* remains one of the best instances of the three-strip technicolor process which became obsolete in the mid–1950s, while its fairytale, romantic and virile content is hard to fault on any level even if the comedy interludes jar here and there. A peerless cast is in top form in every case, and Flynn and de Havilland have some of their best love scenes together, showing Curtiz's unerring instinct for balance between hectic pace and character development. The climactic fencing duel between Flynn and Rathbone in the castle is unlikely ever to be bettered.

With a profit of almost two million dollars despite its high cost, *The Adventures of Robin Hood* proved to be Warners' biggest 1938 money spinner. It was nominated for the best film Oscar but lost to Capra's *You Can't Take It With You*, although Oscars went to Korngold, Weyl, and Dawson. Over the years it has lost none of its contemporary attraction and is the movie upon which Flynn's place in cinema history will mostly rest. Above all it is the film against which every screen portrayal of Robin Hood has to be measured, and thus far it has not been toppled from its perch, certainly not by Kevin Reynolds's *Robin Hood, Prince of Thieves* in 1991. Keighley's contribution to this outcome was by no means slight, but it was Curtiz who was responsible for the overall stunning impact and, as so often, his taut direction caused players to rise well above their usual performances. Even Flynn overcame his initial distaste for Curtiz's replacement of Keighley, for the daily progress reports from the unit manager show no hint of friction between them and reveal that Flynn was co-operative, especially over time-keeping. If Jack Warner and Wallis had calculated that, despite Curtiz's known tendency to over-shoot action material, he would be more likely to recover the already heavy expenditure with the finished production than Keighley, they were proved correct. However, what they could not have foreseen was that Curtiz would be able to adapt to another director's style to accommodate his own and in the process create a classic film, for the replacement of one director by another except for illness was a rare and possibly unprecedented Warners event.

From April to June 1938 Curtiz directed *Four Daughters*, for which by mid–1937 producer Brown and Julius Epstein had put together an outline script with a contribution from Lawrence Kimble. Subsequently Lenore Coffee had amended this script and Epstein had rewritten some of the dialogue, but active casting preparations had not begun until early 1938 when the film was envisaged as a Flynn vehicle. Curtiz became the assigned director in March when he commenced tests for the other main parts, especially the Lane sisters for the four daughters. One of these, Leota, was rejected and replaced by Gale Page, while Curtiz apparently favoured Charles Winninger for the role of their father after Rains had taken a test, but Wallis overruled him.[18] Meanwhile Flynn had failed to arrive at the studio from a holiday, and Jeffrey Lynn, previously cast in a minor role, was hastily substituted once it was certain that Flynn would not appear. However, the most sensational piece of casting was that of Jules Garfield, a New York theatre unknown whose name Jack Warner quickly changed to John Garfield,[19] as a ne'er-do-well with an immense chip on his shoulder. Legend has it that Garfield had failed a MGM screen test and was on his way back to New York when Curtiz saw the test and at once cast him in a difficult role. The Warners documents on the film do not expressly confirm this, but certainly Garfield was very suddenly signed for the part on 15 April while Curtiz was carrying out extensive tests and it remained possible that Flynn would star.

As a small-town soap opera *Four Daughters* was ideal to showcase the likeable and lively Lane sisters (Lola, Priscilla, and Rosemary), but Flynn's absence allowed Curtiz to transform the film into a delightful study of small-town Americana. He was hampered to some extent by Wallis as it fell steadily behind schedule and had to be cut short by nine scenes on 4 June, apart from a retake on 25 July, but this does not show on the screen. The family enjoys stable domestic bliss while each of the four daughters contemplates a romantic future. All four show interest in serious composer Lynn, but when he sends for friend Garfield to help him with his latest composition, family harmony is placed in jeopardy. The unkempt and casual Garfield soon poses a threat to sisterly relations. Eventually he marries Priscilla Lane, proves unable to support her, and commits suicide so that she can marry Lynn. In other hands than those of Curtiz this sentimental hogwash might well have become a disaster, but instead the film exudes flawless romantic entertainment. The narrative moves along briskly in Curtiz's best style, but he dwells long enough on the most heart-rending moments to create a depth of feeling without simultaneously permitting sentiment to dominate too much. Lynn's dullness would never convince anyone that one sister would be attracted to him, let alone all four, but otherwise the cast is beyond reproach. Garfield makes one of the most striking debuts in cinema history, beginning the film as a supporting actor and ending it as a star. He was nominated for the best supporting actor Oscar, while there were also nominations for Epstein and Coffee as well as Curtiz himself, his first. *Four Daughters* was also nominated for best film. Although today its charm has dated, the film still contains some irresistible moments. After its release in August 1938 it raked in more than one million dollars profit, most of which came from American box-office receipts. Coming so soon after the success of *The Adventures of Robin Hood* and LeRoy's move from Warners, the film placed Curtiz at the pinnacle of his studio career beyond challenge.

The release of *Four Daughters* virtually coincided with that of the earlier-filmed, lightweight but amiable Flynn–de Havilland comedy *Four's a Crowd*. This was Warners' contribution to the late 1930s screwball comedy cycle, envisaged for other players and already rejected by Edmund Goulding.[20] In the event, in February 1938 Warners had borrowed Rosalind Russell from MGM for the second female part and Walter Connolly from Columbia, but the production ran into unforeseen problems, and one scene involving Patric Knowles was reshot as late as mid–June a few days after preview. Although Curtiz was ultimately eleven days over schedule, he was under budget by some 12,000 dollars. Flynn plays a high-powered public relations man who is employed to boost the circulation of Knowles's newspaper. To do so, he launches a campaign against mean-minded millionaire Connolly, but then falls for the latter's granddaughter, de Havilland, while simultaneously flirting with Russell, a presswoman in Knowles's employ. In his preparations Curtiz had visited three Los Angeles newspaper offices, and the newspaper sets were almost exact replicas of one of the offices he had seen. This gives the film some sense of realism. Flynn performs moderately well in Cary Grant-style light comedy, and de Havilland is surprisingly good in a rare comedy role, but among the principals Russell is best as the hard-boiled, swift-talking career woman who can mix romance with business. Curtiz fully exploited her exceptional suitability for this kind of part, but the film is stolen by Connolly, who got on well with Curtiz, as the idiosyncratic millionaire who plays with toy train sets and revels in his reputation as the most hated capitalist in the United States. 'Why should I do anything for posterity? Posterity never did anything for me', he asks. Flynn's funniest scenes are one where he is chased by Great Danes, biting one in the paw once he himself has reached safety, and another where he holds two simultaneous telephone conversations with Russell and de Havilland, both intent upon snaring him into a marriage date. At one point all three players appear on the screen at the same time. The drawing power and personalities of its stars saw *Four's a Crowd* through financially. Although most reviews were favourable, one more perceptively noted that the direction of Michael Curtiz was commendable inasmuch as he had endeavoured to inject what little reality and practical dramatization the picture contains.[21] At Warners the film enhanced Curtiz's reputation, for he had salvaged a medium-budget project, intended for another director, with some ill-cast players.

Even before the release of *Four Daughters*, Warners appreciated that it would probably make Garfield a star, and he was hastily cast for the lead in William McGann's B feature *Blackwell's Island*. This story of a crusading reporter's one-man war against a crime syndicate and his decision to go to jail in order to expose mobster leader Stanley Fields had been filmed before the release of *Four Daughters*, but it was held back until Garfield's anticipated stardom was assured. Consequently in September 1938, Curtiz was called upon to improve it with additional footage after he had completed his next film. His contribution was slight overall, but he shot a striking jail-break scene towards the end and other externals, which partly explains a curious combination of B feature-type comedy and fast-moving action. The release of *Blackwell's Island* was again delayed until 1939 after Garfield's star status had been confirmed by Busby Berkeley's boxing drama *They Made Me a Criminal*.[22] Although the extra footage took *Blackwell's Island* over budget, it made a 349,000 dollar profit – a very high figure for a B feature – and Jack Warner awarded Curtiz a 2,500 dollar bonus.

Angels With Dirty Faces, filmed from June to August 1938, deals with the rise, fall, redemption, and execution of hoodlum William 'Rocky' Sullivan. Rowland Brown, who had written and directed crime movies in the early 1930s, had composed the scenario in August 1937 for LeRoy as a vehicle for the recently signed Dead End Kids. However, LeRoy had refused to pay Brown's price, and when the latter hawked it around other studios, Grand National bought it for Cagney. Immediately afterwards Grand National collapsed, and with Cagney's return to Warners the Brown script accompanied him at William Cagney's suggestion. When LeRoy left Warners, it was intended to allow Brown to direct, but he was soon dropped in favour of Curtiz. Warren Duff and John Wexley were instructed to amend Brown's story, but Cagney himself wanted the restoration of some of Brown's material. Wallis, associate producer Sam Bischoff, Curtiz, Duff, and Wexley all agreed, and filming on this basis began under a medium budget with plum parts for Pat O'Brien as Sullivan's boyhood pal turned Roman Catholic priest, Ann Sheridan (after some reluctance on Curtiz's part) as another childhood acquaintance who falls for Sullivan, Bogart as a crooked lawyer, and George Bancroft as a gang boss.[23]

The theme of two boyhood friends growing up on opposite sides of the law was not a Hollywood innovation in 1938, but *Angels With Dirty Faces* reached loftier heights than any of its predecessors. A top-notch cast with performances to match were supported by Polito's outstanding photography, Robert Haas's excellent sets, a vivid Steiner score, and above all Curtiz's decisive and fast-paced direction. The film broke fresh ground in that such dramas had never before allowed the central gangster to redeem himself. Cagney not only attempts to pass over a large donation to O'Brien's church funds to aid deprived boys, but he also feigns cowardice on his way to the electric chair to deter the hero-worshipping kids of his old neighbourhood from following in his footsteps. The execution sequence, in which Cagney is seen only in shadow as he shrieks, sobs, begs for mercy, and tries to claw his way out of the chair, exudes tremendous power, while the crackerjack verbal Bogart–Cagney encounters in their first film together make for a strong impact. Moreover, the warehouse gun battle scene in which the police ultimately capture Cagney is magnificently staged and handled. This scene and the death-row walk sequence were largely responsible for Curtiz going seven days over schedule. But, despite the speed of the plot, Curtiz did not neglect subtlety on the way. The energy of the warehouse battle sequence, for instance, sharply contrasts with the delicacy of one where Cagney pauses in the church to listen and silently remember the hymn which a boys' choir is singing.

Angels With Dirty Faces brought in a profit of more than 1,700,000 dollars, more than any previous Cagney vehicle. In a decade rich in crime classics his role as Sullivan stands out as the definitive gutter-sharp gangster portrayal for which he received an Oscar nomination. Brown and Curtiz himself were also nominated for Oscars, but although neither won, for Curtiz 1938 was an excellent year. Without *The Adventures of Robin Hood, Four Daughters*, and finally *Angels With Dirty Faces*, Warners would have lost considerably more money than was actually lost during the only year of this period without an overall profit. By directing these three large money-spinners within such a short time Curtiz had elevated himself, at 50 years of age, to a position far above that of even very competent studio colleagues like Bacon, Goulding, Keighley, and Litvak.

Curtiz's next film early in 1939 was the technicolor *Sons of Liberty*, which earned him his first Oscar for the best 1939 short film. This deals with Polish Jew Haym Solomon's (Rains) dedication to the colonists' cause during the American Revolution and had been under consideration as a full-length screen biography since 1937, possibly as a Muni vehicle. However, Harry and Jack Warner had been doubtful whether Solomon was sufficiently famous for such a film to make money, and they also feared that it might be attacked in the United States as blatant pro-Jewish or anti-British propaganda. During 1938 the Patriotic Foundation of Chicago had launched a public campaign for recognition of Solomon's financial contribution to the American victory over Britain, but while the Warner brothers were anxious to assist the campaign, they knew that a satisfactory full-length feature could not be produced in time. A compromise had been reached in September 1938 whereby Warners seriously considered fitting a film on Solomon into an existing 'patriotic shorts' series under Bryan Foy's supervision. Crane Wilbur, the first Solomon scriptwriter in 1937, was associated with the series as director and writer, but still the studio had hesitated until January 1939. Then suddenly Curtiz, Rains and Gale Sondergaard, who plays Solomon's wife, were assigned to a unique colour twenty-minute short – a suspect move economically in that all three were diverted from a potentially more profitable feature film.

Although *Sons of Liberty* in 1937 was designed to make Americans more aware of a specific Jewish contribution to their achievement of independence, the delayed timing of the production suggests that the final impetus had come from European events. Warners had practised a foreign policy of a kind after Harry and Jack Warner had first met Franklin D. Roosevelt in 1932 just before he had been elected president, but although the Nazis in 1934 had murdered Warners' chief representative in Germany (a Jew), the studio had refrained from producing open anti-Nazi material. However, Nazi persecution of Jews had intensified during 1938, culminating in the notorious 'Crystal Night' pogrom of early November, and the decision finally to make *Sons of Liberty* soon afterwards perhaps had one eye upon Nazi domestic anti-Semitism. The film's link between Jewry and resistance to tyranny is too glaring to be missed, while it is significant that the British are partly personified by Hessian mercenaries. *Sons of Liberty*, which does not seem to have been distributed outside the United States, was in effect Curtiz's first American patriotic film, for which Jack Warner awarded him a 3,000 dollar bonus.[24]

Curtiz's versatility was further extended when he moved on to *Dodge City*, his first real traditional western. Westerns had declined in popularity by 1933, after which they had figured primarily as cheap serials or conveyor-belt B features with former stars, character players or unknown newcomers. By 1938 there had been a tentative revival among the major studios, but the relative failure of *Gold is Where You Find It* had made Jack Warner wary of westerns and of technicolor in general. However, by late 1938 the studio had been running out of suitable parts for Flynn. Although Flynn himself was dubious about playing American heroes,[25] his reservations were overcome by his conversion in the film into an Irish-American when early in 1939 the success of John Ford's *Stagecoach* for United Artists had compelled all the major studios to review their westerns policy. As a result Curtiz was given an A budget for *Dodge City* as well as technicolor and a strong cast including Olivia de Havilland, Ann Sheridan, and Bruce Cabot. The tale of trail boss Flynn's reluctant but successful efforts to clean up a lawless railroad terminus town by defeating villain Cabot represents writer Robert Buckner's interpretation of the real-life exploits of Wyatt Earp in Tombstone, Arizona, during the early 1880s, and as part of his preparation for the film Curtiz had read Earp's book *Frontier Marshal*.[26] Via the camera of Polito and Rennahan, Curtiz brings out the scenic side of the American west and simultaneously gives full rein to his talent for action and spectacle. The highlights are a race early in the film between a railroad steam engine and a stage-coach against the background of a vast and beautiful prairie, a fearsome cattle stampede, a bar-room mass brawl which for a long time afterwards was the most lively ever filmed, a near-lynching sequence, and a showdown set on a moving train which Cabot has set on fire. Released in April 1939, *Dodge City* returned a handsome profit of 1,451,000 dollars. Along with the success of *The Adventures of Robin Hood*, *Dodge City* went far to set aside Jack Warner's reluctance to invest in major technicolor productions.

The success of *Four Daughters* had prompted Warners to seek material for a follow-up, which was located in a Dorothy Bennett/Irving White play. Julius and Philip Epstein were set to work on a script, and much the same cast was assembled for the new film, *Daughters Courageous*. This fable of prodigal father Rains who, after deserting his family, returns and helps it to resolve problems, bears a surface resemblance to its predecessor, but in fact it is very different, far superior, and unjustly neglected. The adolescent bubbliness of the daughters soon disappears, Garfield's sneering cynicism is replaced by sheer cockiness, and middle-aged love as between Rains and deserted wife Fay Bainter as well as between her and intended second husband Donald Crisp – a very rare subject indeed in 1930s Hollywood – is treated very sympathetically. This particularly stands out in two discussions between Rains and Bainter, the only two scenes in which they alone feature. The ending whereby Rains and Garfield, both afflicted with incurable wanderlust, decide to leave before they inflict too much damage upon family unity, avoids the over-sentimentality trap that it might easily have fallen into. Particularly telling is the doubt cast upon a happy outcome when mother and daughter, as the former is marrying Crisp, exchange looks as they hear the whistle of the train carrying Rains and Garfield out of their lives, presumably forever. This tacit admission of loss on their part nicely rounds off the film's consistent theme of inevitable compromise between youthful idealism and real life, with no guarantee that one has decided correctly. Not the least of this film's considerable merits is its use of small-town exteriors, admirably filmed by James Wong Howe in his first collaboration with Curtiz, while the cast is without exception irreproachable. Its very maturity was possibly its greatest drawback in box-office terms, for its profit of 643,000 dollars was disappointing in relation to *Four Daughters* and it slumped into a prolonged backwater from which it has never fully recovered.

Curtiz next directed *The Private Lives of Elizabeth and Essex*, a historical melodrama which encountered personnel problems as a result of studio policy. Chosen to play Queen Elizabeth I of England in her first technicolor movie following her 1938 best actress Oscar for Wyler's *Jezebel*, Bette Davis had already starred with Flynn, selected as the Earl of Essex, in Litvak's 1938 *The Sisters*. Although her personal relations with him were amicable, she held a low opinion of his acting and vainly tried to have Laurence Olivier replace him as the dashing nobleman whose rebellious streak leads him to the executioner's block. In addition, Olivia de Havilland was simultaneously playing in David O. Selznick's *Gone With The Wind* and was miffed at yet another insubstantial Warners role as a lady-in-waiting which failed to acknowledge her full talent range. For once she was inclined to be temperamental while filming. Curtiz thus faced above average difficulties, but considering that he was at his peak and that he was backed by a lavish budget and a strong cast, *The Private Lives of Elizabeth and Essex* is disappointing. Many have attributed this to off-screen frictions, yet Davis gives an impressive performance as the tempestuous queen torn between love and duty and, once she had accepted that Olivier would not be her co-star, she was co-operative. Flynn was not especially well cast, but he was adequate, and de Havilland after initial tantrums settled down to turn in her normal competent performance. The film's chief defect lies in too many love scenes between Davis and Flynn with extended bantering dialogue which add little or nothing to the plot and which Curtiz, perhaps out of deference to his stars' screen personas, uncharacteristically did not control in the interests of a tight narrative. His direction is at its best only at the beginning in Essex's triumphant entry into London and towards the end in the Irish scenes where Essex is starved of military resources, is defeated as a result, and decides upon a seizure of power in London.

Yet, with all its dramatic flaws and lack of conviction, the film remains important if only for Davis's bravura Elizabeth. It is also an excellent example of late 1930s technicolor, superbly photographed by Polito who was nominated for an Oscar. Similarly nominated Korngold composed a strong score, Orry-Kelly's costumes, which graced many a 1930s Warners film, were especially lavish, and Haskin and Nathan Levinson were nominated for the special effects Oscar. The appeal of the stars saw the film through to a profit of over 500,000 dollars, but it was not the smash hit anticipated and American box-office returns were very disappointing.

Curtiz next directed *Four Wives*, a sequel to *Four Daughters* with much the same cast and production crew, even the dead Garfield from the original being resurrected as an apparition. This time Lola Lane and Gale Page are happily married, Garfield's widow Priscilla Lane is engaged to composer Lynn, and fourth daughter Rosemary Lane falls for young doctor Eddie Albert. Priscilla Lane learns that she is to have Garfield's baby but marries Lynn anyway. She achieves happiness while in hospital having a baby girl when she hears her husband on the radio

51

conducting his own orchestra in a symphony he has composed around an unfinished Garfield work. She also becomes the aunt to twin girls, while Rosemary Lane simultaneously becomes engaged to Albert. This story was pulp fiction *par excellence*, but in Curtiz's hands the film is surprisingly lively and less sentimental than one might guess. Steiner's *Symphonie Moderne*, a concerto for one piano or two pianos with a large orchestra, hits the small-town middle-class mood perfectly, while the cast, particularly Rains, rises above the hammy material with great verve and even Lynn is not out of place. Now seldom screened, *Four Wives* is a good example of Curtiz's developing more gentle style in the late 1930s and of his refusal to allow potential mawkishness to spoil a good movie. Although the foreign takings were below those for *Four Daughters* and *Daughters Courageous*, its reception in the United States gained it a profit of more than 850,000 dollars.

In 1940 American federal government anti-trust policy meant that cinema owners no longer had to accept unwanted B features in order to book desired A features. This factor, coupled with the European war, caused a reduced output at Warners as the late 1930s extravagance gave way to comparative austerity with some redundancies and salary cuts. All the stars except Bette Davis had to accept offered parts or be suspended, while all players and directors faced slightly increased daily working hours. These changes worked to Curtiz's advantage, for what the studio lost in quantity it made up for in quality. This trend was helped by the advent of celluloid lacqueurs, which made possible much clearer black and white prints, while new special effects equipment included a fog machine and a deeper water tank.

Curtiz's next assignment, *Virginia City*, made in late 1939 and early 1940, was partly caught up in these changes. The film had been thought up in July 1939 as a follow-up to *Dodge City* and another Flynn vehicle. However, producer Lord would not proceed with Mark Hellinger's script,[27] and later in the year Norman Reilly Raine revised the opening on Curtiz's instructions as Wallis selected Buckner as the writer.[28] Although Buckner was awarded sole screen credit, Raine's opening was retained and other writers were involved, most notably the newly recruited Howard Koch. After the outbreak of the European war, Miriam Hopkins was cast in the female lead role against her will. Flynn did not approve of her,[29] and his reservations and possibly those of Curtiz too were justified in that she blunders through a song-and-dance routine and plays poorly in her love scenes with Flynn. He himself looks bored in his part of a Union officer trying to prevent a gold shipment from reaching the Confederate army during the American Civil War. Location-shooting in desert country near Flagstaff, Arizona, made him unwell, which led him to be unusually abrasive towards Curtiz and perhaps explains his indifferent showing.[30] Bogart was grotesquely miscast as a half-breed bandit and hams it up with a pseudo-Spanish accent, and even the action scenes lack Curtiz's customary flair. Only Randolph Scott as Flynn's Confederate opponent lends the proceedings any distinction, probably because Buckner was a Virginian with strong Confederate sympathies who gave Scott's character high priority in an otherwise leaden script. The plot progresses in fits and starts, which is so unlike Curtiz that it indicates that he must simply have lost interest. The outcome is banality, *Virginia City* ranking as one of his least impressive films as Warners top director. However, at the box-office it pulled in more than 900,000 dollars profit.

Curtiz moved immediately from this artistic low point to one of his highest when he began filming *The Sea Hawk*. Warners had acquired the rights to this Sabatini novel when it had taken over First National in 1929 and had renegotiated them for a sound version in September 1935. In 1936 Harry Joe Brown had been keen to make it as a follow-up to *Captain Blood*, and Delmer Daves had composed a scenario, but when Brown had left the studio in 1937, the project was shelved until the following year when Blanke revived it. Wallis had not liked the resulting Miller script, and Blanke had set Koch to work upon a revision almost as soon as the latter had signed for Warners in March 1939. The Miller script, unlike that of Daves, had been totally unrelated to the Sabatini novel except for the title and had modelled the central personality (Flynn) upon Sir Francis Drake within a broad factual framework of 1580s Anglo-Spanish tension. The characterizations of Drake and Queen Elizabeth I were a combination of fact and fiction, while all the other parts were pure invention.[31] Koch was a devoted anti-Fascist, and the closing stages of his script were written as war had broken out in Europe. Consequently he created it as a political analogy, which met with the approval of Blanke, Curtiz and Flynn.[32] After his experiences with Curtiz over, particularly, *Captain Blood, The Charge of the Light Brigade*, and *The Adventures of Robin Hood*, Wallis in July 1939 had spent several hours with him going over the script sequence by sequence,[33] but since then Koch's script had been written and production delays to *Virginia City* had caused the casting tests for *The Sea Hawk* to be postponed until January 1940. The part of Elizabeth was significantly smaller than in *The Private Lives of Elizabeth and Essex*, so that Warners had to find an actress other than Bette Davis. Flora Robson had already played the part with distinction in William K. Howard's British production *Fire Over England* in 1937, and another director tested her on 4 January for *The Sea Hawk*. She proved unwilling to undertake the role again owing to a simultaneous theatre offer, but Curtiz was instrumental in persuading her to accept.[34] As filmed from February to April 1940, *The Sea Hawk* portrays Elizabeth as an inspiring national leader, the Spanish Armada serving as a historical substitute for the Nazis. However, some of Koch's dialogue was too anti-isolationist to survive, although the anti-Nazi bias is glaring. This is particularly so in the opening scene where the black-attired King Philip II of Spain (Montagu Love) is sitting before a huge map of Spain and her imperial territories and fulminating against England as 'a puny, rock-bound island' offering the only resistance to Spanish world domination.

The Sea Hawk, though, is memorable less for its politics than for its high-quality swashbuckling and performances. Flynn displayed more interest than in his two previous films with Curtiz, and although sporadic clashes between the two occurred and Flynn caused shooting delays through not having learned his lines, he nevertheless turned in his best acting effort since *The Adventures of Robin Hood*. He was fully co-operative only in his few scenes with Flora Robson, filmed out of sequence at the beginning to accommodate her theatre commitment.[35] But in all other respects Curtiz pulled out his best with skilled Polito tilted camera work, shadows on walls, laid-back humour, and tremendous battle sequences. Although the court conspiracies sequences drag a trifle, the action never lets up for any length of time, with Amy's tight editing much in evidence. Robson is a suitably inspirational figure for which Flynn gives his buccaneering all against Spain, even though he knows she will have to disavow him if he is captured. Rains is crafty and villainous as the Spanish ambassador to England, and Henry Daniell is treachery personified as pro-Spanish courtier Wolfingham. Brenda Marshall, then a star prospect, is given little of note to do as the heroine, but she does it capably enough. Apart from the sea battles, in which the new deep water tank came into its own, the spectacle highlight is a Flynn–Daniell fencing clash, in which doubles stood in partly for the former (less nimble than formerly) and totally for the latter (who could not fence at all). Suspense also figures when Flynn and his followers are ambushed in Panama. He and a few of his privateering band escape but are mystified as they row towards his seemingly deserted ship. When they board it, the Spaniards there reveal themselves only at the very last moment so that resistance is impossible. The subsequent escape scene from the Spanish slave ship is also beautifully handled.

The Sea Hawk remains as satisfying a piece of entertainment as when it was filmed, aided by Korngold's rousing score, arguably his finest for the screen for which he gained another Oscar nomination. Other nominees were Grot, Levinson for sound recording, and Haskin for special effects. It was yet another huge box-office draw which demonstrated that Curtiz was without a serious Hollywood rival for action-packed costume dramas. This outcome was remarkable in that filming was plagued with misfortune from the outset and was eventually completed nineteen days behind schedule. The fencing duel occupied eight days on and off, Flynn was genuinely ill for some of the time, Curtiz himself suffered a rare bout of illness, and Brenda Marshall was injured in an off-set riding accident seriously enough not to be able to work for two weeks. In spite of an early Wallis threat to replace him for shooting unscripted material,[36] Curtiz took meticulous care over the battle scenes and over a march by Flynn and his men through swamp and jungle. Blanke protected Curtiz as much as possible from Wallis's wrath, and the box-office result – a 977,000 dollars profit – justified their judgement. *The Sea Hawk* stands as a monument to Curtiz's talent at its zenith.

With *Santa Fe Trail* Curtiz entered controversial screen territory, for Hollywood had always steered well clear of taking direct sides in the question of Civil War responsibility.[37] Even the recent *Gone With The Wind* had ignored the causes of the war as much as possible, although the depicted Southern life style and the contentment of the O'Hara slaves implies that the South wished to be left alone to resolve its own problems, and that therefore the North was to blame. In fact the genesis of *Santa Fe Trail* had no connection with Civil War origins at all. The initiative had come from Wallis who, late in 1939, had already been seeking an epic western to follow *Dodge City* and *Virginia City*, the result being a Buckner script which had envisaged a post–Civil War theme.[38] However, when producer Robert Fellows and Curtiz had brought their influence to bear, the theme had been turned into the opening of the American south-west after 1865 via the Santa Fe Railroad, with a rebellion sub-plot centring upon a character based on John Wilkes Booth, the assassin of President Abraham Lincoln at the end of the Civil War. They then believed that it would be 'a mistake to hang the whole picture on a half-madman'.[39] Somehow over the next few months in early 1940, although it is impossible from the Warners records on the film to determine individual responsibility, the post–1865 idea was transformed into a plot involving Civil War origins and the mid–1850s activities of slave abolitionist John Brown. This script came from a novel entitled *The Grenadiers* which Buckner had then been writing for five years.

Warners was courageous to allow this subject to be tackled at all, but the studio's anxiety can be seen in the retention of the misleading *Santa Fe Trail* title, the over-frequent and out-of-place comic interventions insisted upon by Jack Warner, a superfluous and equally out-of-place romantic rivalry, and Buckner's violently pro-Southern screenplay. To Southerners the determined abolitionist Brown was a mad, murderous fanatic, whereas to Northerners he was a heroic martyr. Buckner painted Brown as an arch villain for his violent anti-slavery actions in Kansas and for his 1859 raid on the federal arsenal at Harper's Ferry, Virginia. Hero Captain James Ewell Brown 'Jeb' Stuart (Flynn), the officer to whom Brown in reality had surrendered at Harper's Ferry, is the personification of slavery as a sectional issue to be settled from within.

Wallis emphasized to Curtiz the importance of keeping within budget on the evening before shooting commenced after the latter had conducted extensive tests,[40] and although Curtiz initially responded with speedy progress, the film fell behind schedule partly because of Flynn's waywardness[41] but mostly because of Curtiz's preoccupation with detail and perfection in the action sequences, especially the Harper's Ferry siege. Completed in mid–September 1940, *Santa Fe Trail* displeased Jack Warner who actually considered cutting out the scene of Brown's execution.[42]

Despite Curtiz's apparent script agreement with Fellows and Buckner, a suspicion lingers that he distorted studio intentions. The action centres upon Brown in Kansas and at Harper's Ferry before his execution, and at times Stuart is reduced to a peripheral figure. Indeed in one scene Flynn actually complained that Raymond Massey, who plays Brown, had too much dialogue.[43] Moreover, the shadow of coming conflict looms over the entire central plot, with two scenes containing prophecies of the Civil War standing out. The first is when six Union officers, including Stuart and his Northern friend George A. Custer (Ronald Reagan), huddle around a Sioux Indian woman's fire as she foretells that a future conflict will convert them into bitter enemies. She ends with the words, 'Somewhere in the east a man is lighting a torch . . .', at which point the screen dissolves into Brown jabbing his finger at a map to indicate the whereabouts of Harper's Ferry. The second scene is the execution where, after Brown's death, Olivia de Havilland tells Flynn that she has a vision of something much worse than Brown's hanging corpse, to the accompanying music of *John Brown's Body*. Both scenes appeared in the Buckner screenplay, but the manner in which Curtiz presents them makes a disproportionate impact on the overall film.

This is another Curtiz film which is underrated. Massey's towering study of obsessive and unstable fanaticism as a god-appointed avenger alone makes it well worth seeing. Flynn's performance in his last western with Curtiz is several notches above that in *Virginia City*, while Van Heflin is good as a discharged anti-slavery officer cadet who joins Brown's followers. An early train gun battle is well staged, and the cavalry charge against Brown at Harper's Ferry (in fact he was captured by a mere dozen troops) is a minor repeat of the assault in *The Charge of the Light Brigade* as Union soldiers advance into murderous fire. *Santa Fe Trail* might have been one of Curtiz's best films but for the irrelevant romantic interludes, the painful Alan Hale–'Big Boy' Williams comedy antics, and the lack of characterization for Reagan and Olivia de Havilland, the latter having little to do either qualitatively or quantitively. Even so, it is no routine western, if only because it is one of the most sombre of its genre in the 1940s with a dark, pessimistic atmosphere throughout, admirably conveyed by Polito's camera and complemented by Steiner's score.

Sombreness was also the dominating tenor in *The Sea Wolf*, Jack

London's already much-filmed novel. Warners had had this film under consideration since September 1937, when it had purchased the screen rights from Selznick as a projected Muni vehicle with LeRoy. However, Muni had rejected the film and when LeRoy left the studio, Wallis had shelved the project.[44] But Blanke pursued it for Edward G. Robinson on the basis of the screenplay by Norman Reilly Raine and Abem Finkel prepared for Muni. Robinson had accepted the part in December 1938,[45] but active preparations did not gain momentum until late in 1939 when Robert Rossen took over the script. By mid–1940 Wallis was ready to go ahead, instructing Blanke to ensure that Rossen's script would not make the film too expensive.[46] By the time Curtiz had become the selected director in September 1940, George Raft was being offered a major role, which he rejected on the eve of filming, but all the other parts remained open. Garfield then stepped into Raft's shoes at very short notice for several reasons: London was one of his favourite authors, Warners had recently refused to loan him to Columbia for Sidney Salkow's *The Adventures of Martin Eden* (another London book), Rossen was a fellow fervent anti-Fascist, and Curtiz was his favourite director. After extensive tests between 20 September and 31 October, Curtiz selected Ida Lupino, a Warners contract player, for the main female part, the unknown Alexander Knox in another major part, and a formidable list of character actors before he began filming on 4 November. The film was completed six days behind schedule on 8 January 1941.

Although Curtiz reduced Rossen's script while filming was in progress,[47] the completed work nevertheless overdoes the verbal philosophizing. However, it is virtually superb from the outset. The opening sequences in a dingy San Francisco bar, together with a collision between a ferry and a larger ship, create a strong dramatic atmosphere even before the main plot unfolds. From then onwards Curtiz's sense of action, conflict and tension combine to shove the obligatory studio love interest between escaped convicts Garfield and Lupino well into the background. Two survivors of the ferry crash, author Knox and Lupino, are picked up by a mystery ship named *The Ghost* captained by the psychopathic but well-read Robinson as 'Wolf' Larsen, who rules with an iron hand. He sails an erratic course, creates unrest among the crew, and then incites incidents to satisfy his cruel streak and simultaneously demonstrate his power. Eventually the crew discovers that he has periodic blind spells, during one of which a mutiny ensues and he is left aboard alone as *The Ghost* lists after it is struck by gunfire from Larsen's brother's ship. The three escaping fugitives take the lifeboat back but Robinson imprisons Garfield. Knox then confronts the blind Robinson and sacrifices himself to ensure Garfield's freedom and the lovers' escape. As *The Ghost* finally sinks, captain and writer go down with it.

Then at the peak of his ability, Robinson gives one of his most masterly performances. A complex mixture of anger and reason, violence and restrained wisdom, Larsen's power-ridden megalomania is convincingly conveyed – 'Better to reign in hell than to serve in heaven' (underlined in Larsen's copy of Milton's *Paradise Lost*) is his creed – in an inordinately difficult role. Particularly striking is the close-up image of Robinson's face contorted with fear when the crew first learns of his blindness. His reduction of Larsen to a vulnerable human being in the closing scenes is an exceptional talent in full flow. He dwarfs the remainder of the cast, but the support of everyone is first class, especially Gene Lockhart as an alcoholic ex-doctor who commits suicide by jumping from the ship's masthead, and Barry Fitzgerald as the ship's cook and Robinson's informer among the crew. Polito's photography incisively captures the moody, fog-encased, doom-ridden atmosphere, admirably bolstered by Grot's sets and Korngold's score. Like *Santa Fe Trail* to a lesser extent, *The Sea Wolf* was far ahead of its time in its study of pathological depravity, but none the less they were both well received with a profit of over one million dollars and 868,000 dollars respectively, primarily due to American takings in both instances. *The Sea Wolf* stands as a permanent tribute to the Warner apparatus at its smoothest and to its chief director as one of his finest films.

During 1941 Curtiz directed two patriotic pieces against a background of the rising American–Japanese friction that led to Pearl Harbor. These films were *Dive Bomber*, released in August, and *Captains of the Clouds*, completed before Pearl Harbor but not issued until January 1942. Both were A budget technicolor movies dealing with aviation, buttressed by excellent aerial and location photography which gained Oscar nominations. The films are above average for what is now a dull genre, but they are of interest as evidence of Warners' resolve to combat complacency and domestic isolationist sentiment. *Captains of the Clouds* is the less intriguing because it is well-worn material with Cagney as an experienced civilian pilot who cannot knuckle down to Royal Canadian Air Force discipline but who ultimately proves himself in action at the cost of his own life. Curtiz delivers the recruiting poster message with his usual efficiency but in such a predictable and stereotyped fashion that the extra spark that might have lifted it to a place among his best work is absent. Cagney, who had a great influence on the script, plays a part made to fit him like a glove for all he is worth, but most of the rest is founded upon stock studio situations and characterizations. Possibly Curtiz was reluctant to disturb a tested studio formula and risk the dilution of its patriotic attraction.

Similar criticism can be levelled against *Dive Bomber*, although to a lesser extent. Overlong at 133 minutes, it none the less contains some unusual features. Flynn's characterization as a doctor interested in pilot blackout problems is more restrained than usual with few devil-may-care exploits. He does not dominate, as Cagney does in *Captains of the Clouds*, but shares the limelight with Fred MacMurray and Ralph Bellamy in the common enterprise among the bombing section of the US Naval Air Corps. The irrelevant sexual exchanges involving Alexis Smith are kept to a bare minimum. No serious romance emerges to interfere with the hunt for scientific progress, as symbolized by a restaurant scene where Flynn and MacMurray discuss an idea for solving pilot blackout and ignore their exasperated lady companions. The superfluous comedy – Allen Jenkins' efforts to avoid paying alimony to his estranged wife by hiding in a hospital isolation ward – is also reduced to three brief interludes. Even the artificial dramatic tensions between the scientists are relatively low-key and quickly phased out in order not to interrupt the propaganda theme more than necessary. The detailed treatment of the experiments aimed at eliminating blackout bestows a technical gloss on the content unique for its time.

In this crucial respect the screenplay of Frank 'Spig' Wead, a former naval pilot forced to retire from the service through injury, is much in evidence. But even in this unprecedented context for Curtiz, he is able to generate tension, particularly in a sequence of pilot experiments in a specially constructed pressure cabin. Location filming at San Diego naval base and aboard the aircraft carrier USS *Enterprise* adds to the general air of service realism. *Dive Bomber* turned out to be the last time that Curtiz and Flynn worked together, for when they were both assigned to *They Died With Their Boots On* in July 1941, they became involved in a fist fight on the set, whereupon Curtiz, then 52 years of age compared to Flynn's 32, refused to direct the star again.[48] Walsh replaced Curtiz on the Custer screen biography. But whatever reservations Curtiz and Flynn had about each other by this time, *Dive Bomber* was another million-dollar plus profit-maker and one of the studio's highest 1941 money-spinners despite its technological slant. The message that the American navy was sparing no effort to modernize itself had struck a receptive chord with the American public. The American entry into the war ensured that *Captains of the Clouds* did equally well financially. Curtiz would probably not have directed this at all but for the unforeseen break-up with Flynn, which possibly helps to explain why at rock bottom it is a standard Cagney vehicle with no special Curtiz stamp upon it.

The extent of Curtiz's directorial supremacy at Warners in these six years can be measured financially. In that time fifteen films of other directors had pulled in profits of more than one million dollars each, but only Goulding, Keighley, and Walsh had managed more than one such success. Goulding with four (three of these Bette Davis vehicles) ran next to Curtiz's nine, but this represented a poor second. By far the largest money-spinner was Hawks's 1941 *Sergeant York*, showing a profit of more than five million dollars which none of Curtiz's films could match. However, Curtiz was well ahead of the field in artistic quality as well as financially. Of the fourteen other than *Sergeant York*, half are now rightly considered comparatively lightweight, hardly fit to be ranked alongside the best Curtiz features of the time – Borzage's 1937 *The Green Light*, Bacon's 1939 *The Oklahoma Kid*, Goulding's 1939 *The Old Maid*, Keighley's 1940 *The Fighting 69th*, Litvak's 1940 *All This and Heaven Too*, Keighley's 1941 *The Bride Came C.O.D.*, and Walsh's 1941 *The Strawberry Blonde*. The other seven were Diertele's 1937 *The Life of Emile Zola*, Goulding's 1938 *The Dawn Patrol*, 1939 *Dark Victory*, and 1941 *The Great Lie*, Wyler's 1940 *The Letter*, John Huston's 1941 *The Maltese Falcon*, and Walsh's 1941 *They Died With Their Boots On*. These are all meritorious films, but only *The Letter, The Maltese Falcon, They Died With Their Boots On*, and possibly *The Life of Emile Zola* can rival *The Charge of the Light Brigade, The Adventures of Robin Hood, Angels With Dirty Faces, The Sea Hawk*, and *The Sea Wolf* as classics in the correct sense of that much misused word. However, war was to afford Curtiz the opportunity to extend and improve upon an already impressive record.

1 Curtiz (right) discusses *Mission to Moscow* (Warner Brothers, 1942–3) with
Joseph E. Davies (left) and Walter Huston, who played Ambassador Davies
in the film

2 From left to right Harry M. Warner, Joan Crawford, Jack L. Warner, and Curtiz, probably taken shortly after Joan Crawford had won the best actress Oscar for the title role in *Mildred Pierce* (Warner Brothers, 1944–5)

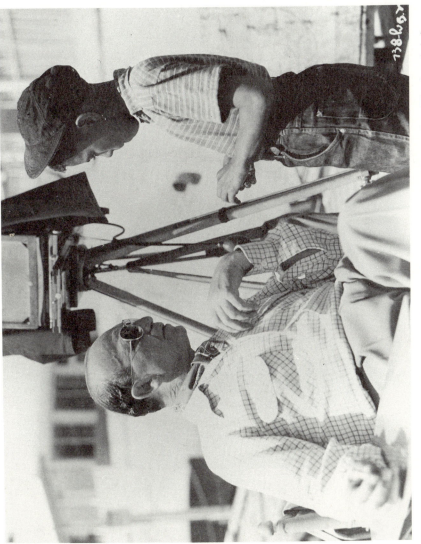

3 Curtiz talking to the real-life son of Puerto Rican actor Juano Hernandez. The boy briefly appeared as Hernandez's son in *The Breaking Point* (Warner Brothers, 1950), Curtiz's underrated masterpiece

4 Curtiz caught in pensive mood while preparing for *Jim Thorpe – All American* (Warner Brothers, 1950)

5 Curtiz locked in earnest conversation with Elvis Presley on the set of *King Creole* (Paramount–Hal Wallis Productions, 1958)

6 Spencer Tracy bids a grim farewell to girlfriend Bette Davis before he goes to the electric chair in *20,000 Years in Sing Sing* (Warner Brothers, 1932). Arthur Byron is the sympathetic warden

7 Errol Flynn wins Olivia de Havilland and the plaudits of grateful sovereign Richard the Lion-heart (Ian Hunter) in *The Adventures of Robin Hood* (Warner Brothers, 1937–8)

67

8 James Cagney as George M. Cohan struts through the *Yankee Doodle Boy* number in *Yankee Doodle Dandy* (Warner Brothers, 1941–2), Curtiz's superb musical biography

9 At the Paris railway station as the Germans move in, Humphrey Bogart as Rick learns that Ingrid Bergman has let him down. A beautifully directed key scene from *Casablanca* (Warner Brothers, 1942). Dooley Wilson plays Sam, Rick's black associate

10 Claude Rains as Captain Louis Renault orders the round-up of all the usual suspects after Major Strasser (Conrad Veidt) has been shot in the famous climactic airport scene from *Casablanca* (Warner Brothers, 1942)

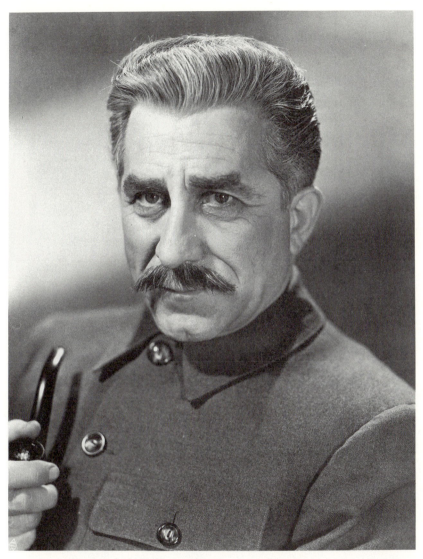

11 Manart Kippen, a real-life anti-Tsarist revolutionary, as Stalin in *Mission to Moscow* (Warner Brothers, 1942–3), one of many examples of Curtiz's meticulous attention to detail when casting even minor parts in his quest for screen realism

12 From left to right Zachary Scott, Jack Carson, and Joan Crawford discuss business in *Mildred Pierce* (Warner Brothers, 1944–5), Curtiz's outstanding *noir* melodrama

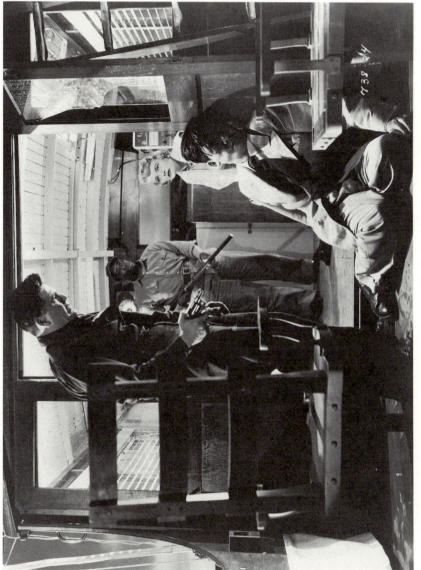

13 John Garfield shoots Victor Sen Yung, while Juano Hernandez and Patricia Neal await developments in *The Breaking Point* (Warner Brothers, 1950)

5

WORLD WAR, December 1941 to August 1945

After Pearl Harbor, as the United States moved over to a war economy, unemployment virtually vanished, and cinema attendances boomed to record levels. This was likewise true of Britain, the chief Hollywood export outlet, these factors more than compensating Warners for the loss of its Far Eastern market. No feature film actually lost money during the war, and the studio profit for this period was massive. However, for war taxation reasons some of the biggest stars would not sign long-term fixed-salary contracts, Cagney and Edward G. Robinson going freelance in 1942. In addition Olivia de Havilland tested the legality of adding player-suspension periods to the lengths of contracts and won her case in 1943–4. Henceforth players were better placed to reject parts which the studio tried to impose upon them. Production dropped from some forty films in 1941 to about half that number by the end of the war. Cutbacks among the directors, producers, technicians, and players inevitably followed, while the diminished output reduced Jack Warner's administrative burdens. His attention returned more to actual film production, which reduced Wallis's authority and created tensions between them, prompting the latter's 1944 departure. Wallis was replaced by the more deferential Steve Trilling, but although the contract system was in the early stages of decline and important studio personnel changes occurred, Curtiz remained unaffected. During the war he completed only eight films. The first five served as the spearhead of the company's war propaganda campaign in accordance with basic themes laid down by the newly formed government Office of War Information (OWI). The first two have deservedly become enduring film legends.

The first was *Yankee Doodle Dandy*, Curtiz's first screen biography. The number of Warners musicals had dwindled in the late 1930s when Harry and Jack Warner had become convinced that they represented box-office suicide. Only two had been made in 1940 and 1941, but *Yankee Doodle Dandy* was a special case because it concerned the legendary George M. Cohan, the actor–author–composer–dancer whose musicals had dominated the Broadway theatre from 1902 to the early 1920s. After his mid–1930s retirement, Cohan had received many offers to film his life, but he had declined them all until he learned late in 1940 that he was dying of cancer. Warners had acquired the screen rights in March 1941, and Cohan had agreed that Cagney should play him, but protracted negotiations involving William Cagney and Buckner had failed to produce an agreed script with Cohan until the end of September. However, the star himself was still not content, and with his contract shortly due for renewal and the studio anxious to retain him, Jack Warner had allowed him to call in the Epstein brothers and James North for further script revision despite the risk of a Cohan contractual veto. On the day after shooting commenced, William Cagney informed the studio that his brother would not sign another contract. In a vain effort to change his mind, Jack Warner sanctioned the reshaping of the film to the Cagneys' specifications and gambled that Cohan would approve. In fact Cohan at first was far from happy, but Edward Raftery, his Hollywood representative and a partner in the New York legal firm which had negotiated the Cohan contract with Warners, saw a rough cut and conveyed his approval to Cohan. Then the latter himself was largely satisfied when he saw the completed film before its release.[1] He lived until 5 November 1942, long enough to know that the film was a smash hit.[2]

Given the many people concerned with the script credited to Buckner and Edmund Joseph, the latter's contribution being minimal,[3] it was predictably indifferent. Cohan himself was responsible for the early emphasis upon the Four Cohans family troupe, but the precise contributions of the Epsteins, North, and the Cagneys cannot be ascertained in detail. Nor is it clear from the Warners archives how deeply involved Curtiz was, but it is unlikely that he was bypassed, for Cagney greatly respected him and knew from experience that he habitually altered and added to scripts during shooting. On top of a shaky script was a cast merely adequate except for Cagney himself and outstanding veteran Walter Huston as Cohan's father. However, the film's deficiencies are completely swamped by the patriotic gloss of the musical numbers, by Huston's touching approach, and above all by a combination of Cagney's magnetic, arrogantly strutting performance and Curtiz's sure-touch direction. The flagwaving element was increased because filming had coincided with the outbreak of war. It symbolized what the new recruits to the forces would be asked to fight and possibly die for, which is why Cagney and Curtiz went all out in the patriotic songs. Officially these were staged and directed by LeRoy Prinz and Seymour Felix, but their sheer scale in many instances indicates a strong Curtiz guiding hand. *Grand Old Flag* sees hundreds of extras, each carrying an American flag, marching on a huge stage as a giant Stars and Stripes is superimposed on to the screen while the curtain is falling. Cagney bombasts his way through *Yankee Doodle Boy* in Cohan's own deliberately adopted dancing style, while *Over There* is set in a First World War American army base where Cagney and Frances Langford lead soldiers in the mass singing as the lights fail. The connection with the Second World War comes only at the end in the *Off the Record* number, and after the president's private award to Cagney of the Congressional Medal, the highest civilian decoration, in Cagney's spontaneous jig down the interior White House steps. When he strolls into the street, he joins a marching military parade singing *Over There*. The introduction of President Roosevelt in person (Captain Jack Young), coupled with Cagney's assertion at one point that democracy means the ordinary citizen having access to the top man, represented a propaganda master-stroke. Despite the heavy patriotic emphasis, Curtiz none the less did not ignore straightforward dramatic opportunities, for Huston's death scene in Cagney's presence is truly moving in traditional Hollywood fashion.

The reviews of the film were ecstatic about both Cagney and the film itself, and it became the star's greatest grosser as well as his favourite movie. It raked in a profit of almost five million dollars for Warners and was by far the studio's largest 1942 money-spinner and Curtiz's most profitable project to date. Cagney deservedly won the best actor Oscar, Levinson did so for the sound effects, and so did Heinz Roemheld and Ray Heindorf for their musical direction and adaptations of the Cohan numbers. The film itself, Buckner, Curtiz, and Huston also received Oscar nominations. It is easy to see why it was such a colossal contemporary success, but although its American chauvinism is now exaggerated, it continues to stand out purely on the strength of its own outstanding cinematic merits. It is difficult to envisage any other Hollywood director of the time who would have achieved the same result with the same material.

Curtiz next began the incomparable *Casablanca*, a much-discussed film now in effect frozen in time. The Warners archive shows that four days after Pearl Harbor a studio story analyst routinely summarized a New York office manuscript of an unproduced Joan Alison/Murray Burnett play entitled *Everybody Comes to Rick's*. The records and various personal recollections suggest that, also as routine, Wallis farmed it out to various studio staff to receive their reactions. This process embraced Curtiz, Lord, Keighley, Rossen, Vincent Sherman, and producer Jerry Wald. Their responses were varied, but by the end of 1941 Warners had purchased the screen rights. Early in January 1942 the project was assigned to writers Aeneas MacKenzie and Walter Kline, but a month later Wallis instructed the Epstein brothers to revise their previous script. After a publicly announced notion of casting Ronald Reagan and Ann Sheridan in the leads for what was intended to be a medium-budget film was swiftly discarded. Bogart was selected as Rick and Wallis was intent upon Hedy Lamarr as the female lead until MGM refused to loan her out. By the end of February, with shooting due to start at the end of April, nobody except Bogart was definitely cast. Even as late as mid-April Jack Warner wished to replace him with George Raft but encountered successful opposition from Wallis and Curtiz, the assigned director in mid-March. They then turned their attention towards securing Ingrid Bergman's services from Selznick, but Wallis also instructed Curtiz to test Michele Morgan, presumably in case Bergman proved unavailable. Selznick agreed to release her, but other roles were still causing difficulties, evidently due to disagreements between Curtiz and Wallis, at least in part, and shooting had to be delayed until mid-May.

Meanwhile the script had also been causing chaos. The Epsteins had been summoned to Washington in late February to collaborate with Capra on the *Why We Fight* documentaries, and although while in Washington they continued to work upon what Wallis had by this time renamed *Casablanca*, their duties there had lasted longer than anticipated. Consequently other writers, Koch and Casey Robinson, were summoned, although when the Epsteins at length returned to California, they remained closely involved. Indeed it was they who personally persuaded Selznick to release Bergman for the film, although it is unclear whether they were following the orders of Jack Warner or Wallis. The upshot of all these developments was that no final script had emerged by the time Curtiz began filming, while the casting, which included many non-contract players, was finalized only at the very last moment.

It is improbable that Bergman would have been cast without Curtiz's approval. All the main characters except Rick and his black pianist Sam (Dooley Wilson) were European (in the play the female lead was American), and one is struck in the film by the large number of European non-contract players or unknowns that American regular character players were readily available for. Curtiz's marked preference for Europeans is clear and in some instances documented. He wanted Dutchman Philip Dorn as resistance leader Victor Lazlo if Austrian Paul Henreid, then with RKO Radio, had been unavailable, and Conrad Veidt was borrowed from MGM as gestapo chief Strasser after Curtiz had tested and rejected Austrian Otto Preminger and German Reinhold Schunzel. The Hungarian Peter Lorre and Briton Sydney Greenstreet figure as local racketeers only in small background roles. Uncredited Frenchman Marcel Dalio appears as Rick's croupier; Russian Leonid Kinskey plays barman Sacha; Austrian Curt Bois (with whom Curtiz had worked in Austria) is the pickpocket; Canadian-born John Qualen had Norwegian ancestry and was thus ideal for Norwegian resistance worker Berger; Hungarian S. Z. Sakall is also on Rick's payroll as Carl; uncredited Helmut Dantine, another Austrian, becomes Bulgarian refugee Jan Brandel; and Frenchwoman Corinna Mura was preferred to Lena Horne and Ella Fitzgerald as the uncredited café singer. The two most prominent unknowns were

Joy Page as Annina Brandel and Madeleine LeBeau as Rick's ex-girlfriend Yvonne. Not much is known about either, for they made no further impact in films, but LeBeau, a recent contract signing, was a real-life escapee from Nazi-occupied France. The Warners records positively confirm that Curtiz personally cast Sakall, Kinskey and Page. They also contain strong circumstantial evidence that he cast all the other minor parts as well, including Austrians Ilka Gruning and Ludwig Stossel as the elderly Austrian or German couple about to emigrate to the United States. Such meticulous casting bears far more the Curtiz hallmark than that of the Warners machinery. A genuine European atmosphere was provided, and among the character parts Americans Dan Seymour and Frank Puglia play Arabs rather than Europeans.[4]

Once filming at last got under way, the main concern of Bogart, Bergman, and Curtiz was a completed screenplay, although Curtiz turned the lack of a known ending to advantage in, for instance, the following dialogue exchange:

Bergman:	Can I tell you a story, Rick?
Bogart:	Has it got a wow finish?
Bergman:	I don't know the finish yet.
Bogart:	Well, go on, tell it. Maybe one'll come to you as you go along.

These lines were spoken with the utmost conviction that only reality can impart. At length Koch and Casey Robinson came up with the famous ending. However, the prolonged debate over who contributed what to the final film is largely pointless, since the vast bulk of the plot was derived from the original play, and the dialogue and situations (excellent though these are) are less crucial than the inspired direction, Arthur Edeson's flawless low-key photography, and the perfection of the players in every case. Curtiz relied upon sheer speed of direction to conceal the plot's numerous holes and an unknown ending, the importance of which has been much exaggerated. It caused anxiety to Bergman and Bogart in particular for the first two-thirds of the film before the ending was decided upon, but it also enhanced their performances, while to Curtiz scripts were never more than a basis for negotiations and he would sometimes film without one.[5] In this instance he frequently consulted on the set with Bogart, the Epstein brothers, and Koch, and although arguments arose, these proved temporary and amounted to nothing out of the ordinary at Warners.

The plot centres upon the activities of refugees from Nazi-occupied Europe in Rick's Café Americain in Casablanca, French Morocco, on the eve of Pearl Harbor. Rick eventually abandons his shattered idealism to rejoin the anti-Nazi cause in aiding Lazlo and his Norwegian wife Ilsa, Rick's former beloved in Paris when she believed her husband to be dead, to escape the Germans and Vichy prefect of police Captain Louis Renault (Rains). This tale represents the purest Hollywood nonsense. No uniformed Germans ever set foot in Casablanca throughout the Second World War, while there was no such thing as letters of transit signed by Free French leader General Charles de Gaulle. On Rick's own admission he is no businessman, yet he has somehow acquired sufficient capital after fleeing from France to establish his fashionable café, to pay its staff for two or three weeks after Renault closes it to placate Strasser, and to sustain a large casino gambling loss to enable Brandel to buy an exit visa. When and how he teams up with Sam, an unlikely combination in real life, is never disclosed. Neither American nor French troops 'blundered into Berlin' in 1918. Lazlo is the Czech with the Hungarian-sounding name. However, these glaring story flaws pale into insignificance within the magic of a film that continues to be a very satisfying cinematic experience long after the political conditions that spawned it have evaporated. Bogart emerged as a first-rate romantic actor, while Bergman, who liked and got on well with Curtiz (they never worked together again), turned in her most memorable Hollywood performance. But the vital element in the film is without doubt Curtiz's spellbinding direction, evidenced even in incidental scenes such as an early police street round-up and one on a station platform in torrential rain. Rick and Sam are waiting to leave Paris when Rick reads Ilsa's letter stating that he will never see her again, the rain on the paper obliterating the written words. Uniquely for Curtiz, personal romance is skilfully woven into the basic propaganda theme, so that neither dominates but both linger in the memory, as they have done for many in the past half-century.

Casablanca was completed in August 1942, eleven days late and at a cost of 1,039,000 dollars – 75,000 dollars over budget. There was then a release delay while Steiner composed his score. During the October preview, audience reaction suggested to Wallis that a scene showing Bogart and Rains together in uniform on a fog-bound freighter discussing their plans to fight the Germans should be added at the end. However, before Wallis arranged for this to be filmed, in early November the allies landed in French North Africa, whereupon the release of the film was speeded up. As a result the planned additional scene was scrapped in favour of a new dialogue line, contributed by Wallis himself. Thus was born Rick's unforgettable closing comment, 'Louis, this could be the beginning of a beautiful friendship.'

The conference between Winston Churchill and Roosevelt in January 1943 at Casablanca, coinciding with the film's general release, provided a welcome but probably superfluous bonus. *Casablanca* proved an instant hit and made a profit of almost six million dollars (American and foreign takings were approximately equal). It has continued to charm audiences ever since. Oscar nominations went to Bogart, Rains, Edeson, and Steiner, although inexplicably not to Ingrid Bergman. Curtiz, the Epsteins, and Koch won Oscars, as did the film itself. These Oscars have stood the acid test of time better than any others, although the unsuccessful nominees, especially Bogart, were hard done by.

Curtiz's next film, *Mission to Moscow*, was his most political. Joseph E. Davies had been American ambassador in Moscow from 1936 to 1938, and after the Soviet Union and the United States had become allies, in December 1941 he had published his memoirs dealing with his spell in Moscow. Warners had bought the screen rights early in 1942, and the assigned producer was Buckner, who had been Moscow correspondent of the London *Daily Mail* in 1934–5. Buckner instructed Koch and novelist Erskine Caldwell to prepare the script for Davies's approval. Jay Leyda was called in to supply technical advice regarding the script and Weyl's sets to create the atmosphere of 1930s Moscow. Both Buckner and Koch conferred extensively in June and September with Davies, who provided them with material not contained in his book and approved the script as well as the actor to play him, Walter Huston, after he had preferred Frederic March.[6] Curtiz approved the script on 24 August. He took scant interest in the political content and expressed reservations about too much dialogue,[7] but he agreed with Buckner at the outset that 'the vital facts should be faced squarely and honestly, without pulling any punches or compromising for any squeamish reason whatever'.[8]

Casting began in late August 1942, but attempted script interventions by Davies and a personality clash between Buckner and Koch[9] complicated Curtiz's task throughout. Shooting commenced on 9 November, and by the end of the month a host of freelance character players had been signed even though there was no dialogue ready to give them.[10] On 13 December, Davies and Jack Warner visited the set and, together with Buckner, Curtiz, and Koch, the entire company discussed the script and the scene order. All the same, in late December players were complaining vigorously to Curtiz that dialogue was being passed on to them too late for it to be learned in time.[11] Furthermore, although Curtiz had tested Dudley Field Malone, a close friend of Davies, for a Churchill cameo part on 28 December, he had still not definitely been cast three days later, probably due to Curtiz's opposition, and was ultimately filmed in the role on 4 January 1943 in the absence of an alternative. This, like Davies's own appearance on the screen to introduce the film, was a sign of Davies's determination to exercise to the full his contractual right of script approval and in effect to shape the final production. Towards the end of January it was even suggested that Curtiz should leave the film to be completed by Don Siegel, who was in charge of montage,[12] ostensibly to allow Curtiz to begin *This is the Army*. Evidently Curtiz demurred, and he finished the film on 2 February when it was 148 minutes long.

Even then Davies was not satisfied. Although he liked the film in general, he wanted it to contain a message for future American–Soviet understanding and forwarded detailed script amendments to that effect.[13] In April, when he was due to leave for Moscow shortly and wished to take a print with him, he tried to have a Chinese scene omitted, although for technical reasons he was unsuccessful.[14] But, possibly at Mrs Davies's insistence, he did succeed in having an additional scene inserted. This was set in a Soviet cosmetics factory and involved Mrs Davies (Ann Harding) and Mrs Molotov, the wife of the Soviet Foreign Minister (Frieda Inescourt). Curtiz filmed this scene on 16 April and with this the film was at last finished.

Apart from Huston as Davies, great care was taken to ensure that the character actors were made up to resemble the famous personalities they were playing. Curtiz himself had selected them, except for Malone as Churchill, with a view to maximum realism, nowhere more evident than in the choice of Stalin. He is played by Manart Kippen, a genuine active revolutionary against Tsarism who had been compelled to leave Russia in 1906 before he turned to acting in the United States in 1910.

Curtiz's direction converted pedestrian material into a fascinating propaganda compilation, given some reality by the insertion of newsreel clips. While in Moscow, Davies had sought closer American–Soviet ties, but he had accepted too unquestioningly much of what he had seen, and his 1941 book was an exercise in retroactive self-justification now that the Soviet Union and the United States were partners against Hitler. When early in the film Davies visits Berlin *en route* to Russia, Germany is projected as full of robot-like peasants ready to endure any hardship for the sake of sufficiency to come, Hitler Youth reading *Mein Kampf* and singing their fatherland's praises, and goose-stepping troops. This sets the tone for the subsequent portrayal of the Soviets as warm-hearted, well fed, noble, and socially emancipated which predominates through-out. Davies accepts the bugging of the American embassy as essential to Soviet security, while all the images of foreign diplomats attending a ball indicate anti-Soviet intrigue on a vast scale. The theme that a Soviet Union surrounded by foes has a right to protect herself against saboteurs, spies, and traitors forms the favourable approach in the film to the notorious 1937–8 show trials of past leading Communists. Although the preceding terror is briefly referred to, the defendants' confessions of treason in open court are interpreted as genuine. Anglo-French appeasement of Hitler before 1939 and betrayal of the League of Nations as well as American isolationism come in for specific condemnation. Curtiz's use of Bert Glennon's camera is at its most superb in a sequence where, when Davies has returned to the United States, he exhorts a Madison

Square Garden mass rally not to be hostile to the Soviet Union. The camera plunges down upon his centre-screen isolated figure in a studio crane shot of incredible inventiveness.

Mission to Moscow was released in late April 1943, whereupon attacks upon it surfaced almost immediately. They began on 9 May when Bosley Crowther's *New York Times* review complained that Warners had cheated with the facts. A letter in the same issue from Professor John Dewey of Columbia University and Suzanne La Follette, chairman and secretary respectively of an international commission of inquiry into the 1937–8 Moscow trials, challenged the film's interpretation of the trials and fancifully charged that the film was basically anti-Congress, anti-democratic, and anti-truth. Eventually in June both Davies and Koch answered the criticisms in print, but the dispute petered out inconclusively as the film itself was registering only a very mediocre box-office profit of 132,000 dollars. However, the press had been divided, while Warners had received many letters of congratulation and only relatively few of disapproval. Jack Warner saw the film's opponents as 'Red-baiters and Facist (sic)',[15] and he defended the film both in public and in private.[16]

There matters rested until October 1947 when the House Un-American Activities Committee (HUAC) investigating alleged Communist subversion in Hollywood received Jack Warner's testimony that the film had been made at President Roosevelt's mid–1942 instigation, a version of events he repeated in his 1964 memoirs. The Warner Brothers archive does not positively confirm Roosevelt's involvement, but the various memoranda indicate that Jack Warner, presumably with brother Harry's authority, was the main driving force behind the film. Buckner reported directly to him, while Wallis was bypassed. This might imply that Jack Warner was acting in accordance with presidential wishes, especially as the Hays Office had expressly warned him before filming concluded that considerable political controversy would result.[17] The whole truth about the derivation of *Mission to Moscow* will probably never be known beyond all doubt, but due to the 1940s furore it remained under a cloud until well into the 1970s. Indeed even then and later it was still capable of arousing political criticism in Britain.[18] The hysterical tone of the critics was an unconscious tribute to the sheer power of Curtiz's film-making. A more detached observer would see *Mission to Moscow* as simply remarkable visual propaganda with a rare insight into world history from one involved personality.

Robust, no-nonsense American patriotism dominated *This is the Army*, based upon the 1941 Irving Berlin musical revue. Although Warners bought the film rights in October 1942, Wallis, Curtiz, and Casey Robinson had met Berlin earlier, and changes were made for the screen version, most notably the introduction of white players where the stage

350-strong cast had all been black, mostly unknowns. The story, such as it is, concerns the production of a mammoth musical by recent army recruits, but, as with *Yankee Doodle Dandy* and unlike the stage revue, this event is linked to the First World War. No fewer than nineteen songs are mostly rendered by ordinary soldiers wholly or in part, while two are sung by Berlin himself. One such was *My British Buddy*, which was not in the stage show and was later added for its British release after being shot in Britain under the direction of George Stevens. The all-black element was partially retained, most conspicuously in the *What the Well-dressed Man in Harlem Will Wear* number, vividly danced and sung to a punch-bag rhythm supplied by black world heavyweight boxing champion Sergeant Joe Louis.

The film was made from February to June 1943 at Burbank where a special military camp was established. Personnel required for filming marched to the studio at 6 a.m. and were made up and costumed by 8.30 a.m. They received a small amount of extra pay, but all the Warners employees contributed their salaries to the Army Emergency Relief Fund. On the set the troops remained under military discipline, the non-commissioned officers collaborating with the assistant directors to ensure swift obedience to Curtiz's requirements. All this is most in evidence in the spectacular finale, *This Time is the Last Time*, carried out in Curtiz's most ostentatious style and the only number in which he supervised LeRoy Prinz's musical direction. A cast of 500 approaches the camera head-on upon the largest stage Warners had ever constructed for any musical. The lighting for this required 200 technicolor arcs, three times more than had ever been used previously, while in the background stands an American eagle, an edifice measuring 150×75 ft. This sequence alone occupied five days of filming and three weeks of rehearsals under officer discipline. As a lavish technicolor military musical, *This is the Army* remains hugely enjoyable within its own undemanding terms, but Curtiz's contribution is largely routine. It pulled in even more money than *Casablanca*, although Warners received back only the cost.

Passage to Marseille, filmed in the second half of 1943, was Curtiz's only stab at war-time realism while the war was actually in progress. It concerns four French convicts who escape from the Devil's Island penal colony to fight with de Gaulle against the Nazis. As in *Casablanca*, Curtiz cast Europeans as much as possible and even tested Helmut Dantine for the lead before accepting Bogart. The only other American actor to play a Frenchman was George Tobias, who had worked with Curtiz in *Yankee Doodle Dandy*. In *Passage to Marseille* Bogart is simply the recognized leader of a group which includes Peter Lorre, Philip Dorn, Dantine, and Tobias. All are convicted criminals who are guilty of the crimes of which they were accused except Bogart, who plays an anti-Fascist publisher framed for murder to silence his newspaper's anti-Nazi editorials.

The convicts escape in a canoe which is picked up by French freighter *Ville de Nancy*, bound for Marseille shortly before the fall of France in 1940. When France concludes an armistice with Germany, the crew and passengers are divided between those who wish to reach France headed by Major Duval (Sydney Greenstreet) and those who wish to sail to Britain, including Captain Malo (Victor Francen) and Captain Freycinet (Claude Rains). Duval attempts to seize the ship, but when he is thwarted after a battle, the pro-Nazi radio operator radios the Germans and a *Luftwaffe* bomber arrives. This is shot down, and the convicts play a leading part in defeating both Duval and the Germans, although Lorre is killed in the process. The rest of the group and Freycinet all reach Britain to join the Free French air force. After a bombing mission Bogart's plane is badly damaged and Bogart himself is killed. The film ends when, over Bogart's grave, Freycinet reads out his letter intended for his young son in France, a son he has never seen.

Warners deferred the release of *Passage to Marseille* in the hope that the allies would open a second front in France, but when this had not materialized by February 1944, the film was then issued. Despite an unnecessarily cumbersome flashback technique, it registers as a strong film, very powerful in Curtiz's best fashion in places. The Devil's Island scenes, greatly enhanced by James Wong Howe's brooding photography in the darkly lit artificial jungle, and Weyl's convincing prison sets are impressive in spite of difficult technical problems in both cases. The two freighter battles are also splendidly staged with the assistance of Don Siegel close-ups. Here and there a semi-documentary approach (rare in Hollywood propaganda features) appears, most conspicuously on the Free French air force station where British war correspondent John Loder interviews Freycinet, the externals for which were filmed at the Army Air Force base at Victorville, California. In the scene where the *Ville de Nancy* picks up the emaciated convicts in the drifting canoe, the camera lingers upon the rescue procedure as though the convicts were in reality survivors of a torpedoed ship in mid-Atlantic. As Howe observed at the time,[19] Curtiz deliberately avoided Hollywood's usual glamorous depiction of war, and it is no accident that both Bogart and Lorre are killed without knowing that the liberation of their country is assured. Conveying the message that pursuit of victory over a merciless enemy might lead to one's own dehumanization, is a risk that Curtiz does not shirk. Immediately after Lorre's death, Bogart machine-guns helpless German airmen on the wings of their downed machine in the sea. Here Bogart's eyes flash with unremitting hatred as he enjoys watching the Germans fall into the sea to die. When Captain Malo calls him an assassin, he responds by asking the captain to look at the death and destruction around him to identify the real assassins. In allowing Bogart to explode in this way in a scene filmed as scripted, Curtiz was perhaps giving expression to his own hatred of Nazism as reports of the Nazi genocide of the Jews in Europe were filtering through to the United States.

As in *Dive Bomber*, romance was bundled aside in favour of the propaganda theme – Michele Morgan's part as Bogart's wife in occupied France is small for a leading lady,[20] and it is made plain throughout that she comes a very poor second to France in her husband's affections. The 1942 Charles Nordhoff/James Hall story had contained no female interest. Co-writer Jack Moffitt had introduced one with Curtiz's acquiescence, but subsequently it seems that Curtiz was unenthusiastic about both first choice Nina Foch and Morgan, and he frequently reduced parts filled by players he did not want. To emphasize the rightness of the Free French cause, the image of pre–1939 France is distinctly unfavourable as presented by Curtiz. French Prime Minister Edouard Daladier is shown as solely to blame for the 1938 Munich agreement with Hitler, while French police stand aside as pro-Fascist thugs smash up Bogart's newspaper office, another powerful scene. Although Duval blames Britain for the 1940 French defeat, no mention is made of the British participation in the pre–1939 appeasement of Germany, in contrast to *Mission to Moscow*.

Passage to Marseille was not the happiest of films off-screen. There was intermittent tension between Curtiz and Howe over lighting and set problems, Bogart and Lorre were sometimes not at their most co-operative, Curtiz had wanted Siegel to film the freighter battle scenes but met successful resistance from Jack Warner and Wallis, and Curtiz himself was too impatient for results when the film fell behind schedule and technical problems were not easily overcome. Only on locations did shooting proceed smoothly.[21] The unit manager wryly reported after Howe had threatened to walk off the set,

> If Mike would only be patient and not try to run the Camera Dept., the Effects Dept., the Electrical Dept., and all the other departments and give orders all day long everyone would be able to function much more efficiently.[22]

However, on the screen Curtiz's perfectionism shows, and the box-office returns gathered in a profit of well over one million dollars.

With the tide of war turning strongly in the allies' favour early in 1944, Warners propaganda output decreased, and Curtiz took charge of *Janie*, an amiable light comedy with a war-time background. This successful Broadway play deals with juvenile Joyce Reynolds's farcical attempts to persuade her respectable middle-class parents Edward Arnold and Ann Harding to welcome the soldiers recently stationed near their small home town. She and her teenage female friends become attracted to the young troops while struggling to remain loyal to their local boyfriends. This dated humour is quintessentially American, a war-time version of the Andy Hardy series without Mickey Rooney's vitality. Curtiz touches are little in evidence, although the small-town atmosphere is as well captured as in *Four Daughters*. Among the adults, Robert Benchley's inimitable brand of wry comedy as the parents' bachelor friend stands out. The overall effect is competent but uninspired, although *Janie*'s profit reached more than 1,700,000 dollars despite poor box-office receipts outside the United States.

Equally in American vein was *Roughly Speaking*. This screen biography of Louise Randall Pierson from 1902 to Pearl Harbor was based upon her own 1943 best-selling autobiography, to which Warners immediately bought the film rights. Pierson's theme in her book was that of an ordinary American woman who never became rich or famous but continually bounced back from adversity. Her screenplay, written in the second half of 1943 in consultation with producer Blanke, maintained the same approach but left out some living persons for legal reasons and toned down the character of others. Beyond that she was resistant to changes, and her contract gave her script approval. Either she or Blanke wanted Bette Davis to play her,[23] but apparently the latter rejected the role, and thereafter matters drifted until Curtiz became the director in March 1944. Shortly after that, Rosalind Russell was contracted from Columbia, and Jack Carson was cast as Pierson's second husband. There is no positive confirmation in the Warners records on the film that Curtiz was responsible for these developments, but Blanke had wanted Ray Milland, Sonny Tufts or George Brent,[24] while a later press article claimed that it was Curtiz who had chosen Carson.[25] It was certainly a typically unorthodox Curtiz selection, for up to this time Carson had almost always been cast as an amiable goon. Russell, too, had contractual script approval, but she was much more flexible than Pierson and generally shared Curtiz's approach to film-making. The eventual script was largely that of Pierson, amended in places by Catherine Turney (uncredited, presumably in deference to Pierson). Under the circumstances, Curtiz's room for manoeuvre was in theory more limited than usual, particularly as Pierson was present on the set every day as a so-called technical adviser.

Shooting began on 26 April 1944 with Polito as cameraman, but the film soon fell behind schedule. There seems to have been no special script friction between Curtiz, Pierson, and Russell, although Pierson stated immediately after the film was completed that he had constantly reduced her to ashes.[26] By mid-June the film was twenty-one days late on a fifty-four day schedule, the budget had been revised from 1,491,000 to 1,723,494 dollars, and Jack Warner was pressing for speedier results.[27] Probably at Russell's request, Joseph Walker from Columbia had replaced Polito on 16 May, a move necessitating retakes, but nothing expedited progress to any significant extent and on 10 August, when shooting ended, the film was as much as thirty-six days behind schedule. Part of the reason was the length of the screenplay, for when the film was submitted for censorship to the Hays Office on 16 September, it was with an added but still incomplete prologue, shot by Haller, and yet the print ran for 151 minutes. At its preview in November 1944, a further six minutes had been added, although about fifteen minutes were cut from the generally released version.

However, despite these cuts and subsequent ones that reduced the film to marginally over two hours, too much is crammed into too short a time, a good example being the brief shot of cheques being signed as the sole symbol of 1920s pre-depression extravagance. None the less, *Roughly Speaking* possesses considerable interest even if the comedy is overstretched. Russell's firebrand who combines a successful business career with intermittent child-bearing and in the process overshadows her two husbands showed for the first time, to her own surprise, that she could tackle dramatic intensity and added a dimension to her later career.[28] Curtiz's influence upon this development is plain. Moreover, of great interest in the light of Curtiz's next film, Carson's performance nearly stole the film, while growing rich is depicted as the complete and only avenue to self-fulfilment. This implied criticism of American social climbing evidently eluded Pierson, although she, Curtiz, and Russell seem to have been united in successfully resisting OWI pressure to depict the aim of the Pierson family's Second World War contribution as the creation of a better world.[29] Box-office takings outside the United States proved disappointing, and the profit of 422,000 dollars was Curtiz's lowest of the war except for *Mission to Moscow*.

Much more promising material for Curtiz emanated from the 1941 James M. Cain novel *Mildred Pierce*, the film version of which was the brainchild of Jerry Wald. He had remained a 1930s Warners writer for seven years, performing much the same machine-like screenplay function that Zanuck had done in the late 1920s. By 1941 he had become a producer, and Wallis's 1944 departure paved the way for his rise to front-rank producer status with Blanke. Wald and Curtiz had been personal friends since at least 1934, but they had never worked together until Wald had grown determined to bring *Mildred Pierce* to the screen with Curtiz as director.

Cain's novel was a sleazy domestic drama without crime or thriller ingredients, unlikely as it stood to be allowed by the Hays Office. Wald had hit upon the idea of introducing a murder at the opening and then a flashback narrative device which would open the way for the 'moral retribution' element so beloved by the censors. Jack Warner had given Wald no encouragement because of the censorship problems, but the latter had persisted to the point where he had approached Cain himself in mid–1943. When Cain had first agreed to write a screenplay and then withdrawn in September, Wald had invited Thames Williamson, a story analyst and an aspiring writer, to try his luck. The resulting script was good enough for Wald to show it to Jack Warner in January 1944. Warner agreed to buy the screen rights, Williamson modified his script to meet Hays Office objections, and by early March the film had received Jack Warner's official blessing. However, Williamson's script had Mildred murder Veda, her daughter, after the latter had been discovered making love with Mildred's second husband. Wald had other ideas for the story and farmed the script out to Catherine Turney, whose strength lay in the conventional tearjerker, and then to Albert Maltz, whose specialisms were action and crime.

At this point various actresses, including Ida Lupino, Ann Sheridan, and Barbara Stanwyck, were considered for the part of Mildred. This seems to have been destined for Rosalind Russell, presumably on the strength of her showing in *Roughly Speaking*, still being filmed. But Joan Crawford, who had not appeared in a major role since signing for Warners, lobbied relentlessly for the part. By degrees her sheer perseverance won over Wald, Trilling, and finally Jack Warner as it dawned on them that her movement into early middle age, combined with the rags-to-riches roles she had so often played at MGM during the 1930s, rendered her more suitable for Mildred than they had previously appreciated. However, while the casting of Mildred had remained uncertain, sometime between July and September 1944 Wald approached Curtiz to direct while he was still occupied on *Roughly Speaking*. Curtiz had already been assigned to direct the Cole Porter screen biography *Night and Day*, but Cary Grant would not give Warners a definite date when he would be available to play Porter. This fortuitously freed Curtiz for *Mildred Pierce*, a project he was more enthusiastic about because of its content and its suitability as a potential *noir* film. Meanwhile Turney had been unable to agree with Wald, and various other writers – including the eventual sole credited one, Ranald MacDougall – were called in to collaborate with both Curtiz and Wald on the final screenplay. Some five years later Curtiz claimed that he personally had telephoned and met Cain to gain his express approval for the basic script that was filmed.[30] The fundamental conception of *Mildred Pierce* had been Wald's, but Curtiz, MacDougall, and other writers greatly contributed to the detailed fulfilment.

Once Curtiz had become the assigned director, the casting became more tentative. As he came close to admitting to the press while the filming of *Mildred Pierce* was in progress, he was not initially keen on Joan Crawford.[31] According to film legend, his first choice was Bette Davis, but this is not borne out by the Warners documentation on the film where there is no evidence that Curtiz or anyone else ever considered her. He thought of Barbara Stanwyck, but she was either unavailable or Curtiz dropped the idea after he had tested Crawford, according to different post-shooting versions which the Warners records do not clarify. Whatever the truth of the matter, he accepted her, and once he became convinced that she was interested only in making a good film rather than playing the former star, they got on famously. According to Crawford herself many years later, Curtiz praised her fulsomely before the entire crew at the end-of-filming celebration.[32] The evidence from the Warners files points in the same direction. The remainder of the casting was a collaborative enterprise between Curtiz, Trilling, and Wald, but Curtiz's influence was clearly considerable and normally decisive. Wald is supposed to have preferred Shirley Temple as Veda, although in fact Selznick had offered Warners her services and been turned down while extensive testing of other young actresses was under way. Virginia Weidler was probably the favourite until 20 and 21 November when Curtiz tested the inexperienced Ann Blyth, who was chosen after only three Universal B movies. It was also no accident that Jack Carson and child actress Jo Ann Marlowe were selected for parts immediately following impressive performances in *Roughly Speaking*. Zachary Scott was soon cast, and the greatest headache proved to be the casting of Mildred's first husband, where Wald and Curtiz favoured Ralph Bellamy but eventually, just prior to filming, accepted Bruce Bennett from a field which at one time had included Dennis Morgan, Donald Woods, Carson, and Scott.[33]

Shooting opened on 7 December 1944. Realizing that Curtiz's skill as a film-maker required maximum freedom, Wald concentrated upon keeping Jack Warner and Trilling, who had wanted Vincent Sherman to direct,[35] at bay. At one point Wald remonstrated strongly with Trilling over a cancelled montage.[35] Although Curtiz and Wald experienced initial qualms over the best cameraman for Crawford, both seeking either Howe or Edeson who were unavailable, the choice finally went to Haller. Everything was then in place except for the script which needed detailed rewriting. Curtiz knew the outline story beforehand and decided to film chronologically, as Crawford desired, leaving the murder and police station sequences until last when, it was assumed, the final script would be ready. Curtiz spent much time on camera angles and lighting, soon incurring Jack Warner's wrath for being a week behind schedule in a project with a budget of 1,342,000 dollars over fifty-four days. Warner's pressure upon Curtiz to forgo what the former saw as visual faddiness persisted, but the daily amount of footage increased towards the end of filming. When shooting was completed in February 1945, Curtiz was nevertheless thirteen days late, and extra exteriors and interiors were filmed on 2 and 3 March.

Mildred feels trapped in her marriage to unemployed husband Bert

(Bennett) and is chiefly concerned to bring up her two daughters, Kay (Marlowe) and Veda (Blyth), to expect the material things of life denied to her. When the marriage breaks up, she becomes a waitress and simultaneously evades the lecherous attentions of Bert's ex-partner Wally Fay (Carson) while using him to secure a house from playboy Monty Beragon (Scott). She converts this into a restaurant with her friend and ex-colleague Ida (Eve Arden). Her restaurant business booms, and she opens a chain of five restaurants as Beragon displays a romantic interest in her. Kay unexpectedly dies, after which Mildred's life becomes centred around the selfish Veda, whose insatiable materialistic excesses are encouraged by Beragon, himself now in money difficulties and a financial parasite upon Mildred. She splits from both Beragon and Veda, but to get the latter back, she marries Beragon at the price of a third share for him of her restaurant profits. This arrangement works temporarily as she and Veda are reconciled, but Mildred then loses her business due to Beragon's underhand dealings. When she goes to his beach house for a showdown, she finds him and Veda in each other's arms. Thereupon Veda informs her mother that she and Beragon will be married after his divorce from Mildred, but just as the latter is leaving he turns upon Veda and tells her that he will not be divorcing Mildred. In her rage Veda shoots him dead. To cover for Veda because she believes that Veda's materialism and selfishness are her fault, Mildred tries to frame Fay for the murder. When the police arrest everyone involved, Bert confesses because of his belief that Mildred committed the murder and Mildred confesses partly to save Bert and partly to shield Veda. However, the police unravel the truth. Mildred and Bert are reunited, although an alternative ending of her leaving the police station alone was also filmed.[36]

Curtiz gave this soap opera plot gleaming treatment. The opening scenes of Beragon's murder by an unseen assailant, Mildred's effort to frame Fay by luring him to the beach house and then locking him in with the dead body, and the policy station exchanges before the main story dissolves into flashbacks, are electric. The 1942 southern California atmosphere is vividly captured through the locales of coastal roads, crowded restaurants, rain-drenched piers and promenades by night, and the avarice of the central figures. Money forms the basis of social class, a repeat dose of the philosophy which dominates *Roughly Speaking*. Curtiz's direction keeps the plot moving steadily, while the players are without exception in top form. Joan Crawford embodies energetic ambition, Eve Arden wisecracking sisterly humour, Jack Carson ruthless opportunism, Zachary Scott smooth but brainless idleness and lust, Bruce Bennett worthy salt-of-the-earth dullness, and Ann Blyth detestable self-centred go-getting heedless of the consequences for others.

Traditional weepies were usually produced during the war for the women left behind at home while their men were drafted into the forces, the principal reason why Wald had set Catherine Turney to work on the script. But Curtiz's approach challenged a way of life and required a different social climate for an ideal release time. The 1945 summer was occupied with the Steiner score, editing, and sound fine-tuning, after which Jack Warner deferred the release in the hope that the war with Japan would end shortly (Germany had been defeated in May), and that the film would fare better in a post-war atmosphere. This would inevitably embrace the anxieties and insecurities about marriage and relations between the sexes which *Mildred Pierce* exploited. On this basis it was released a few weeks after Japan's surrender in September 1945. It raked in a profit of just over four million dollars and gained the best actress Oscar for Crawford, revitalizing her career. Oscar nominations went to Blyth, Arden, and Haller, although it is difficult to see why their contributions were rated above those of Carson, Scott, and above all Curtiz himself. Indeed, behind the scenes he had much impressed Wald by his resolve, whatever the obstacles, to reach maximum cinematic effect.[37] As a result, Wald was keen to work with Curtiz again, a development which was to bring the latter two of his best post–1945 films.

Mildred Pierce, arguably the finest *noir* film of its genre in cinema history, rounded off a very impressive wartime record for Curtiz as Warners acknowledged top director. More than thirty Warners films from 1942 to 1945 inclusive had gathered in a profit of more than one million dollars, but apart from the special case of *This is the Army*, the three largest studio box-office draws were *Casablanca, Yankee Doodle Dandy*, and *Mildred Pierce* in that order. All three have remained classics from a period when high profits from films came too easily due to the war. However, Curtiz himself was fully alive to the danger this trend posed to the achievement of higher standards for films. Soon after the release of *Mildred Pierce*, he told a journalist that he wished to direct better films but doubted whether audiences were ready for them. He caustically added, 'The trouble is picture companies can't lose money today. The very best they can hope for . . . is to break even.'[38] Curtiz's warning fell upon deaf ears everywhere in Hollywood, but post-war events were to show that his fears that a search for long-term quality would be sacrificed to the short-term profit motive within the studio contract system were totally justified.

6

THE TWILIGHT WARNERS YEARS, September 1945 to April 1953

Curtiz's sole contribution to Warners' 1946 releases was *Night and Day*, filmed in the war's closing stages. Jack Warner had first met famous composer Cole Porter on 10 June 1943 to discuss a possible screen biography to follow up *Yankee Doodle Dandy*. Porter had agreed in principle a month later and signed a contract on 29 December. By April 1944 producer Arthur Schwartz had come up with an outline screenplay close to the final film, based upon the idea that Porter's achievements, despite having been a near-cripple since 1937 as the result of a riding accident, would serve as a morale booster to wounded servicemen facing civilian adjustment problems. At that time the war had been expected to last for several more years, Jack Warner in August trying to hurry things along by selecting Curtiz as director with Porter's approval. At the end of September, Porter had agreed to Schwartz's outline script and the choice of Cary Grant to play him, after consultation involving Curtiz. By the end of the year, Warners had borrowed Grant from Columbia, but his marriage to heiress Barbara Hutton was crumbling and he had refused to be tied down to a definite date for starting work on *Night and Day*. Curtiz, whom Grant had accepted as director in August 1944, had meantime been diverted to *Mildred Pierce* and temporarily took little interest in the *Night and Day* script, although he was present on 28 January 1945 when Grant and Schwartz had agreed upon the basic story outline.

When Grant and Monty Woolley had been signed simultaneously, shooting had been scheduled to begin in February, but Porter himself had undergone a lengthy hospital stay until March, which delayed his approval of script amendments. Then Grant had been dissatisfied with the result and refused to appear for work until early May. The unit manager accurately predicted, 'Since Cary Grant has now agreed to come in and work on the story . . . the script will not be out for quite a while.'[1] Grant was determined to have his way on the Porter characterization, thus causing further script delay. More fundamentally, the story was giving rise to difficulties because Porter's life, aside from his music and taboo homosexuality, had been undramatic.[2]

When filming actually started on 14 June, the war was all but over and the production was lumbered with a star who was not only miscast but was also interested in his first colour film mainly as a steadying influence after the collapse of his marriage and the ensuing divorce. Moreover, Grant knew Porter slightly and was unsure how to play the part.[3] Almost from the outset Grant wanted scenes reshot with new dialogue.[4] Curtiz strove valiantly to keep the production moving,[5] but he was handicapped first by Selena Royle's illness, then by a go-slow of technicians which prevented the swift set changes he desired, and finally by a combination of Porter's contractual hold over the script and Grant's obstruction. Curtiz grew uncharacteristically edgy – on 26 June he had cameraman Glennon replaced – while clashes and a divided responsibility with LeRoy Prinz over the musical numbers, a legacy from *Yankee Doodle Dandy* and *This is the Army*, made matters worse. Disputes with Grant persisted, and shooting fell badly behind schedule as the script had constantly to be modified at Grant's insistence. On 25 July, Curtiz replaced Peverell Marley with Haller as a cameraman, but progress remained slow. Although matters went more smoothly for a few days towards the end of August, when location shooting took place at Porter's Long Island home, probably because Porter himself was present, the tense atmosphere resurfaced once the crew returned to the studio.[6] Finally on 28 September, when the film was twenty days behind schedule, shooting went on from 7 a.m. until 4.40 the next morning. At 3.30 a.m. Curtiz blew his top, ostensibly at the sound crew but actually at Grant, and came close to abandoning the film,[7] the only time this happened in his entire Hollywood career. He resumed with reluctance, but then a full-scale technicians' strike from 5 October to 14 November halted the production altogether. When filming recommenced, James Leicester directed Grant's little remaining work.

Eventually no fewer than ten writers were involved on the script, not to mention the input of Porter, Schwartz, Curtiz, and Grant. The result was an uneven, pedestrian film and a dull Porter characterization based all too obviously upon Grant's screen persona. Grant's determination to dominate the script was a large factor in what went wrong, but Warners' administration was also at fault. As a close observer remarked,

> I don't think there has been a set in this picture that has not been changed by Cary. . . . I will say in fairness that Cary Grant pointed these mistakes out, however, before the picture started, but I guess they thought they could get away with it.[8]

The film is only mildly redeemed by Woolley as Porter's friend and ex-professor at Yale and the renowned Porter melodies. Ginny Simms vivaciously delivers *I Get a Kick Out of You*, *You're the Top*, and *I've Got You Under My Skin*, while Mary Martin's *My Heart Belongs to Daddy* is also impressive. However, the tunes on the whole are unimaginatively staged and the film itself is flabbily handled. Moreover, talents like those of Eve Arden, Victor Francen, Dorothy Malone, and Jane Wyman are utterly wasted. As a musical screen biography it lacks all the merits of *Yankee Doodle Dandy* and is untypical of Curtiz. Unsurprisingly in all the filming circumstances, *Night and Day* is unworthy of its subject's music, its star, and its director, yet it gained Warners a profit of close to three million dollars. This was the studio's fourth most successful film of 1946 behind Sam Wood's *Saratoga Trunk*, Hawks's *The Big Sleep*, and David Butler's *The Time, the Place and the Girl*.

The year 1946 was the first of eight years in which Warners amassed a profit of approximately ninety million dollars. Nevertheless the studio was not as well placed as the figures suggested, for almost half of the post-war profit came in the boom years of 1946 and 1947. Later the annual profit dropped in each successive year until in 1953 it had dipped to the 1940 level of approximately three million dollars, actually less in real terms owing to inflation. Profits had been achieved mainly by cutting costs rather than by future quality investment in the light of changes beyond studio control. Post–1945 film trade union restrictive practices, of which the interruptions to *Night and Day* had been an early manifestation, increased production costs. A May 1948 Supreme Court anti-trust decision meant that the studios could handle distribution only film by film rather than in bulk, which greatly increased distribution costs. The anti-Communist moves directed by HUAC in 1947 against Hollywood limited the subject matter which the major studios could safely tackle. Finally in the early 1950s the rise of television produced a challenge to the supremacy of the cinema as a mass-entertainment medium in the United States and the prime export outlets like Britain. Departures, salary cuts or retirements affected many stars, directors, and producers alike, and the Warners personnel was much changed by the early 1950s when annual output remained at just over twenty films. Almost all continued to make a profit, but the film quality suffered, most of the films making one million dollars or more profit being lightweight musicals or routine vehicles for established star names in decline. In this period Curtiz directed seventeen films for Warners, including *Night and Day* and four for his own production unit within the studio structure. Four of these latter Warners films delivered a seven-figure profit, five of the others made more than 700,000 dollars, and none made a loss. However, after 1946 he did not dominate the other directors financially as he had done in the late 1930s and during the war. After *Night and Day* his position at Warners gradually became less secure as he grew older and more difficult film-making economics emerged.

By 1945 Curtiz's salary had risen to 4,200 dollars per week from 1,500 dollars in 1929, and only once in that time, in April 1931, had his salary been reduced. In addition Jack Warner had awarded him hefty bonuses for *The Adventures of Robin Hood*, *Blackwell's Island*, and *Sons of Liberty*.[9] Yet throughout these years Warners had never abandoned its contractual annual option clause upon his services. Even his April 1943 contract had stipulated Warners options up to April 1946, and Curtiz, now in his late fifties, sought a more secure arrangement. He had applied pressure for the formation of his own production company in February 1945 and possibly as early as October 1944.[10] A deal along these lines was finalized in principle during December 1945, but Curtiz was evidently reluctant to commit himself to Warners in writing before his existing contract expired, even though he wrote to Jack Warner in March 1946, 'I agree with you entirely that I will be much happier in my own unit.'[11] In the same letter he referred to a possible link-up with Howard Hawks, while he did not sign another Warners contract in April and at about the same time he received an invitation to join Liberty Pictures, the recently formed directors co-operative company established by Capra, Stevens, and Wyler.[12] Jack Warner seemingly became alarmed that Curtiz might leave the studio after he had completed *Life With Father*, which Curtiz was directing without a contract, for in July 1946 Warner awarded him a huge 50,000 dollars bonus, 25,000 dollars payable immediately and 25,000 payable when the film was finished. In spite of this, Curtiz came very close to leaving Warners in September 1946, and the salary department was actually notified on 7 September that he had left.[13] However, by 7 October the outline bargain of December 1945 was put in writing and legally finalized on 19 February 1947. Perhaps Curtiz had never intended anything else and merely went to the negotiating brink to be sure of obtaining his own production company. This was Michael Curtiz Productions Incorporated with Curtiz himself as president and Amy as vice-president. Curtiz owned 51 per cent of the shares and Warners 49 per cent. He was given a free hand in film selection and casting but undertook to take into consideration production costs, for which Warners remained partially liable, and never to pay more than 300,000 dollars for story rights. No time-limit was placed on the arrangement.[14] In the event Curtiz's company only lasted until 1949, but safeguarded his Warners position for a time even if it did not turn out to be the panacea for artistic autonomy he had imagined.

Given the mid–1946 brinkmanship between Curtiz and the studio and the very trying production circumstances (see p. 96), it is amazing that *Life With Father* turned out to be his best comedy by far. It was based upon family sketches by Clarence Day Junior (Jimmy Lydon in the film), converted to a play by Russel Crouse and Howard Lindsay which had enjoyed a protracted Broadway run. Jack Warner had bought the screen rights late in 1945, but Clarence Day Junior's widow as well as Crouse and Lindsay gained a virtual contractual stranglehold on the film which they exercised to the full. Producer Buckner had to dig deeply into his diplomatic skills to bring the project to fruition at all,[15] and when Jack Warner proposed either William Powell or Frederic March for the father role and Bette Davis or Irene Dunne or Rosalind Russell for the female lead, the New York theatrical trio insisted in November 1945 that Davis should go through a technicolor test in a comedy scene. They also counter-proposed Ronald Colman instead of Powell or March, although they accepted Curtiz as director without any argument.

Curtiz conducted the secret Davis test on 28 November, but she was rejected in New York. In informing her of this on 14 December, after he himself had gone to New York, he blamed 'superior prejudiced critics of the theatre',[16] which has the ring of truth behind it in the light of later events. There is no clear evidence in the Warners files that Davis was Curtiz's first choice, but he accepted Irene Dunne, Warner's second suggestion, although the New York trio first tried Mary Pickford whom Curtiz directed in three tests between 16 and 18 January 1946. He also directed Ronald Colman's test of 23 January, but at length the New York theatre group had to admit defeat and accepted Powell, who refused to take a test and whom Curtiz had probably preferred in the first place. Now a veteran, Powell was borrowed from MGM, had long coveted the role of Father (Clarence Day Senior), was a very accomplished light comedian, and had worked well with Curtiz in the early 1930s. The casting of the other family members – four sons – was carried out with Curtiz's customary fastidiousness, although due to Selznick's intransigence he was unable to secure Shirley Temple to play the eldest son's girlfriend[17] and instead opted for Elizabeth Taylor.

All of this occupied several months of preparation before filming could commence early in April 1946, and tensions were anticipated. Curtiz was at loggerheads with Mrs Day from the outset, while there were exceptional technical problems over sets, costumes and make-up (the entire Day family were to have red hair), exacerbated by a mid-production painters' and carpenters' strike. Intermittent friction between Curtiz and cameraman Marley also occurred, while at various times Powell, Dunne, Taylor, and Edmund Gwenn were all ill. Curtiz himself stood on a sharp spike and had to walk with a cane and without one shoe for a time. To cap it all, despite the film falling behind schedule from an early stage, Mrs Day, Crouse, and Lindsay constantly attempted changes to the Buckner/Donald Ogden Stewart script. The film was eventually completed on 12 August, thirty days over time, and adding the finishing touches occupied until 22 October. *Life With Father* was not one of Curtiz's happiest experiences, especially coming immediately after the incessant altercations with Grant on *Night and Day*.[18]

Set in 1883 New York City, the plot centres upon a crusty but kindly well-to-do Victorian father (Powell) who resists all family efforts, particularly those of his wife Vinnie (Irene Dunne), to persuade him to be baptized. He eventually relents only when Vinnie falls ill from an undiagnosed ailment, but the film is dominated by a succession of comedy sketches in which the father's determination to run his household with the same clockwork efficiency as he runs his successful business is perpetually thwarted. In 1946 this material was dated in its idea that baptism was essential for admission to heaven, but the sharp and witty script was ideal for this type of humour, while the Robert Haas sets, the costumes, and the period details are perfect. The result is a highly watchable entertainment even if the comedy is slightly repetitious. Central to the film is Powell's impeccable portrayal of the irritable old patriarch. Curtiz and Powell strike the delicate balance between bringing to life the overbearing but basically lovable father and not simultaneously relegating the rest of the cast to mere background. Not totally convincing as the financially scatterbrained but otherwise shrewd Vinnie, Dunne none the less conveys an almost saintly air when controlling her husband. The other players render very solid support, especially Gwenn as the local priest whose help Vinnie enlists in the quest for her husband's baptism. Elizabeth Taylor also distinguishes herself in bouts of bubbling puppy love, and with some foresight Curtiz described her as the most promising young dramatic actress in years.[19]

Life With Father was a big hit in the United States upon its deferred release in August 1947, making a profit of over 1,700,000 dollars. Powell received an Oscar nomination, as did Steiner for a hauntingly nostalgic score, and Marley and Bill Skall for their cinematography. Despite the tense off-screen atmosphere, the film does credit to all concerned, but Curtiz's skill is crucial. Powell recognized this, for he wrote an open letter to Curtiz for use by the Warners publicity department which contained a long catalogue of good-natured complaints but ended with the comment that he had loved every nerve-stretching minute of the film.[20]

The latter war years and the immediate post-war period – the culmination of economic hardship and armed conflict going back to 1929 – had produced in the western world a profound cynicism about the supposed inherent goodness of humam nature. In many 1940s *film noirs* this expressed itself in the form of a perverse fascination with evil and evil-doers for their own sake. This mood was influencing Curtiz when his own production company was on the verge of formation and he selected a 1945 Charlotte Armstrong murder tale for his first film as producer–director in Hollywood. This was *The Unsuspected*, for which Curtiz had envisaged Orson Welles and Jennifer Jones.[21] When neither materialized, he fell back upon Claude Rains and Joan Fontaine. The latter was unavailable, and various other casting problems arose before filming eventually began on 20 January 1947 with Rains in a rare leading part.[22] The film was completed on time on 15 March without any major hitch, although a post-preview scene had to be added in June.

In *The Unsuspected* Rains plays a wealthy and cultured radio mystery narrator who plans to murder niece Joan Caulfield to grow even richer but is unmasked before his plan succeeds. The plot is unconvincing, but Rains is excellent as the ruthless epicurean who does not scruple to murder several times simply for material gain when he already has more than enough for his needs. If the theme is a bleaker extension of that in *Mildred Pierce*, the film itself is Curtiz's foremost excursion into *noir* territory. This was founded upon Grot's magnificent sets, for which Curtiz personally wrote to thank him,[23] sharp dialogue in the MacDougall/Bess Meredyth screenplay, and a vast array of camera tricks admirably carried out by Elwood 'Woody' Bredell. The outcome is a broody atmosphere of impending doom similar to that in parts of *The Strange Love of Molly Louvain* fifteen years previously.

The opening sequence at once establishes suspense as a man's shadow is seen moving along the wall of a poorly lit but expensively furnished room. It stops at and then moves over the portrait of a beautiful young woman before a black-gloved hand moves towards a door knob. On the other side of the door sits a woman working alone at a desk when the man's large shadow appears on the wall behind her. As she talks on the telephone, she looks up to see his silhouette in the doorway with a coiled noose in his hand as the camera moves in towards her terrified features. Then her feet are seen standing on a pile of books after the camera follows a glass-topped desk to rest upon Rains's reflection on the shiny surface. His hand then pushes the books from under her feet. Partly because the murderer's identity is disclosed from the outset, this high-suspense standard is not sustained, but among the many illustrious technical accomplishments one stands out. This is early in the film when the camera moves in on a man's reflection in a train carriage window to go out through the window and down an empty city street at night to focus upon one dark hotel room window. Inside, where the room is lit only by a flashing neon sign of Hotel Peekskill, a killer hired by Rains (Jack Lambert) lies on the bed listening to one of Rains's broadcasts and looking at the window where only the 'kill' part of the Hotel Peekskill neon sign is visible. As a study of a demented soul with delusions of divinity – 'I rather enjoy playing God', Rains observes at one point – and as a reflection of post-war disillusion, *The Unsuspected* has long been underrated, although in the final analysis Curtiz's strong direction does not fully compensate for too many implausibilities in the plot. But for these the film might rank with the best of the 1940s *noir* masterpieces. Curtiz himself acknowledged this when he wrote, 'It looks as though I tried to make a great picture out of a story that wasn't basically a great story.'[24] However, after its October 1947 general release, *The Unsuspected* pulled in a profit of 875,000 dollars, a reasonable success in a year when only four Warners films registered a profit of more than one million dollars.

Evidently Curtiz had little faith that *The Unsuspected* would do well financially, for before its release he had decided upon two technicolor musicals, *Romance on the High Seas* (*It's Magic* in Britain) and *My Dream is Yours*. Both were carried by Jack Carson's comedy style and a string of good songs by Doris Day, allied with her naturally vivacious personality. To this and her pleasant voice Curtiz granted full scope, for her songs are filmed mostly in close-up, while her acting, admittedly in none too onerous roles, displays a forthrightness rare in a newcomer. *Romance on the High Seas* conferred an immediate stardom upon Doris Day; Curtiz had taken a chance with an unknown in a part originally meant for a more famous player because even before he had met Doris Day he had written that he did not wish to follow the routine path of musicals with established musical performers.[25] Curtiz finished *Romance on the High Seas* early in August 1947 well within schedule, but he was so confident that the film would make Doris Day a star that he did not wait for its completion before preparing to consolidate her expected new position with *My Dream is Yours*. This was an altogether more meticulous and better cast production, nowadays most notable for a dream sequence in which Carson and Day dance with an animated figure. Although Curtiz was not responsible for the idea in the first place, he had to fight for its retention against Warners pressure for an all-cartoon scene.[26] Both these musicals earned a profit of over 650,000 dollars, respectable but not enough to place them among the big studio money-spinners.

In September 1948 Curtiz embarked upon a project more akin to his best work, *Flamingo Road*. A literary scout had first brought this to the studio's attention soon after the 1942 publication of Robert Wilder's novel, but no action followed, possibly because a theme focusing upon state government corruption was best left until after the war. A theatre version written by Wilder and his wife Sally failed badly in New York in March 1946, but nevertheless Wald had been interested and evidently persuaded Jack Warner to purchase the screen rights in the following October. In spite of resolute censorship resistance from December 1946 onwards over both the theme (considered undesirable in principle while the HUAC hearings were in progress), and implied unconventional sex, Wald pressed ahead with production preparations throughout 1947, Vincent Sherman being his envisaged director. However, Sherman and projected star Ann Sheridan had turned down Edmund North's screenplay, while the censorship obstacles had persisted and Jack Warner's experience with HUAC over *Mission to Moscow* had made him unwilling to give *Flamingo Road* the go-ahead. Early in 1948 Wald had engaged Richard Brooks and MacDougall to improve the script, and Curtiz had become involved in mid–1948 even though he was unenthusiastic about the project.[27] At one point he even publicly announced his rejection of the film when he knew that Warners had signed Joan Crawford for it on the condition that he was the director. All this was perhaps posturing to strengthen his position in the talks then taking place with Warners over the winding up of Michael Curtiz Productions. Eventually matters were smoothed over, and Jack Warner passed over the screen rights to the Curtiz unit in August 1948.

Curtiz retained Wald as producer, and they speedily assigned MacDougall and Wilder to the screenplay, while North amended some of the dialogue once filming actually began on 16 September. Since Zachary Scott as well as Crawford was prominent in the cast, *Flamingo Road* had in effect developed into a *Mildred Pierce* harkback. The theme of money grubbing and social climbing was again much to the fore, but this time it was entangled with corruption and decadence in a steamy small town in the American South. The story centres upon Crawford as a dancer in a tenth-rate itinerant carnival who is accidentally stranded in the town. She soon attracts the attention of rising young politician Scott, which enrages county political boss Sydney Greenstreet, who manoeuvres her first into jail and then into the local bordello run by Gladys George. There she meets Greenstreet's arch opponent David Brian (a compromise piece of casting after Curtiz and Wald had disagreed),[28] who offers her marriage and a mansion among the social high-flyers in the prestige Flamingo Road. She accepts, much to Greenstreet's chagrin, and his various intrigues result in Scott's suicide, Brian's political ruin, and her own social ostracism. She confronts Greenstreet, a struggle erupts, and he is unintentionally shot. She is charged with murder and awaits the jury's verdict as the film ends. Wilder's novel and the script were essentially exposés of local political corruption, but Curtiz's treatment, probably mindful of HUAC probings, converted it into a very well-mounted soap opera with an exciting tale. Crawford plays strongly, and she is well supported by Scott and Brian, but the film is stolen by Greenstreet in a role Wald had first offered to Rains, who had wanted it but was too committed to other engagements.[29] Greenstreet's power-crazy portrayal of Titus Semple, tinged with hints of sexual repression, represents the best by far of his three performances with Curtiz. Equally meritorious is the town's Gothic-style atmosphere, beautifully caught by a subtle combination of Ted McCord's location photography and Leo K. Kuter's sets. Like *The Unsuspected*, *Flamingo Road* is less than it might have been, partly because Crawford was too old for her part and partly because the plot is too improbable. It is also too manifest an attempt to repeat the formula of *Mildred Pierce*, nowhere more glaring than in the final scene where Crawford is shown waiting for the jury's verdict as Brian appears to indicate that he will wait for her if she is found guilty – a ray of hope reminiscent of her leaving the police station arm in arm with her ex-husband as the sun shines in *Mildred Pierce*.

The censorship problems were overcome by making unclear the time in which the story was set and referring to the bordello as a roadhouse. The struggle between Crawford and Greenstreet, in which he hurls into her face a telephone which ricochets on to a mirror, showering glass upon her, is brilliantly staged, while Curtiz's customary jailhouse humour recurs. When Crawford is first in prison, filmed in the Los Angeles County Jail, fellow inmate Iris Adrian tells her she is there because her boyfriend cut himself on a knife she happened to be holding. *Flamingo Road* today is seldom seen and consequently remains undervalued, but it was appreciated in its day, for it was one of six 1949 Warners releases which exceeded the one million dollars profit mark.

Flamingo Road was the last film made by Michael Curtiz Productions. As early as April 1948, when Curtiz had been filming *My Dream is Yours*, Jack Warner had grown concerned that Curtiz, who was notorious for his lack of administrative ability, was spending too much time on non-directorial duties. To remedy this, Warner was edging towards a Warners purchase of Curtiz's shares, payable over several years, and a new seven-year contract for him on the basis of a fixed weekly 3,500 dollars salary and 25 per cent of his film's profits.[30] A deal along these lines was agreed in December 1948, which left Curtiz free to concentrate upon his directing.

During the filming of *Flamingo Road* Curtiz had made a fleeting appearance as himself in David Butler's *It's a Great Feeling*, his first screen acting since before the First World War apart from a one-line bit-part in *Roughly Speaking* when he filled in at the last moment for a Hungarian actor named Lazlo Bartos who had become ill.[31] *It's a Great Feeling* was the only Warners cameo he ever did under another director. As such it was a petty episode in Curtiz's career which was, however, destined to influence his directorial style. He had to deliver a mere twelve words, yet he stayed up all night to learn them and even then got them wrong, which necessitated several retakes by Butler. Afterwards Curtiz openly admitted that he was a poor actor and swore he would never bawl out a player again.[32] Of course he did so, but far less often and by degrees developed a more openly, almost avuncularly, affable approach to players.

After *Flamingo Road* the relationship between Curtiz and Warners had been badly undermined, as events were to show. Jack Warner believed that the Curtiz production unit's failure and the new contract would bind Curtiz to the studio for the rest of his career. On the other hand Curtiz evidently blamed Warners, at least in part, for its lack of moral support for his unit. The rights and wrongs of this disagreement are not easy to fathom from the Warners records, but it seems that Warner harboured no resentment against Curtiz but assumed as a straightforward business proposition that the studio's bargaining position was better, whereas Curtiz was resentful against the studio because he believed that he had been sabotaged.

Tension soon surfaced. Under the terms of his new contract Curtiz was to have two scripts for each film submitted to him, and if he rejected both, Warners could either select one of them for him to direct or assign him to another film. He disapproved of both submitted scripts for the lightweight *The Lady Takes a Sailor* early in 1949 but none the less was compelled to direct it throughout March and April.[33] His lack of commitment to the film communicated itself even to the minor players concerned, for one of these, Allyn Joslyn, correctly observed much later that Curtiz had directed in a surly fashion as though Jack Warner was punishing him.[34] The film itself is a moderately amusing piece of nonsense with Jane Wyman as a successful career woman with a reputation for integrity who goes sailing while resting at the beach house of friend Eve Arden. Wyman's boat is capsized by a weird-looking amphibious tank operated by scientist Dennis Morgan on behalf of the US Navy. He rescues her but, after an encounter with an octopus, he gives her sleeping pills and then dumps her on a beach while she is still asleep in order to conceal his identity and the nature of his work. A coastguard finds her, but she cannot prove her story and as a result loses her job. She meets the scientist again and discovers the truth, but she repudiates her story for national security reasons and because she has fallen for him. Due chiefly to the unpretentious acting by the three principals and Curtiz's unobtrusive direction, the film raises a few laughs here and there, particularly in the octopus sequence, but the script is insipid. The film works best when it concentrates upon the Mack Sennett-style slapstick which inspired it, rendering dialogue irrelevant. *The Lady Takes a Sailor* is a good example of Warners in artistic decline due to a paucity of new ideas. Jane Wyman's talent was squandered, and it was fundamentally an ill-judged enterprise. It was hardly surprising that Curtiz had not wished to direct it, his judgement being vindicated by the meagre profit of 191,000 dollars.

In July and August 1949 Curtiz filmed the much superior *Young Man With a Horn* (*Young Man of Music* in Britain), the trials and tribulations of a professional jazz trumpet player loosely based upon the life of the legendary Bix Beiderbecke as projected in Dorothy Baker's 1945 novel. At Wald's prompting, Warners had purchased the screen rights for Garfield, but after the latter had left the studio, only Wald's persistence had kept the project alive. Towards the end of 1946 he had come into strong conflict with Trilling over the Stephen Longstreet screenplay and offered to withdraw as the producer.[35] In April 1947 Wald had failed to obtain James Stewart for the lead, toyed with Ronald Reagan for a while, and again all but withdrew when Trilling was on the point of casting character actor Dane Clark.[36] However, in November 1946 Wald had managed to cast Hoagy Carmichael and in June 1947 Lauren Bacall. He had also envisaged Doris Day for a serious role while Curtiz was still filming *Romance on the High Seas*,[37] Edmund North had replaced Longstreet as the writer, and North's script had been approved by Dorothy Baker herself.[38] The core of the slow progress on the script was that Jack Warner desired a happy ending, whereas Wald, supported by MacDougall,[39] wished to retain the trumpeter's death of the novel. Deadlock ensued in 1948 over the choice of director and star between Wald and Jack Warner, and the film was on the verge of abandonment until Kirk Douglas's sudden rise to prominence in Mark Robson's boxing saga *Champion* early in 1949. This led Wald to pursue the idea energetically once more when he instructed Carl Foreman to write a screenplay. In May, while still engaged on *The Lady Takes a Sailor*, Curtiz was shown both the North and Foreman scripts and came down heavily in favour of the former. His analysis ran to six typed pages, indicative of his deep interest, and he suggested another director if his ideas were not accepted.[40] He even sent a copy of his analysis to Jack Warner who had asked Foreman to amend the North script in the direction of a happy ending and a hefty reduction of the negro background material.[41]

The choice of Curtiz as director gave rise to problems which Wald had thought solved, for Lauren Bacall tried to withdraw before filming began.[42] Douglas was keen to influence the script in detail,[43] but script compromises were hammered out between Curtiz, Wald, and Foreman, although the issue of the ending was held in abeyance. Filming between 11 July and 27 August progressed smoothly, and the project was completed on time apart from some New York location sequences shot early in September. After the preview Douglas attempted to revive the death ending with Jack Warner,[44] but in fact a typical Curtiz ambiguous ending was retained as a tactful compromise between Warner and himself, backed by Wald.

In the film, pianist Carmichael relates in flashback the life of trumpeter Douglas from his orphaned childhood to his current decline. As a boy he decides to become a great trumpeter and comes under the benevolent influence of black jazzman Juano Hernandez. As a result of Hernandez's expert tuition he achieves his ambition and gains two firm friends in Carmichael and club singer Doris Day. However, neither can break his neurotic obsession with the trumpet, but he meets and falls for selfish playgirl Bacall, marries her, and then starts to lose his outstanding trumpet ability. Hernandez's death in an accident wakes him up to reality, and he leaves his wife, only to slump into alcoholism and depression.

Carmichael and Day seek him out and help him to take the road to personal rehabilitation and a professional comeback.

The real Beiderbecke died in 1931 at 28 years of age and never married. Pianist–composer–singer Carmichael knew him well during his last years and considered him to be the greatest jazz musician of all time. Thus Carmichael's very presence conveys an air of realism about the 1920s jazz scene, the film opening with him seated at his piano as a veteran recalling Douglas. From this Curtiz moves on to create an atmosphere of smoke-ridden dives as well as the itinerant and insecure lives of most jazzmen. This ethos is well supported by the playing of real-life trumpeter and famous bandleader Harry James, Carmichael's own piano work, the Doris Day songs – *Too Marvellous for Words*, *The Very Thought of You*, and *I May Be Wrong But I Think You're Wonderful* (all carefully integrated into the main narrative) – and McCord's photography. However, Curtiz's purpose was neither a straightforward screen biography nor a peep into the jazz world (although at the time this was one of the best films about jazz ever made), but rather a study of the personality dangers arising from any single-minded obsession. Despite several overwrought scenes, most conspicuously the confrontation between Douglas and Bacall after she has smashed his treasured record collection, and the mistaken introduction of the romance and broken marriage, Curtiz handles his theme with great sensitivity. Hernandez is portrayed as considerate, gentle, and talented, while the sequence in which Douglas attends his funeral in an obscure black church and during the ceremony expresses his grief by picking up Hernandez's old trumpet and playing it solemnly, which Jack Warner had sought to have omitted,[45] is as moving as anything Curtiz ever filmed. By contrast Doris Day flits in and out of Douglas's life. She carries a torch for him, but he treats her more like a mother or sister (in the novel she, like Carmichael, was black). Whether or not Douglas makes it back to the top of his profession remains unknown, for the film ends, as it begins, with Carmichael at his piano. He reflects philosophically, 'Rick [Douglas] learned that you can't say everything through the end of a trumpet, and that a man doesn't destroy himself because he can't hit some high note he dreamed up.' Curtiz had taken much trouble over the film, for he personally interviewed 132 boys of between 8 and 10 years old for the part of Douglas as a boy, and he also attended a black funeral and chapel service before filming the Hernandez funeral scene. Released in 1950, *Young Man With a Horn* earned Warners a profit of 994,000 dollars. Only five other Warners releases of that year fared better.

Bright Leaf tells the humdrum saga of Gary Cooper's rise to fame as the builder of an American cigarette empire in the late nineteenth and early twentieth centuries and of the two women in his life. Rising young star Patricia Neal plays aristocratic tobacco planter Donald Crisp's daughter who marries Cooper and almost destroys him in revenge for her father's suicide, while Lauren Bacall is the woman with a heart of gold who loves Cooper but has to play second fiddle to Neal. Both actresses later expressed reservations about Curtiz's direction,[46] although from the film itself it is not easy to understand why, for both are shown to much advantage even if Neal overacts slightly. Uneasy relations with his female leads might explain why so much is seen of Crisp and Jack Carson in supporting roles, the remainder of the cast also turning in highly competent performances. Karl Freund's camera and Victor Young's score bolstered strong production values, which however do not overcome a routine MacDougall screenplay. Curtiz does little more than keep the narrative moving, possibly because Warners had not submitted two scripts to him beforehand, as his contract required.[47] He apparently accepted this situation without protest, but doubtless it induced in him a less than wholehearted attitude towards the film. *Bright Leaf* works as entertainment only when it sticks to melodrama and eschews the romance, as in a brief brawl scene centring upon Carson and one in which a deranged Cooper chases after Neal. In the process he knocks over a table with a lit candle, sets the house on fire, is rescued by a black servant, and decides to allow the house to burn down. Box-office takings produced merely a modest profit of 497,000 dollars.

Curtiz's last 1950 release, *The Breaking Point*, is his finest post–1945 achievement and, from a purely artistic standpoint, arguably his best film of all. On the surface a remake of Hawks's 1944 *To Have and Have Not*, *The Breaking Point* is in fact a much more determined effort to retain the spirit of Ernest Hemingway's 1937 novel to which Warners had immediately bought the screen rights. Producer Wald had been as dedicated to this film as to *Mildred Pierce*. His interest had commenced in July 1948, and he had assigned MacDougall to the script in March 1949. In the following month he had tackled Jack Warner about Garfield for the lead, but Warner had been evasive. Garfield himself was pressing for the role with Curtiz as the director, although he was prepared to accept Fred Zinnemann or Robert Siodmak if Curtiz was unavailable. Wald evidently delayed until Curtiz was available, for by the end of 1949 no decision had been reached about either main casting or director, Curtiz still filming *Bright Leaf* and Garfield threatening to pull out in favour of another film unless decisions were made soon. To complicate matters, Cagney was interested in the same part.[48] However, early in January 1950, when *Bright Leaf* was nearly completed, Curtiz became the designated director,[49] and shortly afterwards Garfield was definitely cast. Curtiz and Garfield read *To Have and Have Not* in mid–January, after which extensive consultations took place over amendments to MacDougall's script. Much to Garfield's surprise, Curtiz invited him to spend a week at Curtiz's ranch with MacDougall for script discussions and other pre-production preparations.[50] This was a sign of the high esteem in which Curtiz held Garfield and of their agreement about script basics in this instance, for Curtiz hardly ever allowed players to influence scripts before filming opened. It was also an indication of Curtiz's exceptional commitment to the project.

Wald and Curtiz disagreed over Garfield's characterization,[51] and Curtiz once wrote to MacDougall, unusually forcefully for him to a writer, to urge him not to introduce 'abstract elements which don't belong to the story',[52] and to stick to straight melodrama without too much deep philosophical and psychological material.[53] To judge from the film, about which Wald was enthusiastic and at one point during filming had seen as another *Casablanca* in the making,[54] he deferred to Curtiz's judgement. He was always highly supportive of Curtiz, and they had taken a substantial risk in plumping for Garfield, then under HUAC scrutiny for his pronounced left-wing views. In this context it is unclear why Jack Warner had allowed the film to be made at all or Garfield to be cast rather than Cagney, but whatever the reason Warners did not mount a high-profile publicity campaign for the film after its October 1950 release. It speedily plunged into a backwater where it has undeservedly remained ever since, apart from occasional television showings. Yet it is far and away the most successful serious attempt to bring the spirit of Hemingway to the screen.

Although true to the ethos of Hemingway's doom-laden, pessimistic novel, symbolic of the late 1930s, *The Breaking Point* is not a literal screen adaptation. The script alters the locales from Cuba and Florida to Mexico and California, transfers the time from the 1930s to the late 1940s, consolidates three minor characters into the one of Wesley Park (Hernandez), Garfield's black partner, substitutes a racetrack robbery by St Louis gangsters for a bank heist by Cuban revolutionaries, and introduces a new character in temptress Patricia Neal. The plot deals with ex-Second World War soldier Garfield whose charter boat business barely gets by and whose relationship with wife Phyllis Thaxter is sexually exciting but contains out-of-bed tensions. Seedy businessman Ralph Dumke and his mistress Neal hire Garfield's boat for a voyage to Mexico with such a large sum of money as to suggest that the 'business' is illegal. Against his better judgement Garfield accepts the deal for the sake of his wife and two daughters, and when Neal tries to seduce him, he all but succumbs due to his declining self-esteem and the pressures of his marriage. Double-crossed and stranded in Mexico, Garfield and Hernandez agree to smuggle Chinese immigrants into the United States for Victor Sen Yung. Garfield is compelled to kill him and set the Chinese ashore, but when the American authorities suspect his involvement and impound the boat, crooked lawyer Wallace Ford obtains its release so that Garfield can transport four criminals to collect cash stolen in a racetrack robbery. *En route* they murder Hernandez, and when Garfield learns that they plan the same fate for him, he decides to get in first. In the ensuing boat battle Garfield kills all the gang, but is badly wounded himself and loses an arm.

As a study in post-war disillusion and fatalism – Garfield is a victim of circumstances rather than of any personality flaw – *The Breaking Point* is superb and a high point of post–1945 Hollywood realism. Much misunderstood in its time as the proletarian anti-hero was going out of Hollywood fashion due to HUAC and American anti-Communism in general, the film explores the question of the individual struggling unsuccessfully against his destiny. Garfield turns in the performance of his career and is supported by a cast in superlative form, especially Hernandez, Ford, and Neal, all selected at the very last moment in much the same fashion as with *Casablanca*. The film is also a rare example of a remake surpassing the quality of the original owing to Curtiz's creation of the fishing town (Balboa, California in reality) with its varied bars and stereotyped canal-side bungalows – 'Two drinks and you can't tell one house from another', complains Garfield – and his relentless portrait of a once-strong and assertively self-confident man in decline. This is due at least partly to a preoccupation with a praiseworthy aim, an honest high living standard for his family. This theme is similar to that in *Young Man With a Horn* and *Bright Leaf* to some extent, and his next film, which perhaps echoed Curtiz's view of his own situation after the winding-up of Michael Curtiz Productions and his deteriorating relations with Warners. 'A man alone ain't got no chance' is Garfield's final utterance. The film was shot between 28 March and 10 May 1950, Curtiz completing it four days ahead of schedule. It made a profit of 580,000 dollars, respectable but well short of the studio's largest 1950 money-spinners.

Jim Thorpe – All American (*Man of Bronze* in Britain) is a standard biography of the Red Indian athlete who won the decathlon and pentathlon at the 1912 Stockholm Olympics, setting new records in the process. Because he had already played professional baseball, he was later stripped of his medals, and his records were expunged from Olympic statistics. In the early 1930s he had written an autobiography with Russell Birdwell, to which MGM had at once bought the film rights but then delayed the project until Louis B. Mayer himself became interested after *Los Angeles Examiner* sports reporter Vincent X. Flaherty had drawn his attention to it. However, Thorpe himself was then in straitened circumstances, and his wife, who possessed power of attorney for her husband, failed to reach agreement with MGM which sold the rights to Flaherty in May 1949 in the hope that another studio would take up the project. A month later Warners purchased the rights from Flaherty, who had by then taken steps to write a screenplay with Douglas Morrow.[55] Warners had more success with Mrs Thorpe than MGM, and a contract was signed in

September. Assigned producer Everett Freeman was deeply committed to the film, for he not only amended the Morrow/Flaherty script but also consulted with Thorpe via his wife and Thorpe's famous coach Glenn 'Pop' Warner. For a time Freeman hovered between Kirk Douglas and Burt Lancaster for the Thorpe part,[56] but by early 1950 he had opted for Lancaster who possessed both the athletic and dramatic ability to play Thorpe. He had recently signed a contract with Warners allowing him to co-produce films at the studio in return for his services purely as an actor in other studio productions.

Freeman seems to have accepted early on a recommendation that the Red Indian aspect should be emphasized in the script as the prime unifying theme,[57] and Lancaster himself was interested in the story's racial aspects. For reasons unknown, production was delayed until mid–1950, when Freeman chose Curtiz to direct at Trilling's suggestion after *The Breaking Point* had just been completed. Curtiz was of an age to remember Thorpe's astonishing 1912 Stockholm feats and had personally selected him as an extra in *Captain Blood*. When Curtiz read the script, he accepted the project, and although he disagreed with Freeman over screenplay details, he began preparations immediately before filming began on 25 August 1950. Since *Captain Blood* Thorpe had hung around Hollywood, securing work as an extra with the occasional bit part, but he was usually in dire financial straits and Warners hired him as a technical adviser to the film. In this capacity he was one of five football coaches who taught Lancaster drop kicking. Warners had earlier initiated a campaign through Thorpe to have his Olympic medals restored in order to obtain the ideal movie personal-triumph ending,[58] but this move had been unsuccessful. Thorpe was to die in obscurity on 28 March 1953 at 64 years of age, but the International Olympic Committee waited until 1982 before restoring his medals.

The film remained reasonably faithful to the outline of Thorpe's life, although his three marriages were compressed to one, his six children reduced to one, and his outstanding prowess at boxing, golf, and swimming was omitted altogether. At the beginning Thorpe's father encourages him to leave the tribal reservation to gain a better education outside. In 1907 he enrols at a Pennsylvania Indian school where, although academically mediocre, he is spotted by sports coach 'Pop' Warner (Charles Bickford, who had consulted the real Warner about his portrayal) as an excellent sporting prospect. Under his guidance Thorpe becomes a multi-event athletic champion and an All-American footballer before sweeping on to his Olympic successes. The Olympics themselves, although spectacularly staged in the best Curtiz manner (they were filmed in the Los Angeles Coliseum, the venue of the 1932 Olympics), occur relatively early and are treated as a mere prelude to Thorpe's personality disintegration after the loss of his medals. His wounded pride and the death of his son lead him to alcoholism and fits of depression, his frequent surly moods causing wife Phyllis Thaxter to leave him. His permanent downfall seems assured until he visits the 1932 Los Angeles Olympics, recalls his past, and decides to pull himself together. He holds down a truck-driving job and turns to the sports-coaching of youngsters in his spare time.

Thorpe was arguably the finest all-round athlete ever, but Curtiz's treatment of his life is more than a personal homage. The very choice of title, made by Jack Warner, placed the film on a par with Bacon's 1940 patriotic *Knute Rockne, All American*, the life of the famed Notre Dame football coach, while Curtiz sensitively probes the problems of a renowned sportsman trying to come to terms with being out of the public limelight and in disgrace as well. Thorpe's own character – obstinacy and a chip-on-the-shoulder conviction that the whole world is singling him out for unjust treatment – is placed as central to his decline, but racialism appears as a supplementary factor. Before the 1912 Olympics he cannot gain a job as a sports coach because of his race, while at his Carlisle Indian school one of his fellow students remarks sardonically, 'White man lick Indian, he win battle. Indian lick white man – massacre.' Both Lancaster and Bickford give strong performances in what remains one of the most admirable sporting films ever made. Although some contemporary reviewers complained about a surfeit of sporting sequences, this criticism holds true only for those totally uninterested in sport, for Curtiz actually strikes a careful balance between the essential sporting and personal narrative contexts. *Jim Thorpe – All American* cleared 938,000 dollars for Warners and is a film of which any director could be proud. Curtiz took great pains over it, for he personally selected for the Indian school site Bacone College in Muskogee, Oklahoma, 1800 miles from Hollywood and one of the most distant filming locations from California ever, where a film crew of over one hundred men spent four weeks. Moreover, the film fell well behind schedule in the closing stages, when Curtiz was filming the Olympics, a sure sign that his interest had been aroused.

Force of Arms was in effect an updated remake of Borzage's 1932 *A Farewell to Arms* for Paramount based upon a Hemingway novel, although in this instance credit was given to Orin Jennings's adaptation of a story by Richard Tregaskis. The film traces the fortunes of American army Sergeant William Holden whose unit in the Second World War Italian campaign is withdrawn from the front for a rest. Holden meets and falls in love with army nurse Lieutenant Nancy Olson, but when his unit returns to battle, he uncharacteristically holds back at a crucial moment, thereby causing the death of his commanding officer, Major Frank Lovejoy, and many of his comrades. He becomes tormented by the thought that he might have failed to attack a German artillery post because of his wish to marry Olson. Although they subsequently marry, he is determined to redeem himself. He thus returns to combat, is wounded, and is left behind presumed dead. Olson refuses to believe in his death, traces his movements into battle, and at length finds him in Rome among freed prisoners-of-war being sent for hospital treatment.

Curtiz read the Tregaskis script in January 1950 and regarded it as dated. It was well written, but the characters had been seen on the screen many times, while although the battle scenes were vivid, they offered nothing new owing to the fact that so many Italian campaign newsreels had already been shown. For these he recommended Italian location shooting, as yet another set-bound war film offered nothing exciting. He also saw the ending as weak, for it did not fulfil early expectations and left the story flat.[59] Over the next three months Wald spent much time on script revision with two basic aims – to create 'an honest and truthful story about the war in Italy as it was, and not as the Hollywood scenario writer thought it was or should have been',[60] and to make the two main characters credible while holding the audience's interest and moving it emotionally.[61] Tregaskis's inability to deliver both these objectives led Wald to replace him with Jennings in mid–1950, but for various reasons the production was not ready to begin until March 1951.

By then the producer was Anthony Veiller who had sought Glenn Ford for the Holden part,[62] but whether he was unavailable or Curtiz preferred Holden is unclear from the Warners records. The latter is more likely, for Curtiz had known Holden since 1940 when he had been on loan to Warners, Holden had frequently visited the set of *The Sea Hawk* while courting Brenda Marshall, whom he had married, and had recently been an Oscar nominee for his performance in Billy Wilder's *Sunset Boulevard* for Paramount. Olson had also appeared in that film as Holden's girlfriend. Jack Warner made a belated effort to replace Holden with Steve Cochran, but Curtiz and Veiller beat this off.[63]

In Curtiz's hands the material became more credible than it reads. The romance rings reasonably true, and a sense of unselfish devotion permeates the Holden–Olson love scenes in their fourth film together as a romantic team. However, what really strike home are the grittily realistic battle scenes and the depiction of man's savagery under fire, the tension of imminent battle which prompts him to simulated merriment while on leave, and the battle carnage itself, splendidly conveyed in McCord's photography complemented by three brief fragments of genuine Italian campaign footage. The battles were filmed in the Santa Susanna mountains, selected for their resemblance to Italian mountains but never previously used for a Hollywood movie because they had no roads. Warners built an entrance road suitable for the access of heavy equipment, which involved 230 men in addition to the players. Twenty explosive experts, known as powder men, climbed hills and cliffs to produce the effect of combat fury and sound involving some 60,000 rounds of live ammunition (nobody was injured), while hundreds of extras were used as American and German soldiers. Curtiz kept in touch with his players, Veiller, and the second unit through an extensive use of 'walkie-talkie' and short-wave radios. One high-angle shot of weary survivors leaving the battlefield stands out. So determined was Curtiz to capture battle realism, in which he brilliantly succeeded, that when Olson turned up to watch as the only woman among several hundred men when she was not required to act, he discouraged her. 'How can I keep my actors in a grim battle mood when they look out of their fox holes and see Nancy', he commented.[64] Holden, who admired Curtiz, was unstinting in his co-operation and frequently risked physical injury. Despite budget and production problems while filming was in progress, Curtiz completed *Force of Arms* on schedule and under budget on 4 May 1951.

Paradoxically the strength of both the battle and romantic sequences is also the film's most significant weakness. They co-exist very uneasily indeed, reflecting Wald's over-ambitious approach, and the overall impact is sufficient rather than totally convincing. All the same it is a worthy film, unduly neglected, even if it does not figure among Curtiz's finest. It brought Warners in a profit of 632,000 dollars, modest compared to the seven greatest 1951 studio hits.

The Story of Will Rogers had first been mooted at Warners several years after the famous American comedian's 1935 air-crash death. Curtiz himself had been Rogers's polo-playing friend during the early 1930s and had always believed that his life would make excellent screen material. However, no concrete steps towards a film had been taken until Mrs Rogers had written her husband's story in the early 1940s. As early as December 1941 Curtiz had been enthusiastic about both the project and a completed script,[65] and with Mark Hellinger he provided the chief driving force over the next three years. However, it had proved hard to find a star name to play Rogers – Frederic March had turned down the chance in February 1944, Gary Cooper evinced no interest six months later, and finally Joel McCrea, after initially having accepted the role in October 1944, had second thoughts in March 1945. He had worked with Rogers in two early 1930s films, had come to know him well, and had eventually felt he could not do justice to Rogers as a performer since the latter was almost a national institution. He withdrew with Curtiz's and Hellinger's understanding if not Jack Warner's,[66] and although Curtiz thereafter kept the idea alive, no solution to the central casting problem had been found.

At length, perhaps in desperation, he hit upon the idea of selecting Will Rogers Junior, a carbon copy of his father in both appearance and mannerisms.[67] Curtiz had tested and rejected him as far back as May

1942, but after he was retested in mid–May 1951 Curtiz was satisfied that he was a good choice provided he was surrounded by good character players,[68] although he was less happy about much of the script.[69] However, the project was put at risk once more when Curtiz was asked to reduce his contractual profit to 10 per cent for this one film. Curtiz refused and went on to propose that his contract should be terminated by Warners either buying out his profit percentage from his last six films and the remaining time of his contract or giving him a new contract based upon 100,000 dollars per film without any profit percentage. He offered to direct the Rogers film for 12.5 per cent instead of 25 per cent of the profit if Warners would re-employ his brother David.[70]

David Curtiz's history is largely unknown, but he had acted in some of Curtiz's Hungarian films and seemingly arrived in the United States under uncertain circumstances in either late 1944 or early 1945. He shot three *Mildred Pierce* exteriors in March 1945, and in June Curtiz had authorized Warners to pay David 250 dollars per week from Curtiz's own salary.[71] Curtiz employed him in various capacities on *Night and Day* and on the four Michael Curtiz Productions films. He had been second unit director of *Flamingo Road* and, much more impressively, of *Young Man With a Horn* and *The Breaking Point*. Curtiz had expected that once his own company had ceased to function Warners might dispense with David. When in 1949 Jack Warner delayed Curtiz's preparations for *Young Man With a Horn*, the latter suspected that this was because David would go on salary.[72] Why Warners was reluctant to continue using David is enigmatic in the light of his good work on *The Breaking Point*, which probably explains Curtiz's irritation. David had subsequently worked with his brother on *Jim Thorpe – All American* and *Force of Arms*, and since Curtiz eventually directed *The Story of Will Rogers*, one must assume that David was again used, at least for a time. He was to die just a few months after Curtiz himself. However, despite Curtiz's personal commitment to Rogers's memory, the background to the film, made in late 1951 and early 1952, and the disagreements over David show that his studio position had weakened, and that the parting of the ways was in prospect.

In the film Jane Wyman plays Mrs Rogers, James Gleason is Bert Lynn, the theatrical agent who started Rogers in vaudeville, and Eddie Cantor appears as himself. Because the script is reasonably faithful to Rogers's life and Curtiz concentrates upon recording a meticulous legend for posterity rather than creating a dramatic story, the film is slow-moving by Curtiz standards and does not explore Rogers's personal character. The effect is a pleasant tribute to Rogers, but the fault lies less in the film than its timing. It simply came too late after Rogers's death, for by the early 1950s a generation had grown up who did not remember him and his humour had dated. As a result the film was not the success it might otherwise have been, although it nevertheless registered a profit of 715,000 dollars.

Filmed earlier in 1951 while Curtiz's differences with Warners over *The Story of Will Rogers* remained unresolved, *I'll See You in My Dreams* relates the life of popular song lyricist Gus Kahn who had a number of big hits during the 1920s and 1930s and made a speciality of film scores. In reality the film is less a biography than a vehicle for Doris Day as Grace LeBoy Kahn, his wife, and a showcase for Danny Thomas, a night club and later television comedian, who played Kahn himself. This was his first Warners film and his first starring role after three supporting parts for other studios, part of Warners' search for new star faces. Curtiz was initially unenthusiastic about the project,[73] but this doubtless reflected his simultaneous disillusion with the studio over the Will Rogers affair. However, once Thomas had been cast instead of Gordon MacRae in deference to Curtiz's wishes,[74] and the film was under way with Grace Kahn as a technical adviser on the set, Curtiz went to work with a will. By early July 1951 he was restructuring the scenario in a way that would take the film above its budget of 1,098,000 dollars.[75]

Once Curtiz had overhauled the script, which traces the up-and-down relationship of Gus and Grace and her influence upon his professional career, it exuded a heart-warming quality between them unmatched in Curtiz musicals, with the possible exception of *Yankee Doodle Dandy*. As usual with Curtiz, the songs are fitted into the various stages of their life together rather than introduced as superfluous set pieces breaking up the main narrative. The night-club scene of the early 1920s effectively captures the musical atmosphere, particularly when waiters busily pile chairs upon tables following an after-hours jam session in a smoke-filled room. Prinz's choreography also provides evocative background for the excellent Doris Day solos, while Curtiz's gentle-toned but incisive direction again exploits her natural ebullience as the foundation stone of her characterization. He soon realized that Thomas was no actor, but covered up this central defect with a portrait of Kahn as a weak man dependent upon his wife, thus allowing Thomas to indulge some of his talent for light-heartedness without a descent into outright comedy. This ploy almost works in that Thomas shows up as merely irritating some of the time and as adequate for most of it instead of miscast throughout. None the less, *I'll See You in My Dreams* exhibits a tenderness that few musicals equal. Aided by Day's superb renderings of *Pretty Baby*, *It Had To Be You*, and *I'll See You in My Dreams*, the film brought Warners in a profit of 1,758,000 dollars upon its delayed release in 1952. This made it the studio's second-largest money-spinner for the year, and it was Curtiz's last great financial success for Warners. Curtiz and Grace Kahn seemingly struck up a good personal rapport which meant that he was subject to less intervention than on his previous musical biographies,

113

and after the film was completed she wrote a warm letter of appreciation to the studio.[76]

Curtiz then moved on to an updated remake of *The Jazz Singer*. Even in the mid–1920s this story of a Jewish son who disobeys his father's wish that he should become a cantor and instead follows a successful showbiz career was outmoded. The triumph of the original had derived from the novelty of sound and the charismatic Jolson presence, but Warners had been planning a remake since 1945. However, various obstacles had prevented this, then and later, until a revival in Jolson's popularity and then his death in the early 1950s led to a more serious effort. Curtiz had hoped to reunite Doris Day with Thomas, but she rejected the idea in mid–1952 and once more the project was faltering until Curtiz heard Peggy Lee sing at a club and talked her into accepting a lead role in her first film. The problem of the film is not the female lead, but a badly dated substance centred upon the unsuitable Thomas as a soldier honorably discharged from the Korean War, then still in progress, which stretches credibility too far. The outcome is pleasantly adequate, but incidental delights are Peggy Lee, the performances of Mildred Dunnock and Eduard Franz as Thomas's parents, and Steiner's score. None of the famous Jolson songs is included, the musical focus partly switching to Peggy Lee who shares with Thomas such golden oldies as *Lover*, *Just One of Those Things*, *I'll String Along With You*, and *The Birth of the Blues*. None of the film's positive merits conceals the basic fact that it was an unwise venture in principle which even Curtiz could not salvage. The tasteful presentation of Jewish hymns and ceremonies also suggest that for once Curtiz allowed a Jewish theme to cloud his cinematic judgement to some extent.[77] It barely passed muster at the box-office with a profit of 263,000 dollars.

Originally known as *Alma Mater*, *Trouble Along the Way* turned out to be Curtiz's most aptly titled film. The script, modelled (one suspects) upon Leo McCarey's populist *Going My Way* (1944) for Paramount, is lively enough, but the film was Melville Shavelson's first as a producer, and he came into conflict with star John Wayne over the script. Curtiz was caught in the crossfire and seems to have lost interest to a certain extent, for the pace of the film is very uneven. Wayne is ill at ease as a famous football coach whom Charles Coburn hires to stave off bankruptcy for a college through improved football results. Wayne accepts only in order to keep custody of young daughter Sherry Jackson from a broken marriage. His ruthless philosophy – 'Winning isn't everything. It's the only thing' – does the trick, while his personal problems are resolved, after initial setbacks, by probation officer Donna Reed. The film is undoubtedly one of Wayne's worst for Warners, probably due to the off-screen friction, but since he allowed Curtiz to direct him again in *The Comancheros* nine years later, he presumably did not blame

Curtiz for what went wrong. None the less, *Trouble Along the Way* is not without merit, especially in the performances of Coburn and Sherry Jackson, and its profit was 771,000 dollars.

The Jazz Singer and *Trouble Along the Way*, both filmed in 1952, had been indifferent films artistically because of poor material, and they hastened Curtiz's final break with Warners. Early in January 1953 he was impressed with the script for *The Boy from Oklahoma*, shot in February and March, but he sought five weeks for filming instead of the allocated four to improve the quality to A feature standard. As Jack Warner had proposed again that Curtiz should reduce his percentage of the profits for this film, Curtiz had concluded that his right to 25 per cent of the profits was the main reason behind the four-week allocation. He went on to state that he regarded the percentage clause of his contract as lying at the root of his differences with the studio, and that he had already indicated to Jack Warner that he was ready to end his contract at any time.[78] The fact that he committed himself in this way on paper shows how much he and Warners had moved apart.

In the event *The Boy from Oklahoma* was Curtiz's last Warners film as a contract director. In the new colour process dubbed Warnercolor, Curtiz achieved in four weeks what he had thought he needed five weeks to do. Will Rogers Junior plays genial, intending law student Tom Brewster who arrives in the lawless town of Bluerock just as the sheriff has been murdered. Although Brewster carries no guns, he is elected as the new sheriff, discovers the murderer, rounds up the villains, and wins dead man's daughter Nancy Olson. This plot is unremarkable, but the tenor is pleasant, with Rogers again in effect imitating his famous father. If Curtiz had had his way in the matter of more time and more experienced supporting players, the film would probably be better than it is. In impact Curtiz harks back to James Stewart's pacifist sheriff characterization in George Marshall's *Destry Rides Again* (1939) for Universal. However, what strikes one most is Curtiz's light-hearted, traditional approach at a time when westerns were on the one hand aspiring to high drama in the aftermath of Fred Zinneman's *High Noon* (1952) for Stanley Kramer and, on the other, indulging in greater visual violence.[79] The outcome is a more entertaining film than many routine westerns. The photography of Robert Burks stands out, and there is an unusual 'who done it' element for a western. *The Boy from Oklahoma* was Curtiz's way of showing that gory, gratuitous violence and new dramatic situations were not necessary to make entertaining westerns. This message did not entirely penetrate through to the box-office, for when the film was released early in 1954, it made a profit of only 454,000 dollars.

Curtiz completed *The Boy from Oklahoma* on 21 March 1953 and was released from his contract on 18 April. This cost Warners 75,000 dollars and the profit percentages from his films since the winding-up of Michael

Curtiz Productions. The application of the latter provision produced a long wrangle, during which Curtiz twice threatened legal action, in September 1953 and April 1954, before Warners settled up. Threats of litigation represented a very sour note for such a fruitful and prolonged association to end upon, but it apparently left no permanent mark on either side. Curtiz attended Harry Warner's funeral in 1958, he returned to the studio for *The Helen Morgan Story* in 1956–7, and Jack Warner's 1964 autobiography contains favourable references to Curtiz.[80]

It has sometimes been suggested that Curtiz left Warners for financial reasons arising from a paternity case by actress Jill Gerrard which went expensively against him.[81] But this did not take place until over a year later, while there were sound career reasons for his move. The quality of Warners films was falling, his last few films having reflected this. The studio personnel with whom he had matured as a director had mostly already gone, the actual film-making having largely fallen into younger hands. His old Warners associates were scattered among the other Hollywood studios, and in a freelance capacity he stood a better chance of being able to select his colleagues and films.

7

HOLLYWOOD NOMAD,
April 1953 to April 1962

When Curtiz left Warners, the Hollywood studio system was under strain. Falling cinema attendances were steadily undermining the economics of traditional Hollywood film-making. Moreover, the second wave of HUAC hearings from 1951 to 1954 kept alive an apprehensive atmosphere into the early 1960s through the ruination of Hollywood careers by blacklisting. This development led to much bland, politically safe film content and a consequent overreliance upon past successful but now outmoded material. Most of the major studios possessed funds in Europe which they had not been able to send to the United States, while European production costs were cheaper, which prompted the studios to use European facilities more and more for film production from the mid–1950s onwards.

The twin reactions of the studios to their changed position were new projection techniques and films dealing with subjects barred to television. The former included large-screen developments such as 3-D, Cinerama, Cinemascope. Vistavision, and the 70mm Todd-AO, whereas the latter advanced into socially controversial areas considered unsuitable for American television family viewing. However, the new large-screen colour films had to have appropriate content to fill them, and the ensuing costume dramas were expensive to produce. Only Cinemascope survived into the 1960s, a relatively small number of post–1954 small scale monochrome so-called permissive dramas proving no more successful in luring mass audiences back into cinemas. By the later 1950s and early 1960s cinema attendances dipped to an all-time low. By 1955 the studios were co-operating with television rather than competing against it by producing television programmes and selling past films to television companies.

Under such changing conditions Curtiz made fifteen films in almost nine years for various studios and remained an active director until his death. His contract details and the financial showing of his films in this period are in most cases unknown, but it seems that he left Warners to sign a seven-year contract with Paramount which allowed him considerable latitude to direct films for other studios. In effect he had become a freelance director, gaining more creative independence than at Warners.

117

Offsetting this were the facts that Hollywood conditions were deteriorating, and that, at 64 years of age in April 1953, he was an ageing director whose health was failing from August 1957.

Curtiz's first film for Paramount was the famous *White Christmas*, a glossy Vistavision reworking of Mark Sandrich's 1942 *Holiday Inn* with Bing Crosby and Fred Astaire for the same studio. Preparations for a near remake had been in progress since 1949 for the same stars, but Astaire had rejected it and been replaced by Danny Kaye just before Curtiz became the assigned director. In fact Paramount had approached Trilling for Curtiz's services on this film just prior to his break with Warners,[1] and the project was so far advanced when he took over that he decided simply to shape the routine musical material into a gentle, well-rounded film to show off the vast array of old and new Irving Berlin songs. In this he totally succeeded. For the most part Kaye's talent is not fully exploited in the story of two successful entertainers who save their revered, retired Second World War commander Dean Jagger's failing winter resort. However, to criticize *White Christmas* in other respects is merely to criticize the entire thin plot/song-based genre from a serious artistic standpoint. Certainly none of the finest Curtiz touches is present, but the film remains very good light entertainment and was reportedly his greatest money-maker.

The Egyptian for Twentieth Century-Fox (TCF) was Curtiz's next and longest film. Finnish author Mika Waltari's 1945 best-selling novel was really too long and too academic for easy adaptation, but TCF boss Zanuck had none the less bought the screen rights in 1952. The screenplay problems had become apparent when Zanuck consulted Casey Robinson on a number of occasions between September 1952 and April 1953, but any doubts that Zanuck might have harboured about the wisdom of the project had been swept away by the success of Henry Koster's *The Robe*. This confirmed Zanuck's resolve to use Cinemascope for a second studio Biblical epic and, with memories of *Noah's Ark* in 1928, to have Curtiz direct it. Within six weeks of Curtiz's departure from Warners and before he had commenced filming *White Christmas*, he became the designated director and was closely involved with Zanuck, Robinson, and later writer Philip Dunne in script preparation. The latter took over from Robinson in August 1953, but script disagreements persisted, and although Curtiz played a part in the casting, Zanuck was the dominating influence. It is not known whether Curtiz approved of Marlon Brando and Bella Darvi in the lead parts, but in any case casting ran into other problems until early in 1954 when the cast included Brando, Victor Mature, Gene Tierney, Michael Wilding, Jean Simmons, and Peter Ustinov. They were supported by *The Robe* cameraman Leon Shamroy, music from top composers Bernard Herrman and Alfred Newman, and stupendous George Davis and Lyle Wheeler sets. The blatant weak link was Darvi, an untalented former Nazi concentration camp inmate, but she could not be removed because she was Zanuck's mistress. At the end of January 1954 Brando left the film, citing Curtiz, Darvi, and his own part as the reasons – all pretexts for his belated realization that the production itself was a mistake. His replacement was Edmund Purdom, then being built up as a star.

The film traces Purdom's rise from a foundling to the position of the Pharaoh's physician in fourteenth-century BC Thebes and his involvement in an assassination plot against his master. There is too little action for 140 minutes running time, but Curtiz contains the overextended narrative while simultaneously keeping it moving and taking opportunities for comedy and spectacle. However, despite his efforts, *The Egyptian* for the most part flounders apart from some epic moments, especially a lion hunt early on and an attack upon Thebes at the end. Acting honours go primarily to Tierney as Pharoah Mature's consort and, as the physician's servant, to Ustinov, who did not enjoy making the film but did not blame Curtiz for the risible result.[2] Both Darvi and Purdom are out of their depth, while the sprawling screenplay was too great a handicap to overcome. Zanuck was pleased with Curtiz, aside from some unauthorized retakes, but he set about editing the film before its completion in a way that did not always meet with Curtiz's approval. Nowadays it is easy to scoff at *The Egyptian*'s imperfections and absurdities, but its lavishness has seldom been equalled and in sheer spectacle Curtiz is at his best.[3]

The first of the three Paramount films which followed was *We're No Angels*, which centres upon escaped Devil's Island convicts Bogart, Aldo Ray, and Ustinov, who hide in a shop run by kindly Leo G. Carroll and wife Joan Bennett. The convicts plan to kill them until greedy relative Basil Rathbone appears. Instead they help Carroll to retain control of his shop through Rathbone's murder and their own voluntary return to prison. The comedy is whimsical, but spark is generally lacking except in the opening sequence, when fierce dogs and prison staff hunt for the convicts in a market street just as a rainstorm erupts.

The Vagabond King is an opulent, set-bound musical remake of Rudolf Friml's famed operetta, which had already been filmed three times, twice in non-musical versions. Francois Villon, the rebel leader of the Paris beggars (Oreste, a Maltese tenor who to date has never made another film), aids King Louis XI against Burgundy as the fall of the city seems imminent. Supposedly a coming star to rival Mario Lanza, Oreste is lifeless, Kathryn Grayson as the female lead has too little to do, and the acting is redeemed by the liveliness of Rita Moreno as Villon's girlfriend and by veteran Walter Hampden in his last film with a clever performance as the conniving French king. In retrospect *The Vagabond King* is not as bad as many contemporary critics believed, but this refurbishment of badly dated material was none the less misjudged. On the whole Curtiz goes through the motions mechanically, but two fencing duels involving Oreste, several crowd sequences, and a spectacular battle after the Burgundian army enters Paris are brilliantly staged.

Produced by Curtiz himself, *The Scarlet Hour* is a smooth, 1940s-style, black and white, eternal triangle thriller in which wife Carol Ohmart and her lover Tom Tryon hijack a jewel thief gang to obtain money for their elopement. Suspecting their affair, husband James Gregory follows the pair, but Ohmart kills him during a scuffle. She is charged with murder, while Tryon goes to jail with new love Jody Lawrance promising to wait for him. Curtiz's direction is slick, but the plot is too conventional, the leads are too inexperienced (they were both making their screen debuts), and genuine suspense occurs only fleetingly. However, a promising debut is made by comedienne Elaine Stritch as a wisecracking showgirl, a performance in the Eve Arden mould.

More memorable is *The Best Things in Life are Free*, the TCF De Luxe color biography of songwriting team Lew Brown (Ernest Borgnine), Buddy de Sylva (Gordon MacRae), and Ray Henderson (Dan Dailey). Zanuck had conceived this for other stars in mid–1955,[4] and the story went through several script stages, but it is unclear from the TCF documentation whether Curtiz became the director before or after Zanuck's subsequent resignation as TCF studio head. However, the film broadly represented Zanuck's idea, and Curtiz's influence was probably concerned with detail rather than basic substance. A bright and breezy, amiable presentation, backed by good 1920s backstage settings and elaborate if disappointing numbers, almost conceals the unsuitability of the material for the irrelevant Cinemascope screen. The story rambles along unevenly and is not helped by the appearance and then sudden disappearance of too many background figures. The most surprising scene portrays the trio, merry from drink at a party, shutting themselves into a room and hastily concocting a deliberately corny song for the pushy Al Jolson, played by Norman Brooks. The song turns out to be *Sonny Boy* which Jolson had made into a hit in the 1928 *The Singing Fool*, the relevant clip from the film actually being seen, although Zanuck had been prepared to film it with Brooks if necessary.[5] The party scene when Jolson telephones was in the script before Curtiz became the director, and it was one that Zanuck had specially wanted, for it was based upon a real incident, slightly falsified.[6] However, the scene was amended after Zanuck's departure, and presumably Curtiz might have omitted it altogether. To that extent its inclusion might have reflected Curtiz's dislike of Jolson arising from *Mammy* in 1929. Despite the film's superficiality, its genial flamboyance, which extends to the gangster portrayals of Murvyn Vye and former heavyweight boxer Tony Galento, shines through the maudlin content.

The Helen Morgan Story (*Both Ends of the Candle* in Britain) marked Curtiz's return to Warners. In the mid–1950s Hollywood had resurrected the 1930s musicals of the 'show must go on' variety, supplemented with lavish sets and striking colour. Parallel to this trend was the musical biography dealing with a central character possessing a self-destructive urge, ultimately cured. *The Helen Morgan Story* falls clearly into neither category, for it is filmed in harsh monochrome close to a 1940s *noir* style (in so far as this applies to Cinemascope) and there is no unambiguous silver lining in a script that for once remained reasonably faithful to real life. Helen Morgan was a blues singer, the height of her popularity being in the late 1920s and early 1930s, but she suffered from chronic alcoholism and died at 41 years of age. A projected biography had been in circulation at Warners ever since her death in 1941, with many writers having been involved with the screenplay, but Jack Warner had held back his final approval because there had never been an obvious choice to play Morgan.

Warner was ready to try again in 1956. Curtiz, a logical choice to direct such nostalgic material, became the director in August with first Richard Whorf and then Martin Rackin as producer, but the central casting problem had still not been settled. Curtiz and Rackin heard, contacted, interviewed or tested many actresses including Olivia de Havilland, Jennifer Jones, Susan Hayward, Doris Day, and Peggy Lee, without success, but the way to a solution was pointed by columnist Hedda Hopper who suggested Ann Blyth to Curtiz. Initially Curtiz and Rackin were reluctant even to test her because they thought her too sweet on the basis of her most recent roles in routine films. Curtiz even maintained in public that he had forgotten about her since *Mildred Pierce*,[7] although in reality he wished to avoid testing her.[8] However, when he did ultimately test her in December 1956, she was selected. To play opposite her as a conventional hoodlum Curtiz chose Paul Newman, who had recently starred as the boxer Rocky Graziano in Robert Wise's *Somebody Up There Likes Me* for MGM, a performance which had impressed Curtiz.[9]

In the film Morgan's alcoholism is played down in favour of problems with men. She is loved by reliable but married Richard Carlson, while she herself loves ne'er-do-well, ambitious crook Newman, with whom she develops a love–hate relationship due to his mental cruelty. She turns to drink, but whenever recovery is a possibility, Newman reappears and her career again declines. Eventually he reforms, finds her in a hospital, and takes her back to a night club where her friends are ready to welcome her back to Broadway. The script is poorly structured, reflecting the many minds involved, but Curtiz's sympathetic approach[10] impressively reconstructs the 1920s background of prohibition, honky tonks, and speakeasys. He also injects high tension into the Blyth–Newman confrontations, but although Blyth is competent, she does not rise to the role's full potential and puts over somewhat mechanically a range of Morgan songs and dances (the voice belongs to Gogi Grant). Newman is better in alternating cynical menace with exploitive smooth-talking charm and sexiness. He brings as much conviction as can be brought to his change of heart arising from his gangland fight wounds and a spell in jail. An enigmatic ending, hinting at Morgan's rehabilitation, was retained against censorship pressure for her to die as the inevitable result of moral waywardness.[11] Curtiz was gratified to return to Warners, however briefly. He was more co-operative on the set than he had been for the most part before 1953, and at the end of filming he wrote a warm letter of appreciation to Trilling, who had evidently smoothed the way.[12] However, the film lost more than 500,000 dollars, a sad and unjust way for Curtiz finally to leave the studio he had served so well.

At the end of August 1957, when Curtiz was preparing for *The Proud Rebel*, he underwent an emergency operation as the first major stage of his fight against cancer.[13] He left hospital just over a week later, but within a few hours he was conducting rehearsals from a wheelchair with stars Alan Ladd and Olivia de Havilland.[14] Such determination shows that he was more than usually keen about the film he was about to direct for Buena Vista under producer Sam Goldwyn Junior. Although it was Goldwyn who had approached Ladd about the lead and about casting Ladd's own son, David, as his screen son,[15] this was unlikely to have occurred without Curtiz's prior approval, while Curtiz himself had sought a renewed collaboration with de Havilland.

The story is concerned with the efforts of Confederate veteran Ladd to find a cure for his son's dumbness, caused by the shock of having seen Union troops kill his mother. They journey with their dog Lance to a Minnesota town where Ladd falls foul of a local family headed by villainous Dean Jagger. Jagger's sons try to steal Lance, and when Ladd prevents them in a fist fight, a judge fines him. The fine is paid by de Havilland, requiring help to run her farm and keep it from Jagger's grasp. She and Ladd manage the farm successfully until Jagger has sheep driven onto it and the barn burnt down. Unknown to his son, Ladd sells Lance to pay for the boy's operation, but when this fails and the boy returns, he turns against his father. Ladd decides to buy Lance back, but Jagger has bought him legally and at first refuses to sell. He then ostensibly relents in order to provoke Ladd into a gun battle which the latter cannot win. At a critical moment during the clash Ladd's son regains his voice to save his father's life, Jagger and his sons perish, and Ladd returns to the farm to marry de Havilland.

Although *The Proud Rebel*'s ending is predictable, it is nevertheless a first-rate western, closely modelled upon George Stevens's 1953 *Shane* for Paramount, also starring Ladd. There is little action before the gun battle climax, the only direct showdown in a Curtiz western, but the narrative always attracts attention and Curtiz maintains a taut control over all the players. McCord's location photography is magnificent, at its best in the fist fight, sheep round-up, and showdown sequences, while David Ladd is perfect as the mute son, especially in a scene where other boys taunt him about his dumbness. None of the 103 minutes is wasted, mawkishness is circumvented, and King as Lance was arguably the most skilled screen dog since Rin Tin Tin.

King Creole, in Vistavision black and white for Paramount, was a reunion for Curtiz with Hal Wallis, who had his own production unit within the studio organization. In January 1955 he had acquired the screen rights to Harold Robbins's 1951 novel *A Stone for Danny Fisher*, but the project had then encountered difficulties with the lead part, script disagreements, and censorship obstacles throughout 1955, 1956, and 1957. Curtiz had read the script as early as May 1955, when he approved of the film in principle but disliked the script and later amendments.[16] In late November 1957 Wallis had signed rock-and-roll idol Elvis Presley and cast him as Danny Fisher, a talented New Orleans singer, with Curtiz's agreement.[17] As a product of the mid–1950s pop revolution and as the natural inheritor of the crazy mixed-up kid legacy left by James Dean's death, Presley plays a teenage vocalist who is poised to become a delinquent under the influence of ruthless gang boss Walter Matthau. When Presley gains a singing job at the rival King Creole night club, attracting patrons away from Matthau's own club, the racketeer initiates an attack upon Presley's ailing father, Dean Jagger. In a noteworthy climax Presley prevails, with the assistance of Matthau's moll Carolyn Jones, whose sacrifice of her life prompts Presley to renounce crime.

A gritty offering, starkly photographed by Russell Harlan, *King Creole* made rapid progress after Presley had been cast. Curtiz was heavily involved in the rest of the casting,[18] and filming took place without a hitch from January to March 1958. He had feared that turning the young hero into a singer would adversely influence his characterization,[19] and consequently, as was his custom, integrated the Presley tunes into the main plot. He guided both the inexperienced youngster and the relatively untried Matthau in only his sixth film into solid performances. The New Orleans French quarter external locations convey a vivid gangland and night club atmosphere, while the climax on a surf-pounded beach as Matthau pursues Presley is gripping. However, at the time Presley fans did not relish their idol as a serious actor, the film reportedly being one of the very few Presley box-office failures.

The Hangman, star Robert Taylor's first independent film under Paramount auspices, saw Curtiz return to 35mm black and white. Taylor plays a federal deputy marshal known as 'The Hangman' for his reputation of always getting his man. In the 1870s south-west he seeks a hold-up man for murder and goes to North Creek to arrest him. However, when he arrives, he finds that suspected outlaw Jack Lord is highly respected and nobody, not even sheriff Fess Parker, will help him. At length Taylor catches up with Lord, who admits he is the man Taylor is after but maintains his innocence of the hold-up murder. Via Lord's ex-girlfriend Tina Louise, Taylor has come to doubt Lord's guilt and thus allows him to escape from jail. He abandons his rigid views on justice and retribution, turns in his badge, and retires to California with Louise.

Curtiz worked well with Taylor, and some contemporary critics praised it, but the film was not a financial success. The passage of time has shown it to stand out as a most unusual western: it contains no climactic shoot-out (not in itself outside the Curtiz pattern) and no real villain, while it avoids the late 1950s western penchant for psychological trimmings. Instead Curtiz pinpoints moral differences and tensions among the principals, a focus sufficiently strong over eighty-six minutes to support the arising situations. Some superfluous mild sexual-comedy interludes suggest that Taylor's image as a hard man makes him attractive to older and younger women alike, while Tina Louise is depicted as a near slut rather than as a conventional heroine. Taylor's change of heart at the end might seem unconvincing, but rarely has a screen lawman been faced with so much evidence that his prey was innocent, although in fact his guilt or innocence is never firmly established. Curtiz's low-key direction fits the slight narrative beautifully, and interest never flags. Although *The Hangman* is now seldom remembered or revived, it deserves respect and is superior to many westerns of its day.

The Man in the Net for Mirisch Brothers stars Alan Ladd as a would-be artist who goes on a day trip to New York and returns to discover that neurotic, faithless wife Carolyn Jones has disappeared. He is suspected of murdering her but establishes his innocence with the aid of children he had painted. Curtiz's heart was probably not in the far-fetched material which is routinely presented, only the children's performances lifting the film in any way. *The Adventures of Huckleberry Finn* is a sturdy version of the 1885 Mark Twain classic novel for MGM in Metrocolor. Eddie Hodges is passable as the irrepressible Huckleberry, but in his solitary film former world champion boxer Archie Moore is surprisingly good as runaway black slave Jim. Although McCord's location photography is beyond reproach, the novel's Mississippi river atmosphere is captured only now and again. Curtiz converts Twain's emphasis upon the fascination of life in the wild into a straightforward if agreeable boys' adventure story. The outcome is no more than workman-like. *A Breath of Scandal* was derived from a 1938 Sidney Howard scenario at MGM which was never filmed. In the late 1950s MGM had sold it to Carlo Ponti who saw it as a vehicle for his wife, Sophia Loren. The play upon which it was based is a barbed satire aimed at the pre–1914 Austrian court, but what emerges on screen is a very feeble sex farce, notable only for the performances of Isabel Jeans and Maurice Chevalier as Loren's parents. Curtiz's motive for taking on this indifferent project was probably the prospect of location filming in Vienna. For the first time since 1926 he directed outside the United States, returning to Vienna for what, in the light of his illness, he must have known would probably be the last time. This perhaps explains Mario Montuori's splendid colour Vistavision photography which dwells upon five Vienna palaces as well as a famous amusement park. These excellent exteriors were Curtiz's final salute to his European career.

However, Curtiz's last European film was *Francis of Assisi* in De Luxe Cinemascope, TCF's contribution to the late 1950s Biblical and religious revival cycle. Curtiz spent three months travelling extensively to find a suitable location, but ultimately he settled upon Assisi itself. Although the village was genuinely medieval, it did not look old enough for Curtiz who had it put through a studio face-lift with the villagers' consent. Many extras in the film came from the village, including some Franciscan monks, and only the Vatican sequences were shot elsewhere, in Rome. Bradford Dillman as the son of prosperous thirteenth-century cloth merchant Eduard Franz takes a vow of poverty, cares for animals, struggles to found his own monastic order and end war, and dies a hermit. This is a legend which Curtiz might have easily turned into a standard Biblical epic. Instead, defying the lavish presentation, he relegates spectacle to second place behind a reverential, somewhat dour, and eventually discomfiting approach. In so doing he achieves a sense of worldly realism seldom seen in religious films, but the impact is marred by a banal, rambling script and an unimpressive central performance. *Francis of Assisi* is unusual in its genre in that idealism suffers a strong buffeting and the hero dies without having achieved success by his own criteria.

By 1961 Curtiz was seriously ill, but he lived long enough to finish *The Comancheros*, a rousing action vehicle for John Wayne. Via TCF producer George Sherman, who was an old friend, Wayne foisted on to the film cameraman Bill Clothier, writer James Edward Grant, Wayne's own son Patrick, and long-standing crony Bruce Cabot. As Clothier remarked many years later, 'Mike was just plain outnumbered',[20] but Curtiz's influence was none the less strong, manifestly so in the casting of the other character parts and the overall impact. During filming he was admitted to hospital at least once, Wayne temporarily taking over, while the action sequences were credited to former 1930s stunt man Cliff Lyons, who had been a double for Curtiz on *Blackwell's Island* in 1938 and had appeared in *Santa Fe Trail* in 1940. On the basis of Lyons's screen credit, it has been believed that Curtiz's direction was confined to the interiors, but in fact he himself filmed at least some of the exteriors, for he was once slightly injured on the southern Utah location while directing an Indian attack upon Wayne.[21] In any case, no matter how ill he was, it would have been most unlike him to have relinquished control of action scenes to a second unit director, and from past experience Lyons was familiar with Curtiz's method of handling such material.

The story is of Texas Ranger Wayne and gambler prisoner Stuart Whitman, arrested for killing a man in a duel. The two men join forces to defeat outlaws and their Indian allies led by megalomaniac Nehemiah Persoff in his canyon stronghold to which there is only one entrance. Through their victory the two men come to admire and respect each other, Wayne allowing Whitman to go free. During the early sequences Curtiz keeps alive the Wayne–Whitman tension while maintaining the flow of the main narrative. Once they gain access to the outlaw hideout, Curtiz switches the main attention to the tyrannical gang leader and then to the action, too similar to Curtiz's style and past films to be the creation of a second unit director. Easy-going, cheerfully violent in its brawls, *The Comancheros* projects vitality and a traditional approach without artistic pretensions, which allow it to retain its high entertainment value today. It opened towards the end of 1961 to favourable reviews, a fitting epitaph to Curtiz's career. Within months the cancer he had fought so resolutely for more than four years had taken its final toll. He died on 11 April 1962 at the age of 73.

8

ASSESSMENT

The foregoing account of Curtiz's career does scant justice to his achievements, which were considerable in his native Hungary alone. From 1912 to 1919, despite absences in Denmark, in the army, and in exile for part of the last year, he not only made the first Hungarian feature film but went on to direct, on the minimum reckoning, more than 10 per cent of his country's entire feature film output for that period. Although his complete Hungarian filmography remains uncertain, it lies beyond question that no other contemporary Hungarian director matched him in either quality or quantity. His only possible rival was Alexander Korda, whose influence at this time extended beyond actual film-making, but he was not Curtiz's equal purely as a director, either then or later, and the latter contributed more than any other single individual to the creation and initial expansion of the Hungarian feature film industry.[1]

Curtiz's part in the expansion of the Austrian film industry during the early 1920s was less striking statistically, for his Austrian films represented approximately only 5 per cent of national output from 1919 to 1926. Nevertheless, under Kolowrat's encouragement and guidance he played a significant role in the emergence of the Sascha studio as one of the foremost in Europe. As in Hungary, he widened the technical horizons of national film-making through location shooting before his departure for Hollywood and Kolowrat's death in 1927 halted the rise of Sascha and of the Austrian film industry in general. More than twenty years after his arrival in Hollywood, Curtiz himself considered his Austrian experience to have been of vital importance to his subsequent career.[2] However, this verdict ignores what he had learned in Denmark in 1913 as well as the development of his Hungarian movies. What little of these survives, together with what is known of them from printed sources, indicates that he accepted traditional Hungarian novels and plays in accordance with Kinoriport, Projectograph, and Uher studio policies but shaped them to his own individual style. When he became head of Phoenix at the beginning of 1917, he turned mostly to adventure, crime, and melodrama for his material, with an occasional incursion into implicit social comment such as *Lu, the Coquette*, a story based upon prostitution. His chief Phoenix scriptwriters were Laszlo Vadja and Ivan Siklosi, who developed their own ideas and plots from outlines supplied by Curtiz himself. The few extant scenes from *The Secret of the Saint Job Forest* bear witness to an outstanding talent for vivid visual images,[3] while his Austrian films, some of which survive,[4] intermittently show the same flair as well as one for slick narrative. Adventure, crime, and melodrama continued to dominate, and the films also grew longer in accordance with international film developments. But nothing he directed in Hungary equalled *Sodom and Gomorrah* and *The Slave Queen* for sheer spectacle, and to that extent his spell in Vienna advanced his professional skills. What influence he possessed in selecting and shaping his Sascha films remains uncertain, but it was probably considerable, for Kolowrat seems to have permitted his directors almost unlimited personal licence, as was customary in Europe at that time. A pointer in the same direction was Curtiz's assertive self-confidence when he joined Warners and at once filmed unscripted material for his first American film, *The Third Degree*.[5]

When Curtiz came to Hollywood in 1926, the scientific management based upon accountancy known as the studio system was largely in place. At Warners that meant Harry Warner, in consultation with his brothers, determined the year's estimated income from films and then how many of the various genres the company would produce at defined budget levels. All this was based upon previous experience, exhibitors' pro-gramme needs, a forecast of the coming year's market, and elementary market research. The total budget could be spread across a large number of films at relatively low budgets or across fewer films with higher budgets or a combination of these two. While Curtiz was there from 1926 to 1953, the studio for the most part concentrated upon the first of these alternatives with the aim of bringing in small but consistent profits. Harry and Jack Warner then planned serials, shorts, and newsreels and sometimes took initial decisions about story selection, director choice, and major casting. After all this groundwork had been laid Jack Warner (following Sam Warner's death in 1927) set in motion actual film pro-duction.

This involved a production department headed by Jack's assistant who acted as the day-to-day economic and management controller and had the power to reduce a script to meet a film's allotted budget. The assistant's deputy on a film, called the assistant director in 1926 and later the supervisor and then the associate producer, usually assumed responsibility for such matters as routine pre-shooting organization, the daily shooting schedule, and the hire of extras. In effect he acted as the liaison between the staff on the set, especially the director, and the production department, always conscious that the lion's share of a film's cost was eaten up by salaries and wages. The fewer people involved in a film and minimum shooting, the less a film would cost to make. The production department normally selected the writers for individual films, although in Hollywood generally it was already rare by the mid–1920s for one writer to carry out the work from start to finish. Instead projects usually travelled through several writers.

Within this production formula a director could influence the script subject to higher approval, but his main function was control of the actual filming. He decided how the film was to be shot, assisted in this task by the camera, casting, costume, make-up, research, and set design (art direction) departments as well as the various technicians. Already film-making had been subdivided into many specialisms – some administrative and financial, some artistic, and some technical – and although the system's basic structure was rigid and there was much pressure for those who did not feel secure in their positions to conform to studio requirements, the system was nevertheless more flexible than is often believed. Everything depended upon individual personalities, their ability to strike up good working relations with superiors as well as subordinates, and their willingness to listen to and possibly compromise with the ideas of others.

In this context Harry Warner saw the studio personnel as one large happy family and was unbending only over a few basic tenets of his extreme cost-consciousness and social conservatism such as his opposition to artistic freedom for players and union rights for film workers. His was always the ultimate studio authority, but he apparently needed to exercise it upon only rare occasions either because that suited his temperament and 'happy family' view of the studio or because he and his brothers mostly saw eye to eye. Jack Warner, too, was not overauthoritarian with regard to his assistant executives and directors within the framework of Harry's policy, while Zanuck's supervision over filming was sympathetic to those on the set, at least until films began to lose money in the early 1930s. To judge from the Warners pre–1931 production records, which consist largely of legal documents, the budget system for individual films was not as thorough and sophisticated as it later became under the impact of heavy film-making losses in the first half of the 1930s. Thus there is no way of establishing whether or not Curtiz or any other Warners director stayed within the prescribed budget or how much latitude he was allowed in the making of his films. This also holds good for the Warners films from 1931 to mid–1935, although for these there is more production documentation and a few budgets. However, Jack Warner always wished directors to have maximum artistic freedom within the constraints of studio policy for the simple reason that this policy would be more likely to produce a better film than over-regimentation. The amount of freedom permitted varied from film to film and from director to director according to many factors such as his studio standing, the financial records of his films, his personal relations with Jack Warner and his assistants, his contractual power, and legal restraints upon film content. Naturally Jack Warner and his assistants selected directors for films according to, as far as possible within film production schedules, their suitability for the particular project concerned and their commitment to it. Although the studio normally had a contractual right to assign a director to a film against his wishes, this was sparingly exercised and directors did sometimes refuse a particular project. There is no doubt that Curtiz was chosen for certain films because he was especially suitable for the subject matter. On present evidence it is impossible to disentangle Curtiz's individual contributions from studio requirements over film content in many of his pre–1935 films, although some of these were almost certainly due solely to studio routine and attracted less than Curtiz's wholehearted zeal. This was probably likewise true of the other Warners directors except LeRoy in the first half of the 1930s when losses at the other studios meant employment there might be hard to obtain. To this extent there might be some substance to the 'studio workhorse' theory of Curtiz until the mid–1930s.

For close to ten years following Curtiz's death the problem of evaluating his European films and attempting to uncover his precise contributions to his early Warners films was compounded by the fact that the latter were all lost, except for a greatly truncated version of *Noah's Ark*. However, a print of *The Third Degree* then came to light in Jack Warner's private collection. This revealed that by 1926 Curtiz was already way ahead of Hollywood directors in camera technique, as corroborated in Jack Warner's autobiography,[6] and in contemporary press reviews of both *The Third Degree* and Curtiz's next film *A Million Bid*.[7] His camera innovations, later to become a Hollywood commonplace, were not confined to the Warners films he himself directed, for ace cameraman Lee Garmes has drawn attention to his revolutionary camera placements for Alfred E. Green's *Disraeli* in 1929.[8]

Throughout his career Curtiz used his directorial authority to pay meticulous attention to camera usage, a characteristic which upset some of his cameramen. However, king of cinematographers James Wong Howe liked him as a person and much admired his versatility when they worked together in the late 1930s and early 1940s.[9] On *The Comancheros* in 1961 cameraman Bill Clothier and Curtiz had never previously collaborated and indeed the former was star John Wayne's choice, but all the same they enjoyed good relations and more than twenty years later Clothier remembered him as a very great director in spite of his poor health during the making of that film.[10] By contrast Hal Mohr seems to have included Curtiz among the directors who treated cameramen as mere photographers rather than as creative partners.[11] Mohr's criticism has to be seen in the light of his 1928 refusal to continue working with

Curtiz on *Noah's Ark* over the lack of adequate player protection against physical danger in the flood sequence, a moral question for which Mohr seemed retrospectively inclined to blame Zanuck as much as Curtiz.[12] Later Mohr worked with Curtiz again, apparently amicably, on *Captain Blood* and *The Walking Dead*, perhaps because other late 1920s and 1930s Hollywood directors were equally neglectful of player physical well-being in their quest for screen realism. After the success of *Captain Blood*, and possibly earlier, Curtiz tried to choose his cameramen and occasionally replaced them in mid-production. As it happened Warners had an exceptional number of accomplished cameramen during Curtiz's time there – for example, Edeson, Gaudio, Haller, Howe, Haskin, McCord, McGill, Marley, Mohr, Polito, Reese, Rennahan, and Skall – and he could expect the best of service in this respect if his first-choice cameraman was not available. In his later Warners years he worked well with McCord who, significantly, also filmed three of Curtiz's post-Warners movies. How far Curtiz consulted his cameramen about his wishes beyond their technical feasibility is unclear, but it is unlikely to have been very far until his latter, more mellowed years.

Writers such as William K. Everson and Joel Finler have argued that, since Curtiz did not have time for full pre-production preparations, he has received credit due to his technicians, particularly his art directors and cameramen. This interpretation is contradicted by all that is known of his methodical, ultra-painstaking approach to film-making, of which there is abundant evidence in the Warner Brothers archive. If Everson and Finler are correct at all, which is doubtful, then their view applies only to his early Warners films, but they both underestimate the director's power within the Warners system, for Grot, who first designed sets for Curtiz on *Noah's Ark* in 1928, confirmed a few years before his death in 1974 that Warners directors approved set design in advance of construction while he was studio art director from 1927 to 1948.[13] Furthermore, the Warners production files show that, from 1935 at the latest, Curtiz regularly inspected sets before shooting commenced and sometimes even altered them while filming was in progress. The truth is more likely that Grot, Carl Jules Weyl, and the other studio art directors designed the high-quality sets that they came to know by experience suited Curtiz's style.

Warners directors varied in the amount of detailed control they employed over the specialist departments, but Curtiz, at least once he became the top studio director and probably earlier, was noted for the close supervision he exercised over all production aspects of his films, as he had done in Hungary from 1917 to 1919 and possibly to a large extent in Austria as well. Not the least of his gifts was his ability to weld players, writers, and technicians into a strong team, usually without lasting resentments despite the varied and sometimes over-sensitive temperaments involved. If it had been otherwise, he could hardly have survived at Warners for as long as he did (longer than most Warners directors and players), much less become the studio's leading director for fifteen years. Moreover, some of his talent rubbed off on to certain studio colleagues and enabled them in turn to become good directors. For instance, Irving Rapper, who acted as Curtiz's dialogue director on many later 1930s and early 1940s films, described Curtiz as his mentor–guide and believed that Curtiz had taught him all he knew about making films.[14] Don Siegel, too, put together montages for Curtiz films, including *Casablanca*, under the latter's guidance and first, very briefly, directed at Curtiz's suggestion part of the freighter battle sequence in *Passage to Marseille*.[15] However poor some of his films were, they can seldom be faulted for their production values within the technical limitations of their time. Indeed the production values were the only redeeming features of the worst of them, a goodly proportion of which occurred in Curtiz's early Warner years. However, during this time he gained valuable experience of the Warners conveyor-belt system and American social values without sacrificing all of his individuality. He managed the transition from silents to sound without losing his natural film-making aptitude, as evidenced by the *Noah's Ark* flood sequence, which rivals anything that Cecil B. De Mille had accomplished. It has been accurately noted that owing to the large number of films he made and the variety of subject matter involved, Curtiz's influence on the development of the early American sound films was considerable.[16]

In the late 1920s he did not see films as a genuine art form. As he told reporter Jerome Strauss in 1928, they were a blend of architecture, literature, music, painting, and sculpture. He feared that cinematic achievement would be only temporary compared to the permanence of Homer's *Iliad*, the Parthenon, and the work of Michelangelo. Their appeal was unchanging, whereas a film of, say, sixteen years earlier possessed an outdated technique which stood out like the ribs of a starving horse.[17] This revealing interview explains his insistence upon the highest possible production values throughout his career and also his apparent readiness until the mid–1930s to accept much routine material.

Players' performances were of course crucial ingredients of quality production values, and Curtiz's directorial philosophy required players to subordinate themselves to his grand design. This demand was accepted Hollywood practice, yet Curtiz has a worse reputation concerning player treatment than most other directors. His disregard of animal and player physical safety was greatly responsible for this, but the trait was also shared with other Hollywood directors. During the 1930s and the first half of the 1940s he adopted an increasingly autocratic stance on the set which was often intimidating. He sometimes experienced morose, remote moods, during which he was virtually unapproachable, but these were exceptional, and for the most part his behaviour was reasonable. When filming did not progress satisfactorily, he tended to rant and rave, sometimes at players and sometimes at technicians. Such a tendency produced sporadic verbal explosions on the set, but on the whole these were no more than one would expect among artistic temperaments and were usually over quickly because everyone held a transcending common interest in desiring to make a good film. Enduring hostility to Curtiz was rare. More typical was the reaction of George Brent, who starred in several 1930s Curtiz movies and much later considered him as a nice man but difficult to work with because he was a screamer and a shouter.[18] However, even in the 1930s, as the Warners unit managers' daily reports disclose, abrasive Curtiz conduct was by no means consistent, and it was eventually abandoned altogether during the 1950s in favour of the Kolowrat family approach of thirty years previously. His manner on the set was at its worst between 1930 and 1935, before the formation of the Screen Actors Guild limited players' daily working hours, and at its best from the late 1940s due to a combination of his own growing mellowness with age and the increased power of the technicians' trade unions. In general Curtiz clashed with players whose professionalism was less than his own utterly devoted one. He had little patience with players who arrived late for work, consistently forgot their dialogue, or otherwise gave him what he saw as unnecessary problems. As he explained in 1947, 'When I see a lazy man or a don't care girl, it makes me tough.'[19] How players and technicians remembered Curtiz thus depended upon how often they worked with him and when, so that it is not surprising that individual impressions of him varied, as will be seen.

His first prolonged clash with a player took place in 1930, the actor concerned being Frank Fay, and their mutual antipathy lasted through their three early 1930s films together. This represented merely a passing episode in Curtiz's long career, but it gained retrospective prominence after Curtiz's death through the publication of incidents during his films with Bette Davis and Errol Flynn. In the 1932 *Cabin in the Cotton* the young Davis was imposed upon Curtiz against his wishes, with the result that he treated her to a sexually insulting verbal abuse from behind the camera as she was actually acting, which she mentioned in her first autobiography, published very soon after Curtiz had died.[20] From then onwards right up until her own death in 1989 she never conceded that in the film he extracted from her the performance that proved to be her initial step towards stardom or his importance in her subsequent career. In that autobiography she had little to say about Curtiz's treatment of her during their five other 1930s films together, although she admitted that *Kid Galahad* had consolidated her position as a rising star.[21] Since she never worked with Curtiz again once she had secured director approval in 1939, many writers have concluded that she disliked him intensely owing to the *Cabin in the Cotton* events and would not work with him again after she had the choice.

However, this was clearly not the case. In a 1974 book, semi-autobiographical in the sense that she supplied a running commentary to a narrative which presumably had her approval, it was pointed out that Curtiz found less fault with her during *20,000 Years in Sing Sing*, although he did not positively help her, that he was gentle with the cast of *Jimmy the Gent*, that he helped her considerably during *Kid Galahad* because he secretly admired her courage in fighting her 1936 British legal case against Warners, and that he did not harry her during *The Private Lives of Elizabeth and Essex*.[22] The Warners unit managers' daily reports on both *Kid Galahad* and *The Private Lives of Elizabeth and Essex* confirm the absence of any Curtiz–Davis friction. Moreover, in 1935 she was critical of *Front Page Woman* (not even mentioned in her own autobiography) only over her particular role.[23] All this evidence suggests that at the time they had arrived at a mutual respect, and that later she recognized his part in her rise to fame but was loath to give him credit openly. Their failure to work together after 1939, when for ten years he was the studio's top director and she its main actress, was accidental. In February and early March 1942 he commenced preparations to direct Rapper's *Now, Voyager* when she was already cast, but he then withdrew in order to direct *Casablanca*, while in 1945 after her secret November test she was not selected for the Irene Dunne role in *Life With Father*. In the first instance Curtiz simply diverted himself to a more attractive film, and in the second he was probably overruled by Mrs Day and the authors of the play, although the evidence on this in the Warners files on the film is not clear-cut. However, it is clear that after 1939 Curtiz and Davis were each prepared to work again with the other. But she, almost certainly mistakenly, had some reason to feel that he had twice rebuffed her, and such a suspicion on her part rather than 1930s filming events might account for her post–1962 reluctance to award him his due over her early career.

In isolation the Davis autobiography might have had little or no influence upon Curtiz's reputation in handling players but for the revelation of his differences with Errol Flynn. Clashes with the excessively hard-drinking, rakish Flynn were inevitable, for his cavalier attitude to film acting and his own career was evident to Curtiz on *Captain Blood*, the outcome being tension between them until matters came to a head in 1941 when they fist fought, not for the first time, on the set of *They Died With Their Boots On*.[24] In refusing to direct Flynn again, Curtiz precipitated the final break. However, their confrontations occurred less often than is generally supposed during their eleven films together and were normally related to the physical dangers Curtiz wished Flynn to undergo in the adventure films. The Warners production records on, for example, *The Perfect Specimen* and *Four's a Crowd* display no sign of disharmony even though in the former early morning work was called for. Even when Curtiz took control from Keighley of *The Adventures of Robin Hood* Flynn was co-operative and on time, possibly because of his wish for a holiday once the film was finished. Furthermore, the antipathy lay more on the impetuous Flynn's side – for Curtiz their differences were purely professional, while for Flynn they were personal – and when Flynn died in 1959 Curtiz attended his funeral long after both had left Warners.[25] Significantly, Flynn's friend and admirer Raoul Walsh followed Curtiz in 1947 in refusing to direct him again. His consistently irresponsible professional behaviour taxed all his directors, especially after 1940, and Curtiz was patient with him, sometimes under extreme provocation, and granted him maximum latitude to exploit his good looks, physical agility, and boyish exuberance as a cover for his lack of natural acting ability. Possibly Flynn himself came to appreciate this as he grew older, for he never questioned Curtiz's prowess as a director and was surprisingly uncritical of him in *My Wicked, Wicked Ways*, Flynn's autobiography written shortly before his death at the age of 50 and published posthumously.

Details of the Curtiz–Flynn on-set clashes did not appear until both men were dead. These revelations, exaggerated for sensationalist effect, together with those of Bette Davis over the treatment Curtiz meted out to her during *Cabin in the Cotton*, have distorted the overall picture of his attitude to players. In any case it has always been impossible to reconcile his supposed harshness towards players with the many outstanding performances in his films. His relations with, for example, Bogart, Cagney, Edward G. Robinson, and Rains were excellent. Cagney's 1976 autobiography expressly praised him, Robinson's 1973 memoirs in no way disparaged him – indeed Robinson held a high opinion of *The Sea Wolf* at the time[26] – and when late in 1946 Warners offered Bogart a fresh contract with director approval, Curtiz was among the five directors he accepted unconditionally.[27] Cagney and Robinson were established stars before Curtiz directed them and thus might have received cosier treatment than lesser mortals. However, he had first directed Bogart while he was still a supporting actor. The common factor was that all three players as well as Rains, who considered Curtiz a great director after their eleven years and eleven films together,[28] were, unlike Flynn, wholehearted professionals whom Curtiz admired and respected. The same holds true for Olivia de Havilland who troubled him only now and again in the late 1930s due solely to studio policy detrimental to her career. When in 1957 Curtiz asked her to appear in *The Proud Rebel*, she agreed even though she lived in Paris and had not been directed by him since 1941, all of which scarcely suggests that she held him in low esteem. Very rarely for an actor, Zachary Scott expressed his appreciation on paper over *Mildred Pierce* before its release and described Curtiz as a truly great director.[29] Curtiz established such good relations with Peggy Lee on *The Jazz Singer* that shortly after its completion he gave her away at her January 1953 wedding to Bradford Dexter. Long-established stars such as Alan Ladd and Robert Taylor entrusted their films to the ageing and manifestly ill Curtiz in the late 1950s, but while their star careers were admittedly faltering, this did not apply to John Wayne over *The Comancheros* in 1961.

Curtiz after all had started his own career as an actor and at times, as with Flynn, was exceedingly flexible and patient, particularly with burgeoning talent and child performers, even if his treatment of the latter sometimes bordered upon cruelty in the 1930s and early 1940s. He was also unorthodox in his casting methods on occasions. Usually he selected from a list of available players submitted to him by the studio's casting department, but he sometimes deviated from this procedure because, as he once put it to a journalist, he did not seek great actors but people who possessed a heart and warmth which could be projected on to the screen, including anyone with an interesting face, plenty of energy, a unique personality, or just plain 'heart and warmth'.[30] His theory of acting was that it was half-trickery, the other half ideally being talent.[31] Such attitudes show why in 1936 he chose David Niven, then an emerging B feature actor, for an important supporting role in *The Charge of the Light Brigade* after Niven had answered him back before a planned test,[33] why in 1938 he plucked John Garfield from obscurity to play a crucial part in *Four Daughters*, and why in 1947, when Doris Day was auditioning for a major part in *Romance on the High Seas* but was preoccupied with her own domestic problems and broke down several times, he insisted upon hearing her out and awarded her the role.[33] These three actions produced star careers, in which respect, as with camera usage, Curtiz contributed more to film history than his own films. Nor should the progress of Jack Carson's career be overlooked after Curtiz had cast him against previous type in *Roughly Speaking* and, more especially, *Mildred Pierce*. Before the release of the latter Carson himself told a reporter that he had become a keen Curtiz fan. He had heard that Curtiz was very tough but had discovered for himself that this was simply malicious gossip.[34]

Curtiz was considerate towards even minor supporting players. As early as 1931 he sent for Boris Karloff to play a minor role in *The Mad Genius* under the impression that Karloff was Russian, but when he found he was in error, he gave him the part anyway just because he was so keen to secure it.[35] At about the same time he unsuccessfully tried to persuade Warners to make *Madame Bovary* with Myrna Loy, then a character actress, in the lead.[36] In 1934 he insisted that Vince Barnett should play a bit part in *Black Fury* against the wishes of star Paul

Muni.[37] In 1943 Dolores Costello, the female lead in *The Third Degree* and several other late 1920s Curtiz films, was given a small role in *This is the Army*. In *The Proud Rebel* Mary Wickes played a one-scene cameo while her career was grinding to a halt – she had earlier worked with Curtiz in much larger parts in *I'll See You in My Dreams*, *The Story of Will Rogers*, and *White Christmas*. Josephine Hutchinson, who had played the lead for Curtiz in the 1936 *Mountain Justice*, had a bit part in the 1960 *The Adventures of Huckleberry Finn*. In *The Comancheros* there were cameo parts for Henry Daniell and Guinn 'Big Boy' Williams (the latter uncredited), both of whom Curtiz had directed in more exalted roles during the 1930s and 1940s, since when their careers had plunged steadily downhill.

Curtiz was the exact reverse of cruel towards players, but, as Carson's comment implicitly acknowledged, he himself bestowed too much credibility upon his contrary reputation by his lack of concern for players' physical security until the mid–1940s and his disposition to lambaste players verbally whenever they did not deliver what he sought. However, his last persistent clashes with a player concerned Cary Grant on *Night and Day* in 1945 when the fault lay with Grant and Warners rather than Curtiz. 'Actor bums' was his favourite form of address to players in his heyday, but in reality even his most severe bark was worse than his bite and he does not seem ever to have had a player replaced for inability once he had cast him or her. However, some players, especially actresses, took his words too much at face value and later recorded what they saw as a lack of rapport with him in their autobiographies. This applies to Lauren Bacall, Michele Morgan, and Patricia Neal, who thus reinforced the unfavourable image of Curtiz first put forward by Bette Davis in 1962. More accurately, James Wong Howe, despite his disagreements with Curtiz on *Passage to Marseille*, conceded that the latter was not as mean as usually supposed. He was pretending most of the time.[38]

Curtiz's conduct on the set at its most irascible has earned him an understandable reputation as an incurable, hard-boiled, foul-mouthed cynic, but in fact his behaviour while directing was a protective outer shell for a highly artistic and hypersensitive nature. Jack Warner, who had a closer and longer contact with him than any player, described him as Bohemian and sensitive.[39] For instance, he was seen to be crying during the filming of the Walter Huston death scene in *Yankee Doodle Dandy*,[40] and Curtiz tears also flowed at times during the shooting of *The Jazz Singer*.[41] Furthermore, some superfluous wry humour in his films, such as Cagney's snappy dialogue exchange with Eddie Foy Junior in *Yankee Doodle Dandy* and the fractured English of the elderly European couple about to emigrate to the United States in *Casablanca* – a likely Curtiz image parody – are inconsistent with intractable cynicism. So also is Curtiz's attendance with other leading European directors on the 1942 Paramount set of *The Major and the Minor* to celebrate Billy Wilder's first day as a Hollywood director.[42] Twelve years later Curtiz was still deeply upset that Bogart had failed to win the best actor Oscar for *Casablanca*.[43] Even when Curtiz's supposed cynicism was at its height in the late 1930s *Four Daughters, Daughters Courageous*, and *Four Wives* oozed sentimentality but tempered it with realism, and the same trait is present in *The Proud Rebel* some twenty years later. The evidence from his films and other sources, as opposed to personal memories of his histrionics on the set, indicates a strong sensitivity camouflaged while filming as terminal cynicism.

Mammy and *A Soldier's Plaything* show that by 1929–30 Curtiz had adapted to American themes with considerable social perspicacity, and there is evidence that he became a naturalized American in 1931 when he had completed the minimum residential qualification. *Mammy* also paved the way for a wide extension of his repertoire into comedy and horror as well over the next few years. From then onwards European film influences dwindled in his work, although these never entirely disappeared and were resurrected from time to time, as in the 1930s horror films, *The Sea Wolf*, and the middle to late 1940s *noir* offerings such as *Mildred Pierce, The Unsuspected*, and *Flamingo Road*. However, he remained fond of the use of shadows for effect along German 1920s expressionist lines to the very end of his life, even in colour films. For example, stars Bette Davis, William Powell, and John Wayne are introduced to the audience in shadow in *The Private Lives of Elizabeth and Essex, Life With Father*, and *The Comancheros* respectively, covering a period from 1939 to 1961.

Curtiz knew that he possessed serious deficiencies as a writer, and he preferred to influence others' scenarios, but he always read them, usually well before production started if circumstances allowed, and engaged in research on the subject matter where appropriate. This was because he regarded the story as one of the three basic elements in a successful film, the others being the players and the director's interpretation of the story.[44] According to him in 1947, he had had few perfect scripts at Warners and much had depended upon the treatment of the story in production.[45] These views reflected the mentality of the true auteur, and it was not surprising that when he met Bess Meredyth at the studio, he found in her a kindred spirit, and after several years of insistent courtship on his part they were married in 1929. According to Wallis many years later, she was shrewd, down-to-earth, and Curtiz's sheet anchor.[46] Although they separated for some months in 1936–7 and again from March 1960 until his death,[47] he nevertheless reportedly left her a considerable sum of money in his will, presumably to express his appreciation of her long support. She evidently subordinated her successful writing career to his, but, it was widely rumoured in Hollywood, she influenced the script of many a Curtiz film without a screen credit. However, even before their marriage he never treated any script as sacrosanct, he almost always altered scripts on the set, and when her health deteriorated in the early 1950s and she was unable to work, he continued to comment on scripts, sometimes at great length, as with *King Creole*. His disagreements with Jack Warner, Wallis, and Trilling, as recorded in the Warners production files, were invariably concerned with scripts and his inclination to embellish stories for cinematic effect.

Certainly Curtiz, and possibly his wife as well, had a decisive impact upon the screenplays of his films even if it is not possible to trace his precise contributions. In his very first Hollywood film, *The Third Degree*, he shot unscripted material retained in the released version.[48] His wishes always prevailed over those of the scriptwriters, the standard Warners procedure, as Howard Koch found on *The Sea Hawk* and *Casablanca*.[49] He was little concerned with dialogue – 'I don't see black and white words on script when I read it – I see action on screen', he once remarked[50] – but concentrated upon character development and the plot's main thrust. Every so often he had to bow to the authority of the producer, as with Buckner over the ending of *Mission to Moscow*,[51] but on the whole his producers gave him his head except when contractual reasons took priority. Blanke, Wald, and Zanuck were particularly supportive of him. So long as Curtiz's films fared well at the box-office, the studio overlooked his idiosyncracies, and in consequence it is often difficult to know within individual films whether he was subordinate to the studio system or the system to him. At least at times, depending upon the depth of Curtiz's interest, it was definitely the latter, apparently with the aid of the unit production staff. For instance, he outmanoeuvred Wallis over *The Sea Hawk*. At one point the latter expostulated,

> It seems to me that I issued instructions to everyone, you Mike [Curtiz], and Tenny Wright, that we were not to shoot any of this sort of thing [battle material], yet the stuff seems to be scheduled every day, the stuff is shot, we keep squawking, the cost keeps mounting, and nobody does anything about it.[52]

Evidently he made little impression, for almost a month later he wrote in much the same tone with even deeper exasperation, finally asking what he had to do to prevent the shooting of unauthorized battle sequences.[53] Although Curtiz had learned to edit in Denmark in 1913, he did not actually edit his American films because editing was considered to be beneath a director's dignity in Hollywood. Some of his films owed much to the editing of George Amy, Ralph Dawson, and Owen Marks, but all the same Curtiz kept a tight grip on the content of his films, even scenes he did not actually direct himself, and influenced the final versions. He once stated, 'A right director cuts on the set, instead of in the cutting room. His individuality should be on the film, not the individuality of a cutter.'[54] He actually selected his editors whenever he could.[55] Although his films were not auteur films in the sense that they were made exactly as he wished in every detail, most films that he directed, particularly after *Captain Blood*, bear his distinctive imprint despite other important contributions.

Curtiz was probably the first director to include reality footage in a feature film – *20,000 Years in Sing Sing* – a ploy which other directors copied after 1933 and he repeated in *Casablanca*, *Mission to Moscow*, and *Force of Arms*. In *Passage to Marseille* he employed flashbacks within flashbacks within flashbacks, a confusing device only rarely emulated. With these two exceptions he invented no directorial techniques, and he also explored no new themes. The best of Curtiz cinema was represented by fast-moving plots with subtle changes of pace, meticulous attention to detail, wonderful control over crowd and mass battle scenes, an ability to weave strong player performances and slick dialogue into an absorbing coherent entity, and the creation of a striking visual atmosphere. No other contemporary possessed all of these qualities. This was what made him such an exceptional director and explains his philosophy that a movie director worthy of the name should be able to direct any genre. Yet in the final analysis what elevated his high competence to greatness was that little extra that most other directors lacked, the intangible natural gift of an instinctive visual sense. Byron Haskin, who worked with Curtiz on many 1920s, 1930s, and 1940s films, recorded this talent and many years later rated Curtiz as the Busby Berkeley of drama.[56] This was the highest possible tribute since Berkeley conceived, designed, choreographed, directed, and often edited his own musical numbers. After the completion of *Casablanca*, Paul Henreid was struck by the fact that Curtiz would occasionally stop shooting for no special reason to say that there was something amiss with that particular scene. Eventually he identified the fault, corrected it, and retook the sequence.[57] In 1947 his prop man of more than fifty Warners films, Herbert 'Limey' Plews, observed that when Curtiz was reshooting a scene two weeks after the original scene, he could remember the exact lighting, the lens and the exposure used, and the positions of the camera and the players from the first take.[58] Fellow director William Diertele recalled that,

> Mike [Curtiz] did everything. . . . He was extraordinarily talented. He didn't always know what he was doing, but he had such an instinct for film, he could do it. I couldn't. If I didn't have my script, I was helpless.[59]

Another Warners director, Vincent Sherman, wrote in 1976 that Curtiz was one of the best ever Hollywood directors.[60]

Curtiz was a camera wizard, a perfectionist in his fastidious oversight

of all production elements, and much more considerate in his handling
of players than his contrary reputation indicates. However, none of these
facts nor his instinctive visual sense proves that he was a great director
until they are placed in the framework of his overall record. His prolific
output in itself points to a most formidable talent, while some of his
films are so good, especially during the 1930s and 1940s, that they cannot
be dismissed as simply the work of a skilled craftsman operating a well-
oiled machine. Moreover, apart from the fact that he gave Niven's career
a hefty push forward and discovered Garfield and Doris Day, he cata-
pulted Flynn and Olivia de Havilland to stardom in *Captain Blood* and
The Charge of the Light Brigade as well as guided Cagney and Joan
Crawford to their only Oscars for *Yankee Doodle Dandy* and *Mildred
Pierce* respectively. In addition the sheer number of different genres he
handled – biographies, comedies, horrors, melodramas, musicals, mysteries, religious epics, swashbucklers, and westerns – has never been equalled, while he proved to be successful in each genre both contempor-
aneously and retrospectively. *Yankee Doodle Dandy* is the best screen
musical biography ever made, *I'll See You in My Dreams* and *The Best
Things in Life are Free* also being better than most for a genre that has
produced very few good movies. *Life with Father* is a well-mounted,
superior, sophisticated social comedy, one of the few of that genre which
remains watchable today even though that style of humour has badly
dated. *Dr X* and *The Mystery of the Wax Museum* are horror classics,
and his only other outright horror movie, *The Walking Dead*, is well
above genre average. *Four Daughters*, *Daughters Courageous*,
Casablanca, *Mildred Pierce*, and the much undervalued *Flamingo Road*
embody exceptionally stylish soap opera and all stand up well nowadays.
The Kennel Murder Case, the prototype of the 1930s 'who done it?'
cycle, is arguably the best of its genre which heavily influenced the
subsequent Thin Man series. The epic sequences of *The Slave Queen*,
Noah's Ark, and *The Egyptian* remain among the most striking ever
filmed. As swashbucklers *Captain Blood*, *The Adventures of Robin Hood*,
and *The Sea Hawk* have never been surpassed, and significantly Flynn
is best remembered for this type of role. *Dodge City* is first rate and
shaped the future development of the traditional western more than John
Ford's 1939 *Stagecoach*.[61] *Santa Fe Trail* and *The Comancheros* are both
several notches above genre average, while *The Boy from Oklahoma*,
The Proud Rebel, and *The Hangman* all look better today than most
other 1950-style non-action westerns. *The Sea Wolf* and *The Breaking
Point* are excellent melodramas by any reckoning, while *20,000 Years in
Sing Sing*, *Black Fury*, *Kid Galahad*, and *Angels With Dirty Faces* all
still carry a very potent punch. *Mission to Moscow* can now be seen as
one of the most fascinating and riveting propaganda pieces of all time.
No other Hollywood director can even approach such a distinguished

record of high-quality versatility in depth. This was partly recognized in Hollywood during his lifetime, for in addition to his Oscars for *Sons of Liberty* and *Casablanca*, Curtiz gained Oscar nominations for *Four Daughters*, *Angels with Dirty Faces*, and *Yankee Doodle Dandy*.

This record of quality combined with quantity was derived from a life dominated by film-making. In 1956 his wife said of him that he slept every night for only five hours, during which he often talked about films.[62] Once, when hosting a dinner party, he rearranged the guests and their food as a trial run for a dinner party sequence in *The Unsuspected* that he was due to shoot next day.[63] He frequently watched films at home or in the cinema and always had a very firm grasp of current Hollywood on- and off-screen developments. In this context he has gained a reputation for working exceptionally long hours, but this seems to apply only before 1935, when the formation of the Screen Actors Guild brought about regulated working times. Even before then it is by no means clear that he worked longer hours with players than the other Warners directors, and when the post–1935 basic day became 9 a.m. until 6 p.m., the Warners daily time-sheets reveal that Curtiz honoured these hours more or less, other than when a film fell badly behind schedule or there were special circumstances related to location shooting. He was normally on the set at least one hour before any of the players and technicians and almost always left after the last of them. Despite this, he was very seldom ill enough (until *The Comancheros*) to be absent and hold up shooting. However, he was sometimes reluctant to break off in mid-scene for meal breaks – he himself did not usually eat lunch – and for the end of the day, which partly explains his reputation for working his crews unduly strenuously. Over the filming of the warehouse shoot-out scene in *Angels with Dirty Faces*, the unit manager noted that 'He would rather play cops and robbers than eat.'[64] One star remarked,

> Mike is a real taskmaster but his own willingness to work harder than anyone else takes away any possible feeling of resentment a player might have over his insistent demands and his constant efforts to attain perfection in every scene, every sequence, every production.[65]

However, his drive for perfection alienated him from less devoted colleagues, and in his early Warners years he was easily diverted from a day's filming schedule. Haskin has confirmed that he was so unmethodical that he once sent for 500 cowboy extras in the middle of a desert and then kept them idle while he spent most of the day shooting a close-up of wagon wheels in the sand.[66] However, when players and then technicians gained trade union rights, Curtiz became more systematic and more tolerant. In July 1947 the unit manager of *Romance on the High Seas* reported that he was three days ahead of schedule and stated,

'Mike himself plans his work so well and knows exactly what he is going to do several days head (sic) of time, which most directors on this lot do not do.'[67] In his later Warners years he filmed at a very fast rate and usually finished ahead of schedule. Such adaptability well into middle age, evident also in his handling of technicolor after 1937, showed a professional single-mindedness so exceptional that it led Peter Lorre to remark that Curtiz ate films and excreted them.[68]

By 1945, in contrast to seventeen years earlier,[69] Curtiz believed that film was after all an art form, and following the success of *Mildred Pierce* he consciously attempted to improve the artistic quality of his movies. By so striving he rose to well above average competence with *Life With Father, The Unsuspected, Flamingo Road, Young Man With a Horn, The Breaking Point, Jim Thorpe – All American,* and *Force of Arms,* but, as he had feared in 1945,[70] audiences were insufficiently perceptive and it has taken time for the true worth of these films to show up. When he left Warners, the other studios knew his full ability, and he experienced no problems in finding productions with top stars and adapting to large-screen innovations. The studios' knee-jerk reaction to the onset of television and plummeting cinema attendances, however, resulted in a dearth of good projects in the 1950s. Some of Curtiz's films in these years, such as *The Egyptian, The Vagabond King, The Man in the Net,* and *A Breath of Scandal,* represented commercial and critical setbacks, but this was due to misguided studio policies rather than to him. It is possible that his interest was waning, and that he undertook such projects purely for the money in order to meet 1954 maintenance agreements he had signed in connection with illegitimate children he had allegedly fathered. On the other hand the careers of other older Hollywood directors were also wavering at the same time for the same reasons – for instance, William Wellman retired after the financial disaster of *Lafayette Escadrille* for Warners in 1957. Curtiz retained the ability to turn out noteworthy films like *The Best Things in Life are Free* and *The Helen Morgan Story,* and when the material moved him sufficiently, he remained a formidable film-maker, as evidenced by *The Proud Rebel, King Creole,* and *The Comancheros* in particular, remarkable for a man of his age, poor health, and prodigious output. These now stand up better than some late 1950s financial successes like *Sayonara,* directed by Joshua Logan, solely because of Curtiz's unwillingness to compromise upon cinematic quality. Curtiz proved himself to be a born survivor over a long period of economic and technological change within the film industry.

Not the least remarkable aspect of his career was that his Hollywood films were made within a foreign culture subordinating artistic inventiveness to profit and in a language not his own. His English was spoken with a thick guttural accent which during the Second World War some people in Hollywood mistook for German. His malapropisms on the set and address of players by a distortion of their real names – 'Earl Flint' for Errol Flynn is the most famous instance – were legendary in his lifetime and have grown more so since his death, yet they were a conscious device to call attention to his individuality, for he spoke and understood the language before he reached the United States. There is no indication that Harry Warner spoke either German or Hungarian, so that his 1925 conversation with Curtiz in Paris was almost certainly conducted in English, while Curtiz's 1926 Warners contract was drawn up only in English. His letters and memoranda in the Warner Brothers archive are couched in very good English. In 1945 a reporter interviewing Curtiz noted that not once did he perpetrate a malapropism. The reporter concluded that the famous misuse of English was born in the minds and typewriters of press agents.[71] In the early 1950s columnist Louella Parsons stated after an interview with Curtiz that he had spoken perfect English.[72]

Owing to Curtiz's large output and varied genres his auteurism is harder to pinpoint than that of other directors, but in any case because of the studio system no contemporary director was able to express his auteurism in every one of his films. What, for example, can be seen of Alfred Hitchcock's suspense auteurism in his 1941 *Mr and Mrs Smith* for RKO Radio? Curtiz is different only in degree, and his auteurist instincts are discernible upon a close analysis. The police are corrupt, imbecilic or ineffective in *The Third Degree, Dr X, The Mystery of the Wax Museum, The Kennel Murder Case, The Perfect Specimen, Casablanca, Passage to Marseille*, and *Flamingo Road*, and only in *Mildred Pierce* is a police character given credit for perceptiveness. In *The Hangman* a US deputy marshal releases a suspect rather than allow a jury to judge his guilt or innocence, while in *The Comancheros* the Texas Rangers release a murder suspect because he has helped them to defeat an outlaw gang. A devastating and still powerful indictment of the American penal system was delivered in *20,000 Years in Sing Sing*, with a side swipe at capital punishment repeated in *Front Page Woman, The Walking Dead*, and *Angels With Dirty Faces*. *We're No Angels* is dominated by the do-good activities of hardened criminals. Contemporary cinematic fashions, the genres involved, and studio policies arguably dictated such material, which appears in other directors' work, but an ambivalent attitude to the law and to law-enforcement agencies is so consistent in Curtiz films and carried over into his post-Warners years that it can hardly be accidental. It is epitomized in the image of the helpless prisoner appearing before a biased and merciless court in *Captain Blood, The Sea Hawk, Passage to Marseille*, and *The Egyptian*. Curtiz's distrust of the law and the police, not unlike that in some Hitchcock films, might have originated from his 1919 Hungarian experiences or from a distaste for American police methods, which he first observed for himself at close quarters before filming *The Third Degree* in 1926.[73] It is also possible that its genesis occurred in 1927 during the shooting of *The Desired Woman* in Yuma, Arizona. There Curtiz and technical adviser Michael Romanoff decided while filming to remove most of their clothes because of the intense heat and were arrested for indecency by the local police before considerable Warners pressure secured their release.[74]

Curtiz's scepticism about the law, the penal system, and the police fitted in well with the emerging Warners early 1930s decision to go in for socially realistic films as the great depression tightened its grip on the United States. Cynicism tended to surface in such films with action plots centred upon the law and law breakers, and Curtiz was undoubtedly selected for such movies because they were perfectly suited to his cinematic style and personality. Until well into 1932 the studio's social realism features offered gritty, almost unredeemed gloom, but even by early 1930s Warners standards the undiluted disillusion and pessimism of *The Strange Love of Molly Louvain* and *20,000 Years in Sing Sing* were severe. However, in the 1932 presidential election campaign Harry Warner supported successful Democratic candidate Roosevelt because he regarded the latter's so-called New Deal reforms as the only antidote to outright revolution while American unemployment was climbing relentlessly. From then onwards Warners' socially realistic dramas usually ended upon an unconvincingly optimistic note, the major flaws of both *Cabin in the Cotton* and *Black Fury*, otherwise stark and worthy social problem films. Nevertheless Curtiz's reservations about the law persisted after 1932 against the general studio trend. For example, in *The Case of the Curious Bride* lawyer Perry Mason was portrayed by Warren William as more lacking in principle than Curtiz's studio superiors wished, while the entire ethos of the film was significantly more cynical than that of *The Kennel Murder Case* which had been made less than two years previously. Furthermore, uniquely for 1930s Warners films after 1932, *Front Page Woman*, *The Walking Dead* and *Angels With Dirty Faces* continued with the implied attack upon American legal executions begun in *20,000 Years in Sing Sing*.

When Zanuck left the studio in April 1933, Warners' film losses were at their height and a tighter budget and production control system than earlier was being instituted. The main responsibility for carrying this through was assigned to Zanuck's successor, Wallis. A by-product of these changes was the exercise of his and Jack Warner's authority through a number of supervisors such as Blanke, each of whom tended to specialize as far as production schedules allowed in particular genres. Direct production department supervision over progress on the set was to be carried out henceforth by unit managers, each answerable to the production manager, T. C. 'Tenny' Wright. These reforms appear to have been phased in by stages between 1932 and 1935, but although Wallis was an excellent executive producer and he and Curtiz respected each other, their different functions in the Warners organization made some friction between them highly probable. In fact Curtiz gave Wallis more trouble than any other Warners director. The sharp tone of many 1930s Wallis memoranda to Curtiz while filming was in progress, taken at face value, suggest that they were at daggers drawn, which logically should have meant one or other was about to quit the studio. However, Wallis's efforts to keep Curtiz in line over shooting schedules were more frequent in some films than others. Indeed there lingers a suspicion that at least some of the restraining memoranda to Curtiz were composed to cover the writer with Harry and Jack Warner if the film concerned went too high over budget rather than genuinely to keep Curtiz in check, for no action was ever taken against Curtiz for disobeying Wallis's instructions. How far Curtiz went his own way differed from film to film according to circumstances, but by 1941 Jack Warner and Wallis had come to acquiesce in Curtiz's waywardness, Wallis's post–1940 memoranda to Curtiz being less shrill in substance and tone than earlier.

By then until the early 1950s Curtiz's position at Warners was too strong for more than limited supervision by Wallis or his successor, Trilling. But in any case Curtiz's disagreements with the studio executives were about means, not ends, for everyone involved at the studio had a common interest in making a maximum-quality film. Given the number of people participating in the film-making process, compromises were normally the order of the day, although on occasions Curtiz was less willing to compromise than most directors, depending upon the type of film content. On the whole he was at his most disobedient and obdurate over what can now be seen as his best films, those which aroused his keenest interest.

Harry Warner also supported Roosevelt's foreign policy during the 1930s. The foundation stone of the latter's approach was continued American non-involvement in war, usually dubbed isolationism, with American diplomacy designed to avert crises between major powers in other hemispheres, especially Asia and Europe. In 1933, as Hitler was consolidating Nazi power in Germany, the United States recognized the Soviet Union, but Roosevelt's overall policy was endangered during 1933 and 1934 by a British plan to resurrect the defunct pre–1914 Anglo-Japanese alliance. This would have facilitated further rises in Japanese power and thus rendered an American–Japanese clash over Asian questions more likely. In the event the British cabinet at the end of 1934 proved unwilling to jeopardize Anglo-American relations for the sake of closer ties with Japan, but while the issue lay unresolved two of Curtiz's films, *The Key* and *British Agent*, contained anti-British material, while the latter was also highly sympathetic to the Russian Bolsheviks, to the point where their 1917 revolution was in effect condoned. It is impossible to say whether Curtiz simply implemented studio policy in support of Roosevelt or shaped the material to reflect his personal convictions.

From 1934 onwards the political ideology implicit in Warners films touching upon foreign affairs remained largely dormant until Nazi anti-Semitism grew more extreme during 1938 and German territorial expansion was set in motion. However, in the interim Curtiz and his writers, almost certainly with some tacit higher studio authority or acquiescence, gave indirect expression to concern at international developments where this would not embroil Warners too blatantly in American domestic politics or too openly call into question American isolationism. In this respect Curtiz had never permitted villains to share, much less steal, the limelight in his films, but there was a steady move in this direction as the Second World War drew closer. In *Captain Blood* Basil Rathbone has a relatively small part as the treacherous French pirate Levasseur, as in the book, and little is seen of his bloodthirstiness in action or its results. However, in *The Charge of the Light Brigade*, although C. Henry Gordon's Surat Khan is relegated to not much more than a bit part, his cruelties, especially the massacre of the Chokoti garrison with their wives and children, are visually dwelt upon. This difference reflected the intervening real-life barbarism of the Italian forces against the primitive Ethiopians early in 1936. In the same film the emphasis upon the tensions endured by men under siege with little hope of relief was probably inspired by the heroic but futile Ethiopian resistance against overwhelming odds between January and May 1936. In *Mountain Justice*, filmed immediately afterwards, Curtiz draws attention to the dangers for individual freedom of a tunnel-visioned life philosophy, with religious fanaticism serving as an analogy with European fascism via Robert Barrat's dogmatically fierce portrayal of the father who is determined to thwart his daughter's secular ambitions. *The Adventures of Robin Hood* lingers in places upon brutal oppression by the Normans of the Saxons, a racially inspired personal violence and smashing-up of property very similar to Nazi actions against the Jews. Here both Rains as Prince John and Rathbone as Sir Guy of Gisbourne are given the same scope to project charactered villainy as Barrat in *Mountain Justice*, which links community persecution to a philosophical creed.

Until 1938 Hitler had not revealed that he was a menace to international stability in Europe. However, by the time *Dodge City* was filmed in 1939, Germany had annexed Austria, carried out the anti-Semitic 'Crystal Night' pogrom, and occupied the whole of Czechoslovakia. Consequently Warners grew openly anti-Nazi, although not yet anti-isolationist, and as a Jew Curtiz was content to project studio policy. In *Dodge City* he allowed the 'heavy', Bruce Cabot, to take a place on a par with star and hero Flynn. Villainy was moved to centre stage, but it was of a relatively gentle sort, scheming within an outward framework of law to control a community striving for salvation from outlaws. When *Santa Fe Trail* was made in mid–1940, war had broken out and Hitler had become the master of much of Europe. Knavery was then elevated to dominating obsession as Raymond Massey's anti-slavery John Brown became in effect a ruthless freedom fighter indistinguishable from the slave owners he abominated. Massey's frighteningly perverted idealism was a portrayal consciously based upon Hitler,[75] which Curtiz did nothing to water down. The film itself has puzzled many who have tried to interpret it in its 1850s American context, yet it makes much more sense if related to 1940 instead, a divided United States refusing to face up to the prospect of an inevitable war. Curtiz directed *The Sea Wolf* in late 1940 when German might was directed against an isolated Britain and was penetrating into the Balkans. As a result Massey's John Brown is carried one stage further by Edward G. Robinson's 'Wolf' Larsen – a mentally sadistic psychopath controlling the destinies of everyone around him within the closed world of the ship he has deliberately isolated. He is made even more menacing than Brown without the latter's highmindedness. The ship serves as an allegory for Nazi-occupied Europe, while, as Robinson noted in his autobiography, Larsen himself is a Nazi in all but name.[76] Curtiz's preoccupation with merciless rascality as a warning to American audiences about Hitler, stronger and more persistent than in the works of other Warners directors, ended only when it became submerged in American patriotic themes. This was also in line with studio policy as the pressure of international events before Pearl Harbor, particularly Hitler's conquest of the Balkans and subsequent invasion of the Soviet Union prior to rising American–Japanese tension in the Pacific, moved Warners towards 'the nation in peril' themes underlying films like *Dive Bomber* and *Captains of the Clouds*. In the latter, lip service was paid to isolationism, still Roosevelt's official policy, in that Cagney plays a Canadian who joins the Royal Canadian Air Force, but the film is highly sympathetic to the British cause and there are references in a passing-out parade scene to Americans who have joined the Royal Canadian Air Force. Warners had effectively abandoned isolationism on the eve of Pearl Harbor.

Curtiz's strident pro-Americanism matched that of his studio. As Jews he and the Warner brothers were naturally hostile to Nazism as soon as Hitler came to power in 1933, but this hostility deepened into alarm as German power grew and seemed to pose a threat even to the United States. His American patriotic films opened in 1939 with *Sons of Liberty* and closed in 1943 with *This is the Army*, but his admiration for the United States is evident, if less directly expressed, in films before and after those dates. Beneath the comedy veneer of *A Soldier's Plaything* in 1930 lies a patriotic layer, while his ability to capture the atmosphere of American small-town middle-class family life is displayed from *Four*

Daughters in 1938 to *Janie* in 1944. Moreover, during the 1950s there is more than a whiff of nostalgia for the American inter-war years in *I'll See You in My Dreams*, *The Story of Will Rogers*, *The Best Things in Life are Free* and *The Helen Morgan Story*. In 1944 he described the United States as the wonderland of the earth and continued,

> But most of you were born here. To you, it's just home . . . it's commonplace. But I come from Europe. There it is different. The struggle is hard . . . But how different in this country . . . . There is the excitement of success [but] . . . there is the American idealism, which you find in even the humblest home . . . . I see [these things] against the background of the old world, and in contrast they are bright and shining.[77]

However, when this sentiment was applied to the needs of American foreign policy in *Mission to Moscow*, it ran into such strong anti-Communism that Curtiz took it personally[78] and vowed never again to direct a political film.[79] He was as good as his word and was prompted perhaps as much by memories of 1919 Hungary as by the *Mission to Moscow* controversy. If after the war he ever questioned this self-denying ordinance, the HUAC hearings probably confirmed its wisdom as they pulled both Jack Warner and Howard Koch into their net over *Mission to Moscow*.

Curtiz was noted in Hollywood for his apolitical attitude,[80] but although his 1945–9 films were all either featherweight entertainments or soap operas in dramatic guise, he commented subtly upon American social issues in the 1950s even if he prohibited to himself open allusions to party politics and international affairs. In *Young Man With a Horn* black jazz musician Art Hazzard is portrayed as considerate, educated, gifted, and sensitive, while black Wesley Park in *The Breaking Point* is a staunch friend of sorely pressed white John Garfield. In this respect both films were ahead of their time (apart from the special circumstances of the Second World War) in their treatment of black–white personal relationships, if only in a small way, even though the screen persona of the actor concerned in both cases, Puerto Rican Juano Hernandez, had already taken shape in Clarence Brown's *Intruder in the Dust* for MGM in 1948. The pro-black material in *Young Man With a Horn* was included against the wishes of Jack Warner, which possibly explains why, as Burt Lancaster has pointed out, Curtiz did not crusade too pointedly on behalf of underprivileged Red Indians in *Jim Thorpe – All American*.[81] On the other hand, in the film Lancaster is married to Phyllis Thaxter, and a marriage between a Red Indian and a white woman was a very rare Hollywood phenomenon at the time. Furthermore, the difference between them is intentionally emphasized in that Lancaster initially believes, when he falls for her, that she is a Red Indian.

After 1951, as racial tension gathered momentum parallel to rabid anti-Communism in the United States, Curtiz continued to steer well clear of direct political or social topics, but at the same time he did not pass up an opportunity for implicit social comment – for instance, *The Adventures of Huckleberry Finn* calls attention to the evils of slavery in a fashion absent from the novel. Moreover, in *The Proud Rebel, King Creole*, and *The Comancheros* the villains, portrayed by Dean Jagger, Walter Matthau, and Nehemiah Persoff respectively, are projected as utterly ruthless, milder versions of John Brown and 'Wolf' Larsen without any high-mindedness or ideology, which was perhaps Curtiz's oblique method of warning against McCarthyite intolerance.

Many central figures in Curtiz's American films function, as Curtiz himself functioned, in an alien environment. Irene Rich plays a British officer's wife in a desert unit station in *The Desired Woman*. William Powell is a British officer in Ireland in *The Key*. Kay Francis is a Russian in Burma in *Mandalay*. Leslie Howard is a Briton spying in Russia in *British Agent*. Paul Muni is a miner of Polish origin in the United States in *Black Fury*. Errol Flynn is transported as an English convict to Jamaica in *Captain Blood*, is a British army officer in India and Russia in *The Charge of the Light Brigade*, is a high-born outlaw in *The Adventures of Robin Hood*, and a cattle-trail boss operating in urban surroundings in *Dodge City*. James Cagney leaves his criminal fraternity to return to his old neighbourhood in *Angels With Dirty Faces*. Alexander Knox, John Garfield, and Ida Lupino are captives aboard 'Wolf' Larsen's ship in *The Sea Wolf*. Humphrey Bogart languishes in self-imposed exile in *Casablanca*, is a Frenchman who cannot return legally to France in *Passage to Marseille*, and is a Devil's Island convict in *We're No Angels*. Joan Crawford moves into a higher social circle in *Mildred Pierce*, and is a carnival itinerant stranded in a small town in *Flamingo Road*. Burt Lancaster stars as a Red Indian who leaves his reservation in *Jim Thorpe – All American*. William Holden is an American soldier in Italy in *Force of Arms*. Alan Ladd is an ex-Confederate in the immediate post-Civil War North in *The Proud Rebel*. Bradford Dillman deserts his prosperous family background for poverty in *Francis of Assisi*. John Wayne is a Texas Ranger operating far from home in *The Comancheros*. Some of this was determined by cinematic fashion or star image, but the trend appears too consistently over more than thirty years and matches Curtiz's own life too closely for it to be a sheer coincidence. For all his successful adaptation and gratitude to the United States, he obviously felt his long absence from Hungary very keenly to the end of his life. It was symptomatic of this that in the twilight of his life he returned to Hungarian material by Ferenc Molnar in *A Breath of Scandal*.

Signs of Curtiz's sense of being an exile can be seen in the high number of misfortunes or sticky ends which befall his heroes or heroines, sometimes against Warners trends, especially in the 1930s. Spencer Tracy winds up in the electric chair for a crime he did not commit in *20,000 Years in Sing Sing*. Errol Flynn is killed in battle in *The Charge of the Light Brigade*, and executed for treason in *The Private Lives of Elizabeth and Essex*. Edward G. Robinson loses his life in a shoot-out and Bette Davis faces a wrecked life (signified by the final unscripted shot when she walks out into the street, tagged on by Curtiz to follow Bacon's *Marked Woman*) in *Kid Galahad*. James Cagney goes to the electric chair in *Angels With Dirty Faces*, and dies in an air battle in *Captains of the Clouds*. John Garfield commits suicide in *Four Daughters*, and leaves the woman he loves in *Daughters Courageous*. Humphrey Bogart loses his girl and remains in exile in *Casablanca*, and dies fighting with the Free French air force in *Passage to Marseille*. Joan Crawford finds that her beloved daughter is both a bitch and a murderess in *Mildred Pierce*, while she herself faces a murder charge in *Flamingo Road*. Kirk Douglas suffers alcoholism in *Young Man With a Horn*, and Burt Lancaster likewise in *Jim Thorpe – All American*. Humphrey Bogart, Aldo Ray, and Peter Ustinov are escaped convicts who return to their Devil's Island prison in *We're No Angels*. Ann Blyth is all but destroyed by love in *The Helen Morgan Story*. Bradford Dillman dies without having achieved his religious ideals, which some monks in his own order have betrayed, in *Francis of Assisi*.

Upon close examination even many of Curtiz's 'happy' endings are found to be at best highly ambiguous. Kay Francis in *Mandalay* gets away with murder to confront probable death from fever with her doctor lover. Errol Flynn in *Captain Blood* wins Olivia de Havilland yet remains in exile as the newly appointed governor of Jamaica. He wins her again in *Dodge City* and *Santa Fe Trail*, but his future as a husband is threatened by, respectively, a potential spell as marshal of lawless Virginia City and looming civil war. Lovers John Garfield and Ida Lupino in *The Sea Wolf* escape from tyrant Edward G. Robinson, but they remain prisoners on the run. In *Casablanca* Humphrey Bogart leaves his American café for the prospect of fighting against Nazi Germany. Joan Crawford returns to her dull marriage, which might or might not work out, in *Mildred Pierce*, and she is last seen awaiting the verdict as the accused in a murder trial in *Flamingo Road*. It is never made explicit that Kirk Douglas, Burt Lancaster, and Ann Blyth recover sufficiently from their problems to resume successful lives in *Young Man With a Horn, Jim Thorpe – All American*, and *The Helen Morgan Story* respectively. John Garfield avoids death only at the cost of an amputated arm in *The Breaking Point*. The wounded William Holden and bride Nancy Olson are about to return to an uncertain American future in *Force of Arms*. Robert Taylor and Tina Louise make for California without secure prospects in *The Hangman*.

Within this catalogue of woe often lies frustrated idealism, a misplaced faith in human nature, and obsessional ambition. Errol Flynn becomes a convict through having practised his profession as a doctor in *Captain Blood*. Having experienced superior officer incompetence, Flynn loses his betrothed to his brother and then his life on the battlefield during a suicidal attack in *The Charge of the Light Brigade*. James Cagney's nostalgia for boyhood haunts and loyalty to his old friend Pat O'Brien lead him to the electric chair in *Angels with Dirty Faces*. Cagney's patriotism leads to his death in *Captains of the Clouds*. John Garfield commits suicide in *Four Daughters* and becomes an itinerant in *Daughters Courageous* to enable the girl he loves to achieve happiness. Humphrey Bogart's devotion to the cause of freedom brings about the loss of his beloved and his political security in *Casablanca* and his death in *Passage to Marseille*. Joan Crawford's social climbing in *Mildred Pierce* is not sufficiently successful to satisfy her materialistic daughter, upon whom she dotes and whom she loses through a murder, while a similar trait draws her into a killing and a homicide charge in *Flamingo Road*. Kirk Douglas's trumpet single-mindedness and talent produce emotional immaturity and depression in *Young Man With a Horn*, while Burt Lancaster and Ann Blyth prove to be their own worst enemies in *Jim Thorpe – All American* and *The Helen Morgan Story*. Robert Taylor's excessive devotion to the cause of law and order causes him to abandon his career as a deputy marshal in *The Hangman*. Fatalism and pessimism, frequently depicted as a road to hell paved with good intentions, permeate much of Curtiz's best cinema. This was another 1930s and 1940s Warners characteristic which is, however, evident in some of Curtiz's post–1953 work as well. It thus appears too persistently over a long period to be a mere coincidence even after due allowance is made for Warners' tendency to assign him to such projects because of his suitability for them.

Curtiz was twice married: in Europe from 1915 to 1923 to ballet dancer Lucy Doraine, who starred in some of his Austrian films, and to Bess Meredyth. His first marriage produced one daughter who was living in the United States when Curtiz died. In September 1923 an Austrian court decided that he was the father of a boy born in November 1920 to a married Viennese bank employee and awarded her the child's maintenance costs from Curtiz's salary. Later she pursued him in the United States until he signed a maintenance agreement for her son in July 1931.[82] It is possible that this liaison cost Curtiz his first marriage. In his later years there was much Hollywood gossip about his lechery with young actresses, although nothing concrete has ever emerged beyond all doubt. In 1954 he signed at least two agreements which in effect acknowledged that he had sired illegitimate children, but these were repudiated in his will. Whether his separation from Bess Meredyth in 1960 was connected with his alleged extra-marital activities is unknown. However, after his death actress Jill Gerrard won a paternity suit against his estate, but the court heard evidence that he had been sterilized just before his second marriage in 1929 and the accuracy of the verdict is questionable.[83]

How all of this moulded Curtiz's attitude to screen women is hard to know, but prior to the 1950s on the few occasions women were projected in his films as positive personalities, they were usually outright bitches or incurably hard-bitten, except where star image dictated otherwise. Whenever they were not bitches or cynics, they tended to be so demure and purely decorative as to be scarcely credible in accordance with Warners general practice. However, even in his 1930s halycon days there were exceptions. For example, Bette Davis in *Kid Galahad* is both high-minded and of strong character, although, typically Curtiz, the basis of her life collapses when she loses the man she loves to another woman and then her longtime man friend to his death in a shoot-out. Apart from such isolated instances, it is virtually impossible to disentangle Curtiz's contributions from Warners policy over the characterization of women until 1950 when signs emerge from Curtiz of a more uniformly sympathetic approach, beginning with Doris Day as Kirk Douglas's long-suffering girlfriend in *Young Man With a Horn* and Phyllis Thaxter as John Garfield's wife in *The Breaking Point*. This change of emphasis allowed women to be nice people without simultaneously being nonentities or purely supportive partners to a central male figure. The best examples are Olivia de Havilland in *The Proud Rebel* and Ann Blyth in *The Helen Morgan Story*.

There is some slight evidence that Curtiz in pre–1919 Hungary developed radical left-wing, perhaps even Communist, views. A few of his early Hollywood films, particularly *Tenderloin* and *The Strange Love of Molly Louvain*, show a concern with the lower depths of American urban life. Furthermore, some of his films, most notably *The Madonna of Avenue A, Roughly Speaking, Mildred Pierce, The Unsuspected, Flamingo Road*, and *The Breaking Point*, are by implication critical of American upper-crust values centring upon money. Although both of these characteristics fell into the Warners studio style, some contribution in his films unquestionably came from Curtiz himself, who in 1947 once complained that Hollywood was all money at the expense of everything else.[84] During the 1950s his films also occasionally side with the American racial underdogs in their struggle for equality with whites, while his 1934 *British Agent* foreshadows *Mission to Moscow* nine years later in its implicitly favourable treatment of Soviet Communism. However, both these films represented Warners support of Roosevelt, and it is by no means certain either that Curtiz was a Communist before 1919 or that even if he was, he held firm to such a belief later. From his films it seems more likely that he was a humanitarian liberal, but he remained secretive about his political leanings, as about so much else personal, until the day of his death.

Cinematically Curtiz was an extraordinary man. His large-scale versatility is unique in cinema history and unlikely ever to be rivalled, much less surpassed. He never forgot that he wanted to capture an audience, and that his prime aim was to supply superior mass entertainment. In this he succeeded more comprehensively than any other contemporary director, for many of his films disdained by critics and film historians were smash hits and only four represented box-office failure until the 1950s. The greatest enduring tribute to his talent is the frequency with which many of his films over the years have appeared on television as well as the sheer number of these.[85] Moreover, many of the same films are also available on video cassette.[86] From this it is all too easy to overlook that Curtiz was exclusively a cinema screen director, and it is significant that despite his 1950s inability after *White Christmas* to deliver a hugh money-spinner, he never directed for television. One suspects that he despised the upstart new medium, for one *White Christmas* sequence shows Bing Crosby appearing on monochrome television, followed by an immediate cut to Crosby in colour within the television studio – Curtiz's way of asserting the superiority of the large screen over the small one.

Nevertheless the current accessibility and continuing popularity of Curtiz films has converted him into a bridge-builder between different generations of movie fans and is a fitting epitaph to his career, one of which he would undoubtedly have wholeheartedly approved. He himself once stated that his aim was to give audiences their money's worth, and to please himself as much as possible without forgetting that audience pleasure took priority. He regarded these considerations as his only substantial contribution to the art of motion pictures.[87] This unduly modest assessment ignored the multi-faceted nature of his own gifts. In particular *Casablanca* was not a fortuitous accident, as its production circumstances led Sarris to conclude. These were in fact very little different from other Warners A budget features of the late 1930s and early 1940s. Frequent script revisions and the involvement of several writers were normal at this time, and if *Casablanca* varied from the routine at all, then it was only in the delay of deciding upon an ending. But even this is doubtful, for the endings to *Mildred Pierce* and *Young Man With a Horn*, for example, were left to a late stage. Nor was *Casablanca* an especially exceptional phenomenon in Curtiz's career, for many of his other films both before and after rate much more than a passing nod of appreciation, and arguably he forged more near masterpieces and good movies from undistinguished script material than any other Hollywood studio system director. As John Baxter believed, he is inescapably one of the best directors ever to emerge in the cinema,[88] and from the formidable body of work he left behind this should have been recognized long ago.

NOTES

INTRODUCTION

1 I. Nemeskürty, *Word and Image: History of the Hungarian Cinema*, Budapest, 1965, enlarged edition 1974, pp. 25–6.

2 Quoted in E. Goodman, *The Fifty-Year Decline and Fall of Hollywood*, New York, 1961, p. 212.

3 'The American cinema', *Film Culture*, 1963, no. 28, pp. 35–6.

4 H. Dienstfrey, 'Hitch your genre to a star', *Film Culture*, 1964, no. 34, pp. 35–7.

5 Arkadin, 'Film clips', *Sight and Sound*, 1968, vol. 37, no. 4, pp. 210–11.

6 *Hollywood in the Thirties*, London, 1968, p. 52.

7 J. E. Nolan (1970), J. Davis and T. Flinn (1971–5), K. Canham (1973), C. Viviani (1973), P. Leggett (1975–6). For full details, see select bibliography.

8 *Swordsmen of the Screen*, London, 1977, p. 253.

9 *American Silent Film*, New York, 1978, p. 307.

10 *The Hollywood Story*, London, 1988, pp. 7, 246. For a contrary 1980s view, see R. Graves, 'Michael Curtiz', *Classic Images*, 1983, no 91, pp. 17–18, 38, and R. Kinnard and R. J. Vitone, *The American Films of Michael Curtiz*, London and Metuchen, New Jersey, 1986.

11 See pp. 5–6.

12 Sascha Film A.G., *Dreissig Jahre Sascha-Film*, Vienna, 1948 (pamphlet), no page number.

13 'Talent shortage is causing two-year production delay', *Films and Filming*, 1956, June, p. 9.

14 E. Goodman, *Bogey: the Good-Bad Guy*, New York, 1965, p. 122.

15 Goodman, 1961, op. cit., p. 415.

1 EUROPE, 1888 to 1926

1 Hal Wallis publicity hand-out headed 'Michael Curtiz – Biography'. 26 November 1929, *Los Angeles Examiner* clippings on Curtiz, Hearst newspaper collection.

2 P. Martin, 'Hollywood's champion language assassin', *Saturday Evening Post*, 2 August 1947, p. 64.

3 Ibid., p. 64.

4 *New York Times*, 13 June 1947.

5 Hal Wallis publicity hand-out, op. cit. and Martin, op. cit., p. 64.

6 I. Nemeskürty, *Word and Image: History of the Hungarian Cinema*, Budapest, 1965, enlarged edition 1974, p. 20.
7 Curtiz's Hungarian and Austrian films are referred to by English translations of their titles. None of the Hungarian films has apparently ever been shown in Britain or the United States.
8 Martin, op. cit., p. 64.
9 Nemeskürty, op. cit., p. 14.
10 For Curtiz's German in 1919, see the 1973 testimony of Austrian screenwriter Walter Reisch in E. W. Cameron (ed.), *Sound and the Cinema*, Pleasantville, New York, 1983, p. 110.
11 The full version is a few minutes short of two hours. The print in London's National Film Archive runs for only eighty-four minutes.
12 *The Times*, 12 November 1924.
13 J. L. Warner and D. Jennings, *My First Hundred Years in Hollywood*, New York, 1964, pp. 160–1.
14 Warner Brothers archive, Curtiz legal file no. 2845, Warners to Curtiz, 13 June 1929.
15 Ibid., Warners, Hollywood to Warners, New York, 24 June 1926.

2 HOLLYWOOD BAPTISM, 1926 to 1929

1 The author's comments on the financial performance of Warners films are based upon the confidential official figures in the papers of William Schaefer, Jack Warner's private secretary for almost fifty years.
2 P. Martin, 'Hollywood's champion language assassin', *Saturday Evening Post*, 2 August 1947, p. 64.
3 J. Davis and T. Flinn, 'The Third Degree', *The Silent Picture*, 1973, no. 18, pp. 37–42.
4 For a more detailed analysis of the film, see Davis and Flinn (ibid).
5 Warner Brothers archive, Curtiz legal file no. 2845, Jack Warner to Curtiz, 24 January 1927.
6 The film industry was reportedly outraged at Curtiz when rumours circulated that several actors had been drowned. Injuries were certainly numerous, but there is no firm evidence of any deaths.
7 J. Davis, 'Notes on Warner Brothers foreign policy, 1918–1948', *Velvet Light Trap*, 1972, no. 4, p. 24.
8 Here the author is indebted to information presented at a restoration seminar at the Museum of the Moving Image in London, 3 August 1990.
9 *Sunday Express*, 9 October 1960.
10 Warner Brothers archive, Curtiz legal file no. 2845, Curtiz to R. Obringer, Warners' lawyer, 14 November 1956.
11 H. G. Goldman, *Jolson: The Legend Comes to Life*, Oxford and New York, 1988, p. 193.
12 M. Freedland, *Al Jolson*, London and New York, 1972, p. 163.

3 AN EXPANDING REPERTOIRE, 1930 to 1935

1 See N. Zierold, *The Hollywood Tycoons*, London, 1969, p. 267.
2 T. Schatz, *The Genius of the System: Hollywood Film-Making in the Studio Era*, New York, 1988, pp. 140–1.
3 C. Bickford, *Bulls, Balls, Bicycles and Actors*, New York, 1965, pp. 254–6.
4 K. Kay, *Myrna Loy*, New York, 1977, p. 42.

5 T. Flinn, 'William Diertele, the plutarch of Hollywood', *Velvet Light Trap*, 1975, no. 15, pp. 25–6.

6 W. Schelly, *Harry Langdon*, London and Metuchen, New Jersey, 1982, p. 157.

7 R. Kinnard and R. J. Vitone, *The American Films of Michael Curtiz*, London and Metuchen, New Jersey, 1986, pp. 14–16.

8 For a more detailed analysis, see J. Davis, 'When will they ever learn?: a tale of mad geniuses, scientists, artists, and a director (also mad)', *Velvet Light Trap*, 1975, no. 15, pp. 11–12. For Barrymore's high opinion of the sets, see D. Deschner, 'Anton Grot, Warners art director, 1927–1948', *Velvet Light Trap*, 1975, no. 15, p. 19.

9 *New York Times*, 14 August 1932.

10 For a more extensive discussion, see Davis, op. cit., pp. 13–14.

11 Discussions appear in N. Roddick, *A New Deal in Entertainment: Warner Brothers in the 1930s*, London, 1983, pp. 126–8; J. Shadoian, 'Michael Curtiz's *20,000 Years in Sing Sing*', *Journal of Popular Film*, 1973, vol. 2, no. 2, pp. 165–79; and A. Moran, '*20,000 Years in Sing Sing*', *Australian Journal of Screen Theory*, 1977, no. 3, pp. 36–46.

12 *New York Times*, 18 February 1933.

13 Warner Brothers archive, *Female* file no. 1887, Blanke to Wallis, 14 September 1933.

14 R. Behlmer, *Inside Warner Bros. (1935–1951)*, New York, 1985, p. 14. Wallis to Curtiz, 21 October 1933.

15 Ibid., p. 15. Wallis to supervisor Robert Presnell, 21 October 1933.

16 J. C. Robertson, *The British Board of Film Censors: Film Censorship in Britain, 1896–1950*, London, 1985, pp. 125–6.

17 Warner Brothers archive, *British Agent* file no. 1735, Howard to Jack Warner, undated.

18 Directors Guild of America, *Byron Haskin*, London and Metuchen, New Jersey, 1984, pp. 120–4.

19 M. B. Druxman, *Paul Muni: His Life and His Films*, London and New York, 1974, p. 138.

20 J. Lawrence, *Actor: the Life and Times of Paul Muni*, New York, 1974, p. 201.

21 W. R. Meyer, *Warner Brothers Directors*, New Rochelle, New York, 1978, p. 84.

22 Edward G. Robinson papers, box 36:20, Warners to Robinson, 17 January 1935.

23 Behlmer, op. cit., p. 18. Wallis to supervisor Harry Joe Brown, 6 July 1934.

24 See *The Times*, 15 July 1935.

25 Behlmer, op. cit., p. 19. Jack Warner to Wallis, 11 January 1935.

26 *The Observer*, 14 July 1935.

27 Edward G. Robinson papers, box 36:10, Warners to Robinson, 1 October 1934.

28 Behlmer, op. cit., p. 20. Jack Warner to Hearst, 20 February 1935.

29 Behlmer, op. cit., p. 21. Brown to Wallis, 11 June 1935.

30 Warner Brothers archive, *Captain Blood* file no. 1788, Jack Warner to Wallis, 27 March 1935.

31 Ibid., Brown to Wallis, 20 July 1935.

32 Behlmer, op. cit., p. 23. Wallis to Curtiz, 18 August 1935.

33 Behlmer, op. cit., pp. 23–5. Wallis to Curtiz, 18 August and 9 September

1935; Wallis to producer Robert Lord, 10 December 1935 (when the film was due for imminent release).

34 Warner Brothers archive, *Captain Blood* file no. 1788, Wallis to Jean Negulesco, 24 October 1935.

35 Haller was the uncredited cameraman for other scenes when Mohr was later ill.

36 For a full review of the film, see J. Davis, '*Captain Blood*', *Velvet Light Trap*, 1971, no. 1, pp. 26–31.

4 NEAR AND AT THE SUMMIT, 1935 to 1941

1 This paragraph is based upon Warner Brothers archive, *The Walking Dead* file nos. 1793, 2359, and 2882.

2 N. Roddick, *A New Deal in Entertainment: Warner Brothers in the 1930s*, London, 1983, p. 55.

3 R. Behlmer, *Inside Warner Bros. (1935–1951)*, New York, 1985, p. 31. Wallis to Curtiz, 17 April 1936.

4 Warner Brothers archive, *The Charge of the Light Brigade* file no. 1792, Curtiz to Wallis, 17 April 1936.

5 Ibid., T. C. 'Tenny' Wright, studio production manager, to Wallis, 29 June 1936.

6 R. Nielsen, 'Reviewing the classics', *Cinemaeditor*, 1982, Summer-Fall, pp. 23–4. E. Goodman, *The Fifty-Year Decline and Fall of Hollywood*, New York, 1961, p. 311.

7 See C. Higham, *Errol Flynn: the Untold Story*, London, 1980, pp. 92–3.

8 *New Statesman*, 27 March 1937.

9 This paragraph is based upon Warner Brothers archive, *Stolen Holiday* file no. 2880, W. MacEwen, Wallis's executive assistant, to Obringer, 14 April 1937; file no. 1018, M. Bowman, Wallis's secretary, to Brown, 18 July 1936; file no. 2061, Wallis to Curtiz, 30 June and 20 August 1936; Brown to Wallis, 11 July 1936.

10 Warner Brothers archive, *Kid Galahad* file no. 2019, Wallis to M. Arnow, head of the casting department, 16 September 1936.

11 H. B. Wallis and C. Higham, *Star-Maker: the Autobiography of Hal B. Wallis*, New York, 1980, p. 47. E. G. Robinson and L. Spigelgass, *All My Yesterdays*, London and New York, 1973, p. 183.

12 Edward G. Robinson papers, box 36:20, Wallis to Robinson, 13 and 14 August 1936 (telegrams).

13 Although Gaudio was the sole credited cameraman, Polito shot the boxing climax and Arthur Edeson the early Florida suite internals. Edeson fell ill in mid-production, while the fight scenes were filmed some weeks after the film was otherwise completed.

14 B. Davis, *The Lonely Life: an Autobiography*, New York, 1962, p. 172. C. Higham, *Bette: a Biography of Bette Davis*, London, 1981, p. 86.

15 Warner Brothers archive, *The Perfect Specimen* file no. 2166, Jack Warner to Wallis, 16 July 1936.

16 See Warner Brothers archive, *The Adventures of Robin Hood* file no. 1709, Wallis to Curtiz, 15 December 1937.

17 Ibid., Wallis to Wright, 11 January 1938.

18 Warner Brothers archive, *Four Daughters* file no. 2277, Wallis to Blanke, 22 April 1938.

19 Ibid., Arnow to R. Taplinger, head of publicity department, 3 May 1938.

20 Warner Brothers archive, *Four's A Crowd* file no. 1495, Wright to Wallis, 6 January 1938; MacEwen to Wallis, 26 January 1938.
21 *Motion Picture Herald*, 16 July 1938.
22 G. Morris, *John Garfield*, New York, 1977, pp. 43–4.
23 See Behlmer, op. cit., pp. 66–8.
24 Warner Brothers archive, *Sons of Liberty* file nos. 1017, 2403, and 2786; Curtiz legal file no. 2845, Jack Warner to Obringer, 1 February 1939.
25 Behlmer, op. cit., p. 80. N. Gurney, Flynn's agent, to Jack Warner, 1 September 1938.
26 Warner Brothers archive, *Mission to Moscow* file no. 1015, Herman Lissauer, head of research department, to Mrs Curtiz, 9 March 1943.
27 Behlmer, op. cit., p. 101. Lord to scriptwriter Mark Hellinger, 18 July 1939.
28 Behlmer, op. cit., p. 101. Buckner to Wallis, 23 October 1939.
29 G. Eells, *Ginger, Loretta and Irene Who?*, New York, 1976, p. 111.
30 See Higham, 1980, op. cit., pp. 145–7.
31 Behlmer, op. cit., p. 108. Blanke to Warners, New York, 25 September 1939.
32 H. Koch, *As Time Goes By: Memoirs of a Writer*, London and New York, 1979, pp. 42–4.
33 Warner Brothers archive, *The Sea Hawk* file no. 2230, Wallis to Blanke, 24 July 1939.
34 J. Dunbar, *Flora Robson*, London, 1960, p. 211.
35 See Higham, 1980, op. cit., p. 147.
36 Warner Brothers archive, *The Sea Hawk* file no. 2230, Wallis to Blanke, 2 February 1940.
37 See L. J. Easley, 'The *Santa Fe Trail*, John Brown and the coming of the Civil War', *Film and History*, 1983, vol. 13, no. 2, pp. 25–33.
38 Warner Brothers archive, *Santa Fe Trail* file no. 2226, Wallis to producer Robert Fellows, 2 January 1940.
39 Ibid., Buckner to Wallis, 3 January 1940.
40 Ibid., Wallis to Curtiz, 28 June 1940.
41 Ibid., Fellows to Wright, 10 September 1940.
42 Ibid., Buckner to Wallis, 28 November 1940.
43 Ibid., Fellows to Wallis, 3 September 1940.
44 Behlmer, op. cit., pp. 131–2. Muni to his agent, 1 November 1937.
45 Edward G. Robinson papers, box 36:9, Obringer to Robinson, 22 December 1938.
46 Warner Brothers archive, *The Sea Wolf* file no. 2248, Wallis to Blanke, 11 July 1940.
47 Ibid., Wright to Wallis, 10 December 1940.
48 T. Schatz, *The Genius of the System: Hollywood Film-Making in the Studio Era*, New York, 1988, p. 308.

5 WORLD WAR, December 1941 to August 1945

1 Cohan believed that he was portrayed too pugnaciously as a child and was irked by the scene between Cagney and Eddie Foy Junior, which he considered out of place and uninteresting. The latter had been added at the last moment. See Warner Brothers archive, *Yankee Doodle Dandy* legal file no. 2733, Cohan to Jacob Wilk, Warner story editor in New York, 12 April 1942 and Jack Warner to Wilk (cable), 13 February 1942.
2 See R. Behlmer, *Inside Warner Bros. (1935–1951)*, New York, 1985, pp. 178–82 for further details of the talks with Cohan over the script.

3 According to Buckner in 1943. See Warner Brothers archive, *Yankee Doodle Dandy* legal file no. 2733, Obringer to Warners, New York, 18 May 1943. The film credits Buckner with the original story.

4 The previous paragraphs are based upon Warner Brothers archive, *Casablanca* file nos. 1011, 1486, and 2870. Many of the relevant documents appear in Behlmer, op. cit., pp. 194–207.

5 T. Flinn, 'William Diertele: the plutarch of Hollywood', *Velvet Light Trap*, 1975, no. 15, p. 26.

6 Warner Brothers archive, *Mission to Moscow* file no. 2085, March to Davies (copy), undated, and Davies to Jack Warner, 30 July 1942.

7 H. Koch, *As Time Goes By: Memoirs of a Writer*, London and New York, 1979, pp. 113–14, 128.

8 Warner Brothers archive, *Mission to Moscow* file no. 2785, Buckner to Jack Warner, 24 August 1942.

9 Ibid., file no. 2085, Buckner to Jack Warner, 11 February 1943.

10 Ibid., file no. 1486, Al Alleborn, unit manager, to Wright, 20 November 1942.

11 Ibid., Alleborn to Wright, 31 December 1942.

12 Ibid., Alleborn to Wright, 26 January 1943.

13 Ibid., file no. 2085, Davies to Jack Warner, 17 February 1943.

14 Ibid., Davies to Jack Warner, 17 April 1943.

15 Ibid., file no. 2785, Jack Warner to Buckner, 22 May 1943.

16 Ibid., file no. 2085, Jack Warner to William Randolph Hearst (cable), 21 May 1943.

17 Ibid., Joseph I. Breen to Jack Warner, 23 December 1942.

18 See G. Wheatcroft, *The Spectator*, 2 September 1978 and R. West, *The Spectator*, 26 February 1983.

19 *New York Herald Tribune*, 13 February 1944.

20 She was pregnant unknown to Curtiz who, according to her many years later, was the most disagreeable director of her career. See M. Morgan and M. Routier, *With Those Eyes*, London, 1978, p. 175. At the time it was reported that she 'did not seem to be in very good shape' in Warner Brothers archive, *Passage to Marseille* file no. 1487, Eric Stacey, unit manager, to Wright, 23 October 1943.

21 This account is based upon Warner Brothers archive, *Passage to Marseille* file nos. 1016, 1487, and 2878.

22 Ibid., file no. 1487, Stacey to Wright, 2 October 1943.

23 Warner Brothers archive, *Roughly Speaking* file no. 2189, Blanke to Davis, 20 December 1943.

24 Ibid., Phil Friedman, head of casting department, to Curtiz, 23 March 1944 and Blanke to Curtiz, 15 April 1944.

25 *Chicago Sunday Tribune*, 1 April 1945.

26 Quoted in W. R. Meyer, *Warner Brothers Directors*, New Rochelle, New York, p. 98.

27 Warner Brothers archive, *Roughly Speaking* file no. 2189, R. A. Pease to Trilling, 5 June 1944 and Jack Warner to Curtiz, 20 June 1944.

28 N. Yanni, *Rosalind Russell*, London, 1975, p. 85.

29 Warner Brothers archive, *Roughly Speaking* file no. 2189, Office of War Information, Los Angeles, to Warners, 21 March 1944.

30 For the genesis of *Mildred Pierce*, see Behlmer, op. cit., pp. 254–61. See also Warner Brothers archive, *Mildred Pierce* file no. 2876, T. Chapman, assistant story editor, to Obringer, 13 February 1950.

31 *Seattle Times* and *Evening World Herald*, 5 January 1945.
32 R. Thomas, *Joan Crawford: a Biography*, London, 1978, pp. 148–9.
33 See S. Temple-Black, *Child Star*, London, 1988, p. 366. Warner Brothers archive, *Mildred Pierce* file no. 2086 provides extra details.
34 Warner Brothers archive, *Mildred Pierce* file no. 2086, Trilling to Wald, 22 June 1944.
35 Ibid., Wald to Trilling, 18 January 1945.
36 Joan Crawford in *New York Sun*, 9 September 1945. The *Mildred Pierce* post-production file in the Warner Brothers archive bears her out.
37 Warner Brothers archive, *Mildred Pierce* file no. 2086, Wald to Curtiz, 28 September 1945.
38 *New York Post*, 1 November 1945.

6 THE TWILIGHT WARNERS YEARS, September 1945 to April 1953

1 Warner Brothers archive, *Night and Day* file no. 1487, Stacey to Wright, 4 May 1945.
2 This and the previous paragraph are based upon Warner Brothers archive, *Night and Day* file no. 2124, Schwartz to Jack Warner, 29 January 1945; file no. 2877, Obringer to Ralph E. Lewis of Freston and Files, a legal firm, 7 August 1943, Schwartz to Jack Warner, 13 April 1944 and 6 August 1944, Jack Warner to Schwartz, 15 August 1944; Cary Grant legal file no. 2830, Jack Warner to Obringer, 17 August 1944.
3 G. Eells, *The Life That Late He Led: a Biography of Cole Porter*, London, 1967, pp. 220–1. W. C. McIntosh and W. Weaver, *The Private Cary Grant*, London, 1983, pp. 42–3.
4 Warner Brothers archive, *Night and Day* file no. 1487, Stacey to Wright, 16 June 1945.
5 Ibid., Stacey to Wright, 20 and 21 June 1945.
6 Ibid., Stacey to Wright, 4, 5, and 7 September 1945.
7 Ibid., Stacey to Wright, 29 September 1945.
8 Ibid., Stacey to Wright, 5 September 1945.
9 Warner Brothers archive, Curtiz legal file no. 2845, Jack Warner to Obringer, 1 February 1939 and Curtiz payroll no. 2.
10 Ibid., Curtiz legal file no. 2845, Jack Warner to Curtiz, 20 October 1944.
11 Ibid., Curtiz to Jack Warner, 12 March 1946.
12 J. Davis and T. Flinn, 'Michael Curtiz', in T. Shales et al., *The American Film Heritage: Impressions from the American Film Institute Archives*, Washington DC, 1972, p. 38.
13 Warner Brothers archive, Curtiz legal file no. 2845, Warners to Curtiz, 8 July 1946 and Curtiz payroll no. 3.
14 Warner Brothers archive, Curtiz legal file no. 2733, contract of 19 December 1947.
15 Warner Brothers archive, *Life With Father* file no. 2043, Buckner to Wright, 6 June 1946.
16 R. Behlmer, *Inside Warner Bros. (1935–1951)*, New York, 1985, p. 269, Curtiz to Bette Davis, 14 December 1945.
17 A. Edwards, *Shirley Temple: American Princess*, London, 1988, pp. 175–6.
18 This account is based upon Warner Brothers archive, *Life With Father* file nos. 1015, 1488, 2043, and 2807.

19 D. Sheppard, *Elizabeth: the Life and Career of Elizabeth Taylor*, London, 1975, p. 43.

20 Warner Brothers archive, *Life With Father* file no. 704, Powell to Curtiz, undated.

21 Warner Brothers archive, *The Unsuspected* file no. 2339, Curtiz to Welles, 3 August and 1 December 1946, Curtiz to Selznick, 23 October 1946.

22 The casting difficulties can be traced in Warner Brothers archive, Curtiz legal file no. 2733, Curtiz to Sam Goldwyn, 2 December 1946 and the ensuing correspondence.

23 D. Deschner, 'Anton Grot, Warners art director, 1927–1948', *Velvet Light Trap*, 1975, no. 15, p. 22.

24 Warner Brothers archive, *The Unsuspected* file no. 2339, Curtiz to producer Charles Hoffman, 16 June 1947.

25 Jack L. Warner papers, box 27, Curtiz to Jack Warner, 27 March 1947.

26 Ibid., box 26, Curtiz to Trilling, 18 May 1948.

27 Ibid., box 23, Curtiz to Trilling, 21 June 1948.

28 Ibid., Jack Warner to Curtiz and Curtiz to Trilling, 10 September 1948.

29 Warner Brothers archive, *Flamingo Road* file no. 1905, Rains to Collier Young, undated but probably late November 1947.

30 Behlmer, op. cit., pp. 304–5. See also Warner Brothers archive, Curtiz legal file no. 2875, for the full details.

31 Warner Brothers archive, *Roughly Speaking* file no. 698, undated.

32 Warner Brothers archive, *Flamingo Road* file no. 699, undated.

33 Warner Brothers archive, Curtiz legal file no. 2875, Trilling to Obringer, 7 September 1949.

34 L. J. Quirk, *Jane Wyman: the Actress and the Woman*, New York, 1986, p. 127.

35 Warner Brothers archive, *Young Man With a Horn* file no. 2379, Wald to Trilling, 15 November 1946.

36 Ibid., Wald to Trilling, 23 June 1947.

37 Ibid., Wald to Trilling, 4 June 1947.

38 Ibid., North to Dorothy Baker, 19 March 1947.

39 Ibid., MacDougall to Wald, 2 December 1946.

40 Ibid., Curtiz to Wald, 15 April 1949.

41 Ibid., Jack Warner to Wald, 16 April 1949.

42 Ibid., Wald to Trilling, 17 May 1949 and Wald to Curtiz, 21 June 1949.

43 Ibid., Wald to Foreman, 19 April 1949.

44 Ibid., Douglas to Jack Warner, 29 September 1949.

45 Ibid., Wald to Curtiz, 23 August 1949.

46 P. Neal, *As I Am*, London, 1988, p. 118. L. Bacall, *By Myself*, New York, 1980 (paperback), p. 236.

47 Warner Brothers archive, Curtiz legal file no. 2875, Trilling to Obringer, 7 September 1949.

48 Warner Brothers archive, *The Breaking Point* file no. 2306, Wald to Jack Warner, 22 April 1949 and Wald to Trilling, 7 May, 8 June, 25 November, and 16 December 1949.

49 Ibid., Wald to Wright, 3 January 1950.

50 *Los Angeles Times*, 16 April 1950.

51 Warner Brothers archive, *The Breaking Point* file no. 2306, Wald to Curtiz, 27 January, 16, and 24 February 1950, Wald to MacDougall, 10 February 1950.

52 Ibid., Curtiz to MacDougall, 10 February 1950.

53 Ibid.

54 Ibid., Wald to Curtiz, 6 April 1950.

55 Warner Brothers archive, *Jim Thorpe – All American* file no. 1761, Flaherty to Jack Warner, 22 November 1950.

56 Ibid., Freeman to Touchdown Club of Washington, 22 December 1949.

57 Ibid., Milton Sperling to Freeman, 1 December 1949.

58 Ibid., correspondence between Thorpe and the US Olympic Association, June to October 1949.

59 Warner Brothers archive, *Force of Arms* file no. 2001, Curtiz to MacEwen and Trilling, 3 January 1950.

60 Ibid., Wald to Tregaskis, 30 January 1950.

61 Ibid., Wald to Tregaskis, 8 March 1950.

62 Ibid., Veiller to Trilling, 26 December 1950.

63 Ibid., Veiller and Curtiz to Jack Warner, 22 February 1951.

64 Ibid., production notes, undated.

65 Warner Brothers archive, *The Story of Will Rogers* file no. 2341, P. Nathan, Wallis's secretary, to Wallis, 1 December 1941.

66 Ibid., McCrea to Hellinger (telegram), 6 March 1945. See also P. McGilligan, 'Interview with Joel McCrea', *Focus on Film*, 1978, no. 30, pp. 21–2, 29.

67 Jack Warner had considered this in 1942. See Warner Brothers archive, *The Story of Will Rogers* file no. 2341, Jack Warner to Hellinger and Trilling (telegram), 26 December 1942.

68 Ibid., Curtiz to Trilling, 17 May 1951. Jack Warner papers, box 28, Curtiz to Trilling, 18 January 1952.

69 Ibid., Curtiz to Trilling, 17 May 1951.

70 Warner Brothers archive, Curtiz legal file no. 2875, Obringer to Jack Warner, 21 May 1951.

71 Ibid., payroll no. 3.

72 Warner Brothers archive, *Young Man With a Horn* file no. 2379, Curtiz to Jack Warner, 23 May 1949.

73 He actually asked to be assigned to another film. See Warner Brothers archive, *I'll See You in My Dreams* file no. 1939, Curtiz to Trilling, 29 May 1951.

74 Ibid.

75 Ibid., Wright to Jack Warner, 5 July 1951.

76 Ibid., Grace Kahn to Jack Warner, undated.

77 Curtiz himself came to recognize this. See Warner Brothers archive, Curtiz legal file no. 2375, Curtiz to Jack Warner, 15 January 1954.

78 Ibid., Curtiz to Trilling, 8 January 1953.

79 Curtiz had referred to both *Destry Rides Again* and *High Noon* when he had first read *The Boy from Oklahoma* script. See ibid.

80 The full details of the disagreement between Warners and Curtiz can be found in Warner Brothers archive, Curtiz legal file no. 2875.

81 For instance, in J. Wakeman (ed.), *World Film Directors, vol. i, 1890–1945*, New York, 1987, p. 179.

7 HOLLYWOOD NOMAD, April 1953 to April 1962

1 Warner Brothers archive, Curtiz legal file no. 2875, Trilling to Jack Warner, 23 March 1953.

2 See T. Thomas, *Ustinov in Focus*, London and New York, 1971, pp. 96–9.

3 This account is based upon the Twentieth Century-Fox papers on *The Egyptian* and the Philip Dunne papers, box no. 6.

4 Twentieth Century-Fox papers on *The Best Things in Life are Free*, conference between Zanuck, Buddy Adler, and Henry Ephron, 16 June 1955.

5 Ibid., conference between Zanuck, Ephron, and writer John Monks Junior, 28 October 1955, p. 10.

6 Ibid., p. 9.

7 *Los Angeles Daily News*, 18 August 1956. *Los Angeles Times*, 1 December 1956.

8 Jack Warner papers, box 24, Curtiz to Trilling, 1 November 1956.

9 Ibid., Curtiz to Trilling, 6 August 1956.

10 Warner Brothers archive, *The Helen Morgan Story* file no. 2099, Curtiz to Trilling, 8 March 1957.

11 Ibid., file no. 2954, Geoffrey M. Shurlock to Jack Warner, 3 January 1957.

12 Jack Warner papers, box 24, Curtiz to Trilling, 22 March 1957.

13 *Los Angeles Examiner*, 27 August 1957.

14 Ibid., 5 September 1957.

15 B. Linet, *Ladd: The Life, The Legend, The Legacy of Alan Ladd*, New York, 1979, pp. 214–16.

16 Hal B. Wallis papers, *King Creole* general (Nathan) folder no. 1, Curtiz to Wallis, 3 May 1955 and folder no. 2, Curtiz to Wallis, 28 September 1955.

17 Ibid., folder no. 1, Curtiz to Wallis, 27 November 1957.

18 Ibid., casting folder.

19 Ibid., general (Nathan) folder no. 1, Curtiz to Wallis, 27 November 1957.

20 S. Eyman, *Five American Cinematographers*, London and Metuchen, New Jersey, 1987, p. 135.

21 *Los Angeles Examiner*, 29 June 1961.

8 ASSESSMENT

1 See K. Kulik, *Alexander Korda: The Man Who Could Work Miracles*, London, 1975, pp. 21–2.

2 Sascha Film A. G., *Dreissig Jahre Sascha-Film*, Vienna, 1948 (pamphlet), no page number.

3 I. Nemeskürty, *Word and Image: History of the Hungarian Cinema*, Budapest, 1965, enlarged edition 1974, pp. 29, 32.

4 The National Film Archive in London holds prints of *The Way of Terror* (1921), *The Slave Queen* (1924), *The Road to Happiness* (1926), and *The Golden Butterfly* (1926). *The Slave Queen* print is the shortened version shown in Britain, while the third reel of six is missing from *The Golden Butterfly*. The Austrian Film Archive has restored *Sodom and Gomorrah* to about half of its original length and filled the missing content with stills and explanatory sub-titles.

5 See note 48 below.

6 J. L. Warner and D. Jennings, *My First Hundred Years in Hollywood*, New York, 1964, pp. 161–2.

7 See *New York Times*, 15 February and 31 May 1927.

8 C. Higham, *Hollywood Cameramen: Sources of Light*, London, 1970, p. 40.

9 S. Eyman, *Five American Cinematographers*, London and Metuchen, New Jersey, 1987, p. 77.

10 Ibid., p. 135.

11 B. Rosenberg and H. Silverstein, *The Real Tinsel*, London, 1970, pp. 364, 370.

12 Ibid., p. 364.

13 D. Deschner, 'Anton Grot, Warners art director, 1927–1948', *Velvet Light Trap*, 1975, no. 15, pp. 18–22.

14 C. Higham and J. Greenberg, *The Celluloid Muse*, London, 1969, p. 199.

15 See p. 85.

16 G. F. Noxon, 'The European influence on the coming of sound to the American film, 1925–40', in E. W. Cameron (ed.), *Sound and the Cinema*, Pleasantville, New York, 1983, p. 155.

17 *Los Angeles Examiner*, 24 June 1928.

18 Quoted in J. R. Parish and D. E. Stanke, *The Debonairs*, New Rochelle, New York, 1975, p. 31.

19 Curtiz quoted in P. Martin, 'Hollywood's champion language assassin', *Saturday Evening Post*, 2 August 1947, p. 66.

20 *The Lonely Life: an Autobiography*, New York, 1962, p. 135.

21 Ibid., p. 212.

22 W. Stine, *Mother Goddam*, New York, 1974, pp. 42, 54, 91, 121.

23 *Film Weekly*, 29 March 1935.

24 T. Schatz, *The Genius of the System: Hollywood Film-Making in the Studio Era*, New York, 1988, p. 308.

25 Warner and Jennings, op. cit., p. 302.

26 Edward G. Robinson papers, box 36:10, Robinson to Jack Warner, 9 February 1943.

27 Schatz, op. cit., pp. 427–8.

28 *Hollywood Citizen*, 24 February 1947.

29 Warner Brothers archive, *Mildred Pierce* file no. 2086, Scott to Wald, 20 February 1945.

30 *Hollywood Citizen*, 25 February 1947.

31 Curtiz quoted in Martin, op. cit., p. 63.

32 D. Niven, *The Moon's a Balloon*, London, 1972 (paperback), pp. 179–80.

33 A. E. Hotchner, *Doris Day: Her Own Story*, London, 1976, revised 1985, pp. 101–3.

34 *Chicago Daily News*, 9 May 1945.

35 P. Underwood, *Horror Man: the Life of Boris Karloff*, London, 1972, p. 54.

36 M. Loy and J. Kotsilibas-Davis, *Being and Becoming*, London, 1987, p. 49.

37 M. B. Druxman, *Paul Muni: His Life and His Films*, London and New York, 1974, p. 138.

38 Eyman, op. cit., p. 77.

39 Warner and Jennings, op. cit., pp. 160–4 assess Curtiz favourably.

40 J. Cagney and D. Warren, *James Cagney: the Authorized Biography*, London, 1983, p. 146.

41 P. Lee, *Miss Peggy Lee: an Autobiography*, London, 1991 (paperback), p. 134.

42 J. R. Taylor, *Strangers in Paradise: the Hollywood Emigrés, 1933–1950*, London, 1983, p. 197.

43 E. Goodman, *Bogey: the Good-Bad Guy*, New York, 1965, p. 123.

44 Warner Brothers archive, *Mildred Pierce* file no. 704, publicity notes on Curtiz, undated.

45 Warner Brothers archive, *The Unsuspected* file no. 2339, Curtiz to Hoffman, 22 January 1947.

46 H. B. Wallis and C. Higham, *Star-Maker: the Autobiography of Hal B. Wallis*, New York, 1980, p. 26.
47 *Los Angeles Examiner*, 9 September 1936, 29 April 1937, and 25 March 1960.
48 Wallis and Higham, op. cit., p. 26.
49 H. Koch, *As Time Goes By: Memoirs of a Writer*, London and New York, 1979, pp. 46, 82.
50 Curtiz quoted in Martin, op. cit., p. 63.
51 Koch, op. cit., pp. 128–9.
52 Warner Brothers archive, *The Sea Hawk* file no. 2230, Wallis to Blanke, 7 March 1940.
53 Ibid., Wallis to Blanke and Wright, 3 April 1940.
54 Curtiz quoted in Martin, op. cit., p. 63.
55 Warner Brothers archive, *Roughly Speaking* file no. 2189, Blanke to Harold McCord, editorial supervisor, 25 March 1944.
56 Directors Guild of America, *Byron Haskin*, London and Metuchen, New Jersey, 1984, pp. 95–6, 151–2.
57 J. E. Nolan, 'Michael Curtiz: thought living to work is better than working to live', *Films in Review*, 1970, vol. 21, no. 9, p. 535.
58 Martin, op. cit., p. 63.
59 T. Flinn, 'William Diertele, the plutarch of Hollywood', *Velvet Light Trap*, 1975, no. 15, p. 26.
60 Letter by Sherman, *American Film*, October 1976, p. 4.
61 See D. Morse, '*Dodge City* and the development of the western', *Monogram*, 1975, no. 6, pp. 34–9.
62 British Film Institute Library microfiche on Curtiz.
63 Hal Wallis as quoted in R. Kinnard and R. J. Vitone, *The American Films of Michael Curtiz*, London and Metuchen, New Jersey, 1986, p. 5.
64 R. Behlmer, *Inside Warner Bros. (1935–1951)*, New York, 1985, p. 70. F. Mattison, unit manager, to Wright, 29 July 1938.
65 Warner Brothers archive, *Mildred Pierce* file no. 704, typed notes by Joan Crawford, undated, probably soon after she had won her Oscar for the film.
66 Directors Guild of America, op. cit., pp. 97–8.
67 Behlmer, op. cit., p. 274. Stacey to Wright, 5 July 1947.
68 Goodman, op. cit., p. 135.
69 See p. 132.
70 See p. 69.
71 Wood Soanes in *Oakland Tribune*, 12 February 1945.
72 *Los Angeles Examiner*, 4 July 1952.
73 See J. Davis and T. Flinn, '*The Third Degree*', *The Silent Picture*, 1973, no. 18, pp. 37–42.
74 Warner and Jennings, op. cit., pp. 162–4.
75 See 'On playing John Brown', in M. R. Werner, *Along the Santa Fe Trail*, a pamphlet of special material issued by Warner Brothers when the film was released, pp. 26–30. In this interview Massey stated that Brown was the embodiment of the single-tracked mind and an embryonic Hitler (p. 26).
76 E. G. Robinson and L. Spigelgass, *All My Yesterdays*, London and New York, 1973, p. 218.
77 Warner Brothers archive, *Roughly Speaking* file no. 698, publicity notes, undated.
78 Warner Brothers archive, *Mission to Moscow* file no. 2785, Buckner to Jack Warner, 20 May 1943.
79 Koch, op. cit., p. 130.

80 Koch, op. cit., p. 112.
81 R. Windeler, *Burt Lancaster*, London, 1984, pp. 63–5.
82 For further details, see Warner Brothers archive, Curtiz legal file no. 2845.
83 See R. Graves, 'Michael Curtiz', *Classic Images*, 1983, no. 91, pp. 17–18, 38.
84 Curtiz quoted in Martin, op. cit., p. 66.
85 As far as the author has been able to trace, more than fifty have appeared on either American or British television. In chronological order these are: *Noah's Ark, Mammy, Dr X, 20,000 Years in Sing Sing, The Mystery of the Wax Museum, The Kennel Murder Case, Mandalay, Jimmy the Gent, Black Fury, The Case of the Curious Bride, Front Page Woman, Captain Blood, The Walking Dead, The Charge of the Light Brigade, Kid Galahad, The Perfect Specimen, Gold is Where You Find It, The Adventures of Robin Hood, Four's a Crowd, Four Daughters, Angels With Dirty Faces, Dodge City, Daughters Courageous, The Private Lives of Elizabeth and Essex, Virginia City, The Sea Hawk, Santa Fe Trail, The Sea Wolf, Dive Bomber, Captains of the Clouds, Yankee Doodle Dandy, Casablanca, Mission to Moscow, This is the Army, Passage to Marseille, Mildred Pierce, Night and Day, Life With Father, The Unsuspected, Romance on the High Seas, Flamingo Road, Young Man With a Horn, Bright Leaf, The Breaking Point, Jim Thorpe – All American, I'll See You in My Dreams, Trouble Along the Way, White Christmas, We're No Angels, The Vagabond King, The Scarlet Hour, The Proud Rebel, King Creole, The Hangman, The Adventures of Huckleberry Finn, A Breath of Scandal, The Comancheros.*
86 To date the following are available on video in both Britain and the United States (alphabetical order): *The Adventures of Robin Hood, Angels With Dirty Faces, Captain Blood, Casablanca, The Charge of the Light Brigade, The Comancheros, Dodge City, King Creole, Night and Day, Passage to Marseille, The Private Lives of Elizabeth and Essex, The Proud Rebel, Santa Fe Trail, The Sea Hawk, We're No Angels, Yankee Doodle Dandy, Young Man With a Horn. Dive Bomber* has been issued in Britain but not in the United States. The following are available only in the United States (alphabetical order): *The Adventures of Huckleberry Finn, Black Fury, A Breath of Scandal, Dr X, The Egyptian, Flamingo Road, Four Daughters, Jim Thorpe – All American, The Kennel Murder Case, Life With Father, Mildred Pierce, My Dream is Yours, The Mystery of the Wax Museum, Noah's Ark, Romance on the High Seas, This is the Army, Virginia City, White Christmas.*
87 Quoted in Kinnard and Vitone, op. cit., p. 7.
88 *Hollywood in the Thirties*, London, 1968, p. 52.

SELECT BIBLIOGRAPHY

UNPUBLISHED DOCUMENTS

Michael Curtiz microfiche, British Film Institute Library, London.
Philip Dunne papers, University of Southern California (USC), Los Angeles, California.
William Randolph Hearst newspaper collection, USC.
Edward G. Robinson papers, USC.
William Schaefer papers, USC.
Twentieth Century-Fox papers, USC.
Hal B. Wallis papers, Margaret Herrick Library (Academy of Motion Picture Arts and Sciences), Beverly Hills, California.
Jack L. Warner papers, USC.
Warner Brothers archive, USC.

JOURNALS AND NEWSPAPERS

The American Film
Australian Journal of Screen Theory
Chicago Daily News
Chicago Sunday Tribune
Cinema (UK)
Cinema Papers
Cinemaeditor
Classic Images
Evening World Herald
Film and History
Film Culture
Film Weekly
Films and Filming
Films in Review
Focus on Film
Hollywood Citizen
Journal of Popular Film
Los Angeles Daily News
Los Angeles Examiner
Los Angeles Times
Monogram
Motion Picture Herald

New Statesman
New York Herald Tribune
New York Post
New York Sun
New York Times
Oakland Tribune
The Observer
Saturday Evening Post
Seattle Times
Sight and Sound
The Silent Picture
The Spectator
Sunday Express
The Times
Velvet Light Trap

OTHER PUBLISHED DOCUMENTS

Books

Bacall, L., *By Myself*, New York, 1980.
Baxter, J., *Hollywood in the Thirties*, London, 1968.
Behlmer, R., *Inside Warner Bros. (1935–1951)*, New York, 1985.
Bergman, I. and Burgess, A., *My Story*, London, 1981.
Bickford, C., *Bulls, Balls, Bicycles and Actors*, New York, 1965.
Bordwell, D., Staiger, J. and Thompson, K., *The Classical Hollywood Cinema*, London, 1985.
Cagney, J., *Cagney by Cagney*, Garden City, New York, 1976.
Cagney, J. and Warren, D., *James Cagney: the Authorized Biography*, London, 1983.
Cameron, E. W. (ed.), *Sound and the Cinema*, Pleasantville, New York, 1983.
Canham, K., *The Hollywood Professionals*, vol. 1, London, 1973.
Davis, B., *The Lonely Life: an Autobiography*, New York, 1962.
Directors Guild of America, *Byron Haskin*, London and Metuchen, New Jersey, 1984.
Druxman, M. B., *Paul Muni: His Life and His Films*, London and New York, 1974.
Dunbar, J., *Flora Robson*, London, 1960.
Edwards, A., *Shirley Temple: American Princess*, London, 1988.
Eells, G., *The Life That Late He Led: a Biography of Cole Porter*, London, 1967.
—— *Ginger, Loretta and Irene Who?*, New York, 1976.
Everson, W. K., *American Silent Film*, New York, 1978.
Eyman, S., *Five American Cinematographers*, London and Metuchen, New Jersey, 1987.
Finler, J. W., *The Hollywood Story*, London, 1988.
Flynn, E., *My Wicked, Wicked Ways*, London, 1960.
Freedland, M., *Al Jolson*, London and New York, 1972.
Fritz, W., *Die Österreichischen Spielfilme der Stummfilmzeit, 1907–1930*, Vienna, 1967.
Gesek, L., *Filmzauber aus Wien*, Vienna, 1966.
Goldman, H. G., *Jolson: the Legend comes to Life*, Oxford and New York, 1988.
Gomery, D., *The Hollywood Studio System*, London, 1986.

Goodman, E., *The Fifty-Year Decline and Fall of Hollywood*, New York, 1961.
—— *Bogey: the Good-Bad Guy*, New York, 1965.
Higham, C., *Hollywood Cameramen: Sources of Light*, London, 1970.
—— *Warner Brothers: a History of the Studio*, New York, 1975.
—— *Errol Flynn: the Untold Story*, London, 1980.
—— *Bette: a Biography of Bette Davis*, London, 1981.
—— *Olivia and Joan: a Biography of Olivia de Havilland and Joan Fontaine*, London, 1984.
Higham, C. and Greenberg, J., *Hollywood in the Forties*, London, 1968.
—— *The Celluloid Muse*, London, 1969.
Higham, C. and Moseley, R., *Cary Grant: the Lonely Heart*, London, 1983.
Hirschhorn, C., *The Warner Bros. Story*, London, 1979.
Hotchner, A. E., *Doris Day: Her Own Story*, London, 1976, revised edition 1985.
Kay, K., *Myrna Loy*, New York, 1977.
Kinnard, R. and Vitone, R. J., *The American Films of Michael Curtiz*, London and Metuchen, New Jersey, 1986.
Koch, H., *As Time Goes By: Memoirs of a Writer*, London and New York, 1979.
Kulik, K., *Alexander Korda: the Man Who Could Work Miracles*, London, 1975.
Lawrence, J., *Actor: the Life and Times of Paul Muni*, New York, 1974.
Lee, P., *Miss Peggy Lee: an Autobiography*, London, 1991.
Linet, B., *Ladd: the Life, the Legend, the Legacy of Alan Ladd*, New York, 1979.
Loy, M. and Kotsilibas-Davis, J., *Being and Becoming*, London, 1987.
Lyon, C. (ed.), *The International Directory of Films and Film-makers*, vol. 2, London, 1984.
McIntosh, W. C. and Weaver, W., *The Private Cary Grant*, London, 1983.
Massey, R., *A Hundred Different Lives: an Autobiography*, London, 1979.
Meyer, W. R., *Warner Brothers Directors*, New Rochelle, New York, 1978.
Morgan, M. and Routier, M., *With Those Eyes*, London, 1978.
Morris, G., *Doris Day*, New York, 1976.
—— *John Garfield*, New York, 1977.
Neal, P., *As I Am*, London, 1988.
Nemeskürty, I., *Word and Image: History of the Hungarian Cinema*, Budapest, 1965, enlarged edition 1974.
Niven, D., *The Moon's a Balloon*, London, 1972.
—— *Bring On the Empty Horses*, London, 1975.
Noble, P., *Bette Davis: A Biography*, London, no date, probably 1948.
Parish, J. R. and Stanke, D. E., *The Debonairs*, New Rochelle, New York, 1975.
Quinlan, D., *The Illustrated Guide to Film Directors*, London, 1983.
Quirk, L.J., *Jane Wyman: the Actress and the Woman*, New York, 1986.
Rainsburger, T., *James Wong Howe: Cinematographer*, London, 1981.
Richards, J., *Swordsmen of the Screen*, London, 1977.
Robertson, J. C., *The British Board of Film Censors: Film Censorship in Britain, 1896–1950*, London, 1985.
Robinson, E. G. and Spigelgass, L., *All My Yesterdays*, London and New York, 1973.
Roddick, N., *A New Deal in Entertainment: Warner Brothers in the 1930s*, London, 1983.
Rosenberg, B. and Silverstein, H., *The Real Tinsel*, London, 1970.
Russell, R., *Life is a Banquet*, New York, 1977.
Sarris, A., *The American Cinema: Directors and Directions 1929–1968*, Chicago, Illinois, 1968.
Sascha Film A. G., *Dreissig Jahre Sascha-Film*, Vienna, 1948.

Schatz, T., *The Genius of the System: Hollywood Film-Making in the Studio Era*, New York, 1988.

Schelly, W., *Harry Langdon*, London and Metuchen, New Jersey, 1982.

Shales, T., et al., *The American Film Heritage: Impressions from the American Film Institute Archives*, Washington, DC, 1972.

Sheppard, D., *Elizabeth: the Life and Career of Elizabeth Taylor*, London, 1975.

Taylor, J. R., *Strangers in Paradise: the Hollywood Emigrés, 1933–1950*, London, 1983.

Temple-Black, S., *Child Star*, London, 1988.

Thomas, R., *Joan Crawford: a Biography*, London, 1978.

Thomas, T., *Ustinov in Focus*, London and New York, 1971.

Underwood, P., *Horror Man: the Life of Boris Karloff*, London, 1972.

Viviani, C., *Curtiz: Anthologie du Cinéma no. 73*, Paris, 1973.

Wakeman, J. (ed.), *World Film Directors, vol. 1, 1890–1945*, New York, 1987.

Walker, A., *Bette Davis: a Celebration*, London, 1986.

Wallis, H. B. and Higham, C., *Star-Maker: the Autobiography of Hal B. Wallis*, New York, 1980.

Warner, J. L. and Jennings, D., *My First Hundred Years in Hollywood*, New York, 1964.

Windeler, R., *Burt Lancaster*, London, 1984.

Yanni, N., *Rosalind Russell*, London, 1975.

Zierold, N., *The Hollywood Tycoons*, London, 1969.

Articles

Arkadin, 'Film clips', *Sight and Sound*, 1968, vol. 37, no. 4, pp. 210–11.

Behlmer, R., 'Erich Wolfgang Korngold', *Films in Review*, 1967, vol. 18, no. 2, pp. 86–100.

Curtiz, M., 'Talent shortage is causing two-year production delay', *Films and Filming*, 1956, June, p. 9.

Davis, J., '*Captain Blood*', *Velvet Light Trap*, 1971, no. 1, pp. 26–31.

—— 'Notes on Warner Brothers' foreign policy, 1918–1948', *Velvet Light Trap*, 1972, no. 4, pp. 23–33.

—— '*The Unsuspected*', *Velvet Light Trap*, 1972, no. 5, pp. 21–4.

—— 'The tragedy of Mildred Pierce,' *Velvet Light Trap*, 1972, no. 6, pp. 27–30.

—— 'When will they ever learn?: a tale of mad geniuses, scientists, artists, and a director (also mad)', *Velvet Light Trap*, 1975, no. 15, pp. 11–17.

Davis, J. and Flinn, T., '*The Third Degree*', *The Silent Picture*, 1973, no. 18, pp. 37–42.

—— '*The Breaking Point*', *Velvet Light Trap*, 1975, no. 14, pp. 17–20.

Davis, J. and Pepper, L., 'John Brown's body lies a'rolling in his grave', *Velvet Light Trap*, 1973, no. 8, pp. 14–19.

Deschner, D., 'Anton Grot, Warners art director, 1927–1948', *Velvet Light Trap*, 1975, no. 15, pp. 18–22.

Dienstfrey, H., 'Hitch your genre to a star', *Film Culture*, 1964, no. 34, pp. 35–7.

Doyle, N., 'Olivia de Havilland', *Films in Review*, 1962, vol. 13, no. 2, pp. 71–85.

Easley, L. J., '*The Santa Fe Trail*, John Brown and the coming of the Civil War', *Film and History*, 1983, vol. 13, no. 2, pp. 25–33.

Flinn, T., 'William Diertele: the plutarch of Hollywood', *Velvet Light Trap*, 1975, no. 15, pp. 23–8.

Graves, R., 'Michael Curtiz', *Classic Images*, 1983, no. 91, pp. 17–18, 38.

Greenberg, J., 'Writing for the movies: Casey Robinson', *Focus on Film*, 1979, no. 32, pp. 7–32.

Hark, I. R., 'The visual politics of *The Adventures of Robin Hood*', *Journal of Popular Film*, 1976, vol. 5, no. 1, pp. 3–17.

Haun, H. and Raborn, G., 'Max Steiner', *Films in Review*, 1961, vol. 12, no. 6, pp. 338–51.

Kay, K. and Peary, G., 'Talking to Pat O'Brien', *Velvet Light Trap*, 1975, no. 15, pp. 29–32.

Leggett, P., 'The noble cynic Michael Curtiz', *Focus on Film*, 1975, no. 23, pp. 15–19.

McGilligan, P., 'Interview with Joel McCrea', *Focus on Film*, 1978, no. 30, pp. 8–33.

McVay, D., '*The Maltese Falcon* and *Casablanca*', *Focus on Film*, 1978, no. 30, pp. 4–7.

Martin, P., 'Hollywood's champion language assassin,' *Saturday Evening Post*, 2 August 1947, pp. 22–3, 58, 63–6.

Moran, A., '*20,000 Years in Sing Sing*', *Australian Journal of Screen Theory*, 1977, no. 3, pp. 36–46.

Morse, D., '*Dodge City* and the development of the western', *Monogram*, 1975, no. 6, pp. 34–9.

Mundy, R., 'Death plays and wax works: Curtiz, Freund, Florey', *Cinema* (UK), 1971 no. 9, pp. 8–10.

Nelson, J., 'Warner Brothers' deviants, 1931–1933', *Velvet Light Trap*, 1975, no. 15, pp. 7–10.

Nielsen, R., 'Reviewing the classics: *The Amazing Dr Clitterhouse* and *The Charge of the Light Brigade*', *Cinemaeditor*, 1982, no. 2–3, pp. 23–5.

—— 'John Qualen and *Black Fury*', *Classic Images*, 1984, no. 106, p. 46.

Nolan, J.E., 'Michael Curtiz: thought living to work is better than working to live', *Films in Review*, vol. 21, no. 9, pp. 525–48.

Richards, J., 'Discoveries: *The Walking Dead* and *Strangler of the Swamp*', *Focus on Film*, 1973, no. 15, pp. 59–62.

—— 'In praise of Claude Rains' and 'Claude Rains: a career to remember', *Films and Filming*, 1982, February, pp. 12–17 and March, pp. 8–14.

Sarris, A., 'The American cinema', *Film Culture*, 1963, no. 28, pp. 35–6.

Shadoian, J., 'Michael Curtiz *20,000 Years in Sing Sing*', *Journal of Popular Film*, 1973, vol. 2, no. 2, pp. 165–79.

Shirley, G., 'Interview with Byron Haskin', *Cinema Papers*, 1975, March–April, pp. 18–23, 86.

Squarini, P., 'The original Rocky: James Cagney', *Classic Images*, 1983, no. 102, pp. 31–2.

FILMOGRAPHY

HUNGARY, 1912–19

1912

Ma Es Holnop (*Today and Tomorrow*). *w* Imre Roboz, Ivan Siklosi; *cast* Curtiz, Arthur Somlay, Ilona Azel.
Az Utolso Bohem (*The Last Bohemian*).
Rabalek (*Captive Soul*). *w* Imre Foldes; *ph* Oden Uhrer; *cast* Alfred Deesy, Sari Fedak, Marton Ratkai.

1913

Marta (*Martha*). *Cast* Marton Ratkai, Sari Fedak, Mihaly Varkonyi.
Hasasidik Az Uram (*My Husband Lies*).
Atlantis (directed by August Blom for Nordisk, Denmark). Based upon a Gerhard Hauptmann story; *ph* Johan Ankerstjerne; *cast* Curtiz, Olap Fonss, Ida Orloff.
Curtiz probably directed a film of unknown title while in Denmark.

1914

Az Ejszaka Rabjai (*Slaves of the Night*). *w* Imre Roboz, Ivan Siklosi; *cast* Sander Goth, Ica Lenkeffy.
A Tolonc (*The Vagrant*). *w* Ede Toth; *cast* Mari Jasznai, Mihaly Varkonyi, Lily Berky.
A Henczengo Pongyolaban (*Princess Pongyola*).

174

Bank Ban. w Jeno Janovicz, following Joszef Katona; *cast* Mari Jasznai, Mihaly Varkonyi, Erzi Paulay, Istvan Szentgyorgy.

A Kolocsonkert Csessemok (Borrowed Babies). w Jeno Janovicz; *cast* Lily Berky, Kate Berky, Aladar Ihasz, Aljos Meszaros; *co-directed* with Janovicz.

Aranyaso (The Golden Spade).

1915

Akit Ketten Szeretnek (Loved by Two). Cast Curtiz, Mici Haraszti, Matild Giosi, Edit Lakos.

A Kathausi (The Carthusian). ph Bela Zsitkovsky; *cast* Kamilla Hollay, Karoly Lajthai.

A Tanitono (The Mistress). Cast Lily Berky, Mihaly Varkonyi, Istvan Szentgyorgy; *co-directed* with Marton Keleti.

1916

A Medikus (The Doctor). Cast Curtiz, Mihaly Varkonyi.

Makkhetes (Seven of Clubs). ph Joszef Becsi; *cast* Eugenia Della Donna.

A Fekete Szivarvany (The Black Rainbow). Cast Vilma Medgyasar, Arthur Somlay.

Az Ezust Kekske (The Silver Goat). ph Aladar Fodor; *cast* Mihaly Varkonyi, Leontine Kulumberg.

A Farkas (The Wolf). Based upon a Ferenc Molnar play; *cast* Mihaly Varkonyi, Arthur Somlay, Ella (or Frida) Gombaszogi, Lucy Doraine.

Doktur Ur (The Apothecary). Based upon a Ferenc Molnar play; *cast* Marton Ratkai, Arpad Latahar.

1917

A Magyar Fold Ereje (The Strength of the Hungarian Soil). Cast Alfred Deesy, Gustav Vandory, Karoly Lajthai, Ilona Kovaks, Lucy Doraine.

Zoard Mester (Master Zoard). Cast Gyula Hegedus, Imre Roth, Geza Orvoczy.

A Voros Samson (The Red Samson). Cast Ica Lenkeffy, Gyula Czortos, Tivadar Uray.

Az Utolso Ajnal (The Last Dawn). Cast Leopold Kramer, Claire Lotto, Erzy B. Marton.

Tavasz A Telben (Spring in Wintertime). Cast Ica Lenkeffy, Sandor Goth, Karoly Husnar.

A Senk Filia (Nobody's Son). Cast Ica Lenkeffy, Gyula Czortos, Karoly Lajthai.

A Szentjoby Erdo Titka (The Secret of the Saint Job Forest). w Laszlo (Ladislaus) Vadja; *ph* Joszef Becsi; *cast* Jeno Torzs, Derszo Kertesz (David Curtiz), Ferenc Peter.

A Kuruszlo (The Charlatan). Cast Ica Lenkeffy, Gyula Czortos, Tividar Uray.

A Halalcsengo (The Death Bell). ph Vilmos Gabriel; *cast* Lajos Gellbert, Gitta Cathy, Derszo Kertesz (David Curtiz).

A Fold Embere (A Man of the Soil). Cast Oskar Beregi, Gisela Bathory, Giza Meszaros.

Az Ezredes (The Colonel). ph Itsvan Eileer; *cast* Bela Lugosi, Karoly Husnar, Sandor Goth, Arpad Latahar.

Huszar A Telben (*Hussars in Winter*). *Cast* Ica Lenkeffy, Sandor Goth, Karoly Husnar.

Egy Krajcar Tortenete (*The Story of a Penny*). *w* Frigyes Karinthy; *cast* Gyula Kovary, Laszlo Z. Molnar, Boke T. Olah.

A Beke Utja (*The Road to Peace*).

Az Arendas Szidoz (*John the Tenant* or *The Tenant Jew*). *Cast* Gyula Gal, Giselle Bathory, Lajos Kemenes.

A Szamarbor (*The Donkey Skin*). Based upon Honoré de Balzac's novel; *cast* Marsen Iza, Lajos Kemenes.

Tatarjaras (*The Tartar Invasion*). *ph* Joszef Becsi; *cast* Kamilla Hollay, Emmy Kosary, Erno Kiraly.

1918

Az Ordos (*The Devil*). *Cast* Mihaly Varkonyi, Claire Lotto.

A Napraforgos Holgy (*The Lady With the Sunflowers*). *Cast* Jeno Torzs, Erzy B. Marton, Lajos Kemenes, Claire Lotto, Jeno Balassa.

Lulu. Possibly based upon the Franz Wedekind novel; *cast* Claire Lotto, Bela Lugosi, Sandor Goth, Karoly Husnar, Zoltan Szeremy.

Judas. *Cast* Leopold Kramer, Gyula Gal, Julisca Nemeth.

Kilencvenkilenc (*Ninety-nine*). *w* Ivan Siklosi; *cast* Mihaly Varkonyi, Gyula Gal, Claire Lotto, Bela Lugosi.

Dudas (*The Bagpiper*). *w* Ivan Siklosi; *cast* Leopold Kramer, Gyula Gal, Claire Lotto.

A Skorpio (*The Scorpion*). *w* Ivan Siklosi.

A Wellington Rejtely (*The Wellington Mystery*). *w* Ivan Siklosi.

A Csunya Filu (*The Wicked Boy*). *Cast* Leopold Kramer, Erzy B. Marton, Jeno Balassa.

Alraune (*Mandrake*). Based upon a Heinz Hans Ewers work; *cast* Gyula Gal, Jeno Torzs, Szollos Roszi, Margit Lux; *co-directed* with Edmund Fritz.

A Vig Ozvegy (*The Merry Widow*). Based upon Franz Lehar's operetta; *cast* Ica Lenkeffy, Frigyes Tarnay, Emil Fenivessy.

Varazseringo (*The Magic Waltz*). *ph* Eduard Hösch; *cast* Margit Lux, Mihaly Varkonyi, Lajos Ujvary.

Lu, A Kokott (*Lu, The Coquette*). *Cast* Margit Lux, Berta Valero.

Jon Az Ocsem (*The Younger Brother*).

1919

Liliom. Based upon a Ferenc Molnar play; *cast* Ica Lenekeffy, Gyula Czortos, Nusy Somogyi; unfinished.

AUSTRIA, 1919–26

1919

Die Dame mit den schwarzen Handschuhen (*The Lady With the Black Gloves*). *w* Ivan Siklosi; *cast* Lucy Doraine, Harry Walden.

FILMOGRAPHY

1920

Der Stern von Damaskus (*The Star of Damascus*). *w* Ivan Siklosi; *cast* Lucy Doraine, Anton Tiller, Svetozar Petrov.

Die Gottesgeissel (*The Scourge of God*). *Cast* Lucy Doraine, Anton Tiller, Svetozar Petrov.

Die Dame mit den Sonnenblumen (*The Lady With the Sunflowers*). *w* Ivan Siklosi; *cast* Lucy Doraine, Anton Tiller, Svetozar Petrov.

Boccacio.

Miss Tutti Frutti. Cast Lucy Doraine, Alfons Fryland, Josef König, Oskar Saks.

1921

Cherchez La Femme (*Find the Lady*). *Cast* Lucy Doraine, Alfons Fryland, Anton Tiller.

Frau Dorothys Bekenntnis (*Dorothy's Admission*). *Cast* Lucy Doraine, Alfons Fryland, Otto Tressler.

Wege des Schreckens or *Labyrinth des Grauens* (*The Way of Terror*). *Cast* Lucy Doraine, Max Devrient, Alfons Fryland, Otto Tressler.

Herzogin Satanella (*Madame Satan*). *Cast* Lucy Doraine, Alfons Fryland, Anton Tiller.

1922

Sodom und Gomorrha (*Sodom and Gomorrah*). *ph* Gustav Ucicky; *w* Ladislaus Vadja; *cast* Lucy Doraine, Georg Reimers, Walter Slezak, Victor Varconi, Willi Forst; two parts, released in 1922 and 1923.

Die Lawine. ph Gustav Ucicky; *cast* Lily Marishka, Victor Varconi, Mary Kidd.

1923

Der Junge Medardus (*Young Medard*). *w* Ladislaus Vadja, Arthur Schnitzler; *ph* Gustav Ucicky; *cast* Victor Varconi, Ferdinand Onno, Josef König; *co-directed* with Count Alexander Kolowrat.

Samson und Dalila (*Samson and Delilah*). *ph* Gustav Ucicky; *cast* Maria Corda, Alfredo Boccolini, Paul Lukas; *co-directed* with Alexander Korda.

Namenlos (*Nameless*). *ph* Gustav Ucicky; *w* Karl Farkas; *cast* Victor Varconi, Mary Kidd, Karl Farkas.

1924

Ein Spiel Ums Leben (*A Gamble for Life*). *ph* Gustav Ucicky.

General Babka. ph Gustav Ucicky; *cast* Mary Kidd.

Der Onkel von Sumatra (*The Uncle from Sumatra*). *ph* Gustav Ucicky; *cast* Mary Kidd, Angelo Ferrari, Julius Szoreghi.

Avalanche. ph Gustav Ucicky; *cast* Mary Kidd, Victor Varconi, Greta Marishka.

Harun El Raschid. ph Gustav Ucicky; *cast* Mary Kidd, Adolf Weisse.

Die Sklavenkönigin (*The Slave Queen* or *Moon of Israel*). *ph* Gustav Ucicky; *w* Ladislaus Vadja; *cast* Maria Corda, Oskar Beregi, Adelqui Millar, Hans Marr, Ferdinand Onno, Lya de Putti.

1925

Das Spielzeug von Paris (*The Plaything of Paris* or *Red Heels*). *ph* Gustav Ucicky, Max Nekut; *cast* Lili Damita (later Errol Flynn's first wife), Hugo Thimig, Eric Barclay, Georges Tréville.

1926

Der Goldene Schmetterling (*The Golden Butterfly*). *ad* Paul Leni; *w* Adolf Lantz; *cast* Lili Damita, Nils Asther, Jack Trevor, Curt Bois.

Fiaker Nummer Dreizehn (*The Road to Happiness*). Based upon Xavier de Montepin's novel; *w* Alfred Shirokauer; *ad* Paul Leni; *ph* Gustav Ucicky; *cast* Lili Damita, Harry Liedtke, William Diertele, Walter Rilla.

Curtiz's European filmography might be incomplete or incorrect owing to the difficulty of distinguishing between films he directed and those he supervised. When in Hollywood, he also claimed to have directed a Swedish film on great women of history with Greta Garbo in a Marie Antoinette sequence in either 1919 or 1920 and a part of Fritz Lang's 1922 *Die Spinnen*. In addition, Curtiz has occasionally been credited with the 1926 *Richthofen, der rote Ritter der Luft* (*Richthofen, the Red Knight of the Air*) with Angelo Ferrari, George Berghardt, and Sybill Morel.

By contrast his American filmography is substantially accurate. Up to April 1953 the production company was Warner Brothers. The American release date is given where the year differs from that of production.

UNITED STATES, 1926–61

1926

The Third Degree. Based upon Charles Klein's play *The Music Master*; *e* Clarence Kolster; *ph* Hal Mohr; *w* C. Graham Baker; *cast* Jason Robards Senior, Dolores Costello, Louise Dresser, Rockliffe Fellowes, Harry Todd; *assistant director* Henry Blanke. US release: February 1927.

1927

A Million Bid. Based upon a George Cameron work; *ph* Hal Mohr; *w* Robert Dillon; *cast* Warner Oland, Dolores Costello, Malcolm McGregor, Betty Blythe, William Demarest; *assistant director* Henry Blanke.

The Desired Woman. Based upon a Mark Canfield (Zanuck) short story; *ph* Conrad Wells; *w* Anthony Coldeway; *cast* Irene Rich, William Russell, William Collier Junior, John Miljan, Richard Tucker; *assistant director* Henry Blanke; *supervisor* Darryl F. Zanuck.

Good Time Charley. Based upon a Zanuck story; *ph* Barney McGill; *w* Anthony Coldeway, Owen Francis, Ilona Fulop; *cast* Warner Oland, Helene Costello, Mary Carr, Clyde Cook, Montagu Love; *supervisor* Zanuck.

1928

Tenderloin. Based upon a Melville Crossman (Zanuck) story; *e* Ralph Dawson; *ph* Hal Mohr; *w* Edmund T. Lowe, Joseph Jackson; *cast* Dolores Costello,

Conrad Nagel, Mitchell Lewis, Dan Wohlheim, George E. Stone, Pat Hartigan; *supervisor* Zanuck; part sound.

Noah's Ark. *ad* Anton Grot; *c* Orry-Kelly; *e* Harold 'Hal' McCord; *ph* Hal Mohr, Barney McGill; *w* Anthony Coldeway, Zanuck, B. Leon Anthony; *cast* Dolores Costello, Noah Beery Senior, Louise Fazenda, Guinn 'Big Boy' Williams, Paul McAllister, George O'Brien, Malcolm Waite, Myrna Loy; *supervisor* Zanuck. US release: March 1929.

1929

Glad Rag Doll. *ph* Byron Haskin; *w* C. Graham Baker, Harvey Gates; *cast* Dolores Costello, Ralph Graves, Claude Gillingwater, Audrey Ferris.

The Madonna of Avenue A. *e* Ray Doyle; *ph* Byron Haskin; *w* Ray Doyle, Leslie S. Burrows, Mark Canfield (Zanuck); *cast* Dolores Costello, Grant Withers, Louise Dresser, William Russell, Douglas Gerrard, Otto Hoffman.

The Gamblers. Based upon a Charles Klein play; *e* Thomas Pratt; *ph* William Reese; *w* J. Grubb Alexander; *cast* George Fawcett, Jason Robards Senior, Lois Wilson, H. B. Warner.

Hearts in Exile. Based upon a John Oxenham work; *e* Thomas Pratt; *m* Howard Jackson; *ph* William Reese; *w* Harvey Gates; *cast* Dolores Costello, Grant Withers, James Kirkwood, George Fawcett, David Torrence.

Mammy. Based upon *Mr Bones* by Irving Berlin and James Gleason; *c* Orry-Kelly; *md* Leo F. Forbstein; *ph* Barney McGill; *w* Gordon Rigby; *cast* Al Jolson, Lowell Sherman, Lois Moran, Louise Dresser, Tully Marshall; part colour. US release: April 1930.

1930

River's End. Based upon a James Oliver Curwood story; *e* Ralph Holt; *ph* Robert Kurrle; *w* Charles Kenyon; *cast* Charles Bickford, Evalyn Knapp, John Farrell MacDonald, Zasu Pitts, Walter McGrail, David Torrence.

Under a Texas Moon. Based upon Stewart White's story *Two Gun Man*; *ph* William Reese; *w* Gordon Rigby, Joseph Jackson, Raymond Griffith; *cast* Frank Fay, Raquel Torres, Myrna Loy, Noah Beery Senior, George E. Stone, Fred Kohler, Betty Boyd; technicolor.

The Matrimonial Bed (aka *A Matrimonial Problem*). Based upon a Yves Mirande/André Mouëzy-Eon play; *ph* Dev Jennings; *w* Seymour Hicks, Harvey Thew; *cast* Frank Fay, Florence Eldridge, Lilyan Tashman, James Gleason, Beryl Mercer.

Bright Lights. *m* Allie Wrubel; *md* Leo F. Forbstein; *ph* Lee Garmes; *w* Humphrey Pearson; *cast* Frank Fay, Dorothy Mackaill, Noah Beery Senior, Inez Courtney, Eddie Nugent, Frank McHugh; *supervisor* Robert North; technicolor.

A Soldier's Plaything. Based upon a Vina Delmar work; *e* Jack Killifer; *ph* J. O. Taylor; *w* Perry Vekroff, Arthur Caesar (dialogue); *cast* Harry Langdon, Ben Lyon, Lottie Loder, Fred Kohler, Jean Hersholt, Noah Beery Senior. US release: April 1931.

Dämon des Meeres (*The Sea Demon*). Based upon Herman Melville's novel *Moby Dick*; *ph* Sid Hickox, Robert Kurrle; *w* H. P. Garnett, Ulrich Steindorff; *cast* Wilhelm Diertele, Lissy Arna, Karl Eltinger; German-language version.

1931

God's Gift to Women. Based upon the Jane Hinton play *The Devil is Sick*; *e* James Gribbon; *ph* Robert Kurrle; *w* Joseph Jackson, Raymond Griffith; *cast* Frank Fay, Joan Blondell, Laura La Plante, Charles Winninger, Alan Mowbray, Louise Brooks.

The Mad Genius. Based upon Martin Brown's story *The Idol*; *ad* Anton Grot; *ballet choreography* Adolph Bolm; *e* Ralph Dawson; *ph* Barney McGill; *w* J. Grubb Alexander, Harvey Thew; *cast* John Barrymore, Marian Marsh, Donald Cook, Luis Alberni, Carmel Myers, Charles Butterworth, Boris Karloff, Frankie Darro.

The Woman from Monte Carlo. Based upon a Claude Ferrer/Lucien Nepoty work; *c* Orry-Kelly; *e* Harold McLernon; *ph* Ernest Haller; *w* Harvey Thew; *cast* Lil Dagover, Walter Huston, Warren William, Robert Warwick, John Wray, George E. Stone. US release: January 1932.

Alias the Doctor. Based upon a Charles Foldes play: *e* William Holmes; *ph* Barney McGill; *w* Houston Branch, Charles Kenyon; *cast* Richard Barthelmess, Laura La Plante, Lucille La Verne, Marian Marsh, Norman Foster, Oscar Apfel, Boris Karloff (American released version only), Nigel de Brulier (British released version only); some sources give Lloyd Bacon as co-director, but this is not supported in the Warner Brothers archive, although he might have directed additional footage for the British version, for it seems as though the medical sequences were refilmed to overcome British censorship objections. US release: February 1932.

1932

The Strange Love of Molly Louvain. Based upon Maurine Watkins's play *The Tinsel Girl*; *e* James Borby; *ph* Robert Kurrle; *w* Erwin Gelsey, Brown Holmes, Maurine Watkins; *cast* Lee Tracy, Ann Dvorak, Leslie Fenton, Richard Cromwell, Guy Kibbee, Frank McHugh.

Dr X. Based upon a Howard W. Comstock/Allen C. Miller play; *ad* Anton Grot; *c* Orry-Kelly; *e* George Amy; *make-up* Max Factor; *ph* Ray Rennahan, Richard Tower; *w* Earl Baldwin, Robert Tasker; *cast* Lionel Atwill, Lee Tracy, Preston Foster, Fay Wray; *producer* Hal B. Wallis; technicolor.

Cabin in the Cotton. Based upon Henry Harrison Kroll's novel; *ad* Esdras Hartley; *c* Orry-Kelly; *e* George Amy; *ph* Barney McGill; *w* Professor Paul Green; *cast* Richard Barthelmess, Dorothy Jordan, Bette Davis, David Landau, Russell Simpson, Tully Marshall, Berton Churchill, Henry B. Walthall, Dorothy Peterson; *producer* Wallis; *assistant director* William Keighley (not co-director, as suggested by some sources).

20,000 Years in Sing Sing. Based upon the book by Warden Lewis E. Lawes; *ad* Anton Grot; *c* Orry-Kelly; *e* George Amy; *ph* Barney McGill; *w* Brown Holmes, Wilson Mizner, Robert Lord, Courtney Terrett; *cast* Spencer Tracy, Bette Davis, Arthur Byron, Lyle Talbot, Louis Calhern, Warren Hymer; *producer* Robert Lord. US release: January 1933.

1933

The Mystery of the Wax Museum. Based upon a Charles Belden work; *ad* Anton Grot; *c* Orry-Kelly; *e* George Amy; *make-up* Perc Westmore; *ph* Ray Rennahan; *wax sculptures* L. E. Otis, H. Clay Campbell; *w* Don Mullaly, Carl

Erickson; *cast* Lionel Atwill, Fay Wray, Glenda Farrell, Frank McHugh, Gavin Gordon, Allen Vincent, Edwin Maxwell; *producer* Henry Blanke; technicolor.

The Keyhole. Based upon Alice D. Miller's play *The Adventuress*; *ad* Anton Grot; *c* Orry-Kelly; *ph* Barney McGill; *w* Robert Presnell; *cast* Kay Francis, George Brent, Glenda Farrell, Allen Jenkins, Monroe Owsley, Henry Kolker; *producer* Wallis.

Private Detective 62. Based upon a Raoul Whitfield short story; *ad* Jack Okey; *e* George Amy; *ph* Tony Gaudio; *w* Rian James; *cast* William Powell, Margaret Lindsay, Ruth Donnelly, Gordon Westcott, James Ball, Arthur Byron; *producer* Wallis.

The Mayor of Hell. Directed by Archie Mayo, starring James Cagney. Curtiz (uncredited) directed additional footage.

Goodbye Again. Based upon an Allan Scott/George Haight play; *c* Orry-Kelly; *e* Thomas Pratt; *ph* George Barnes; *w* Ben Markson; *cast* Warren William, Joan Blondell, Genevieve Tobin, Hugh Herbert, Helen Chandler, Ruth Donnelly, Wallace Ford, Hobart Cavanaugh; *producer* Henry Blanke.

The Kennel Murder Case. Based upon the S. S. Van Dine novel *The Return of Philo Vance*; *ad* Jack Okey; *e* Harold McLarlin; *ph* William Reese; *w* Robert N. Lee, Peter Milne; *cast* William Powell, Mary Astor, Eugene Pallette, Ralph Morgan, Helen Vinson, Jack La Rue, Paul Cavanagh, Robert Barrat; *producer* Robert Presnell.

Female. Based upon a Donald Henderson Clarke story; *ad* Jack Okey; *e* Jack Killifer; *ph* Sid Hickox, Ernest Haller (the latter uncredited); *w* Gene Markey, Kathryn Scola; *cast* George Brent, Ruth Chatterton, Johnny Mack Brown, Ruth Donnelly, Lois Wilson, Douglas Dumbrille; *co-directed* with William Dieterle and William Wellman (the latter uncredited); *producer* Henry Blanke.

Mandalay. Based upon a Paul Hervey Fox short story; *ad* Anton Grot; *c* Orry-Kelly; *e* Thomas Pratt; *ph* Tony Gaudio; *w* Austin Parker, Charles Kenyon; *cast* Kay Francis, Ricardo Cortez, Lyle Talbot, Ruth Donnelly, Warner Oland, Lucien Littlefield; *producer* Robert Presnell. US release: February 1934.

The Key. Based upon a R. Gore-Brown and J. L. Hardy play; *ad* Robert Haas; *ph* Ernest Haller; *w* Laird Doyle; *cast* William Powell, Edna Best, Colin Clive, Hobart Cavanaugh, Halliwell Hobbes, Henry O'Neill, Arthur Treacher, Donald Crisp; *producer* Robert Presnell. US release: May 1934.

1934

Jimmy the Gent. Based upon a Laird Doyle/Ray Nazarro story *The Heir Chaser*; *ad* Esdras Hartley; *c* Orry-Kelly; *e* Thomas Richards; *ph* Ira Morgan; *w* Bertram Milhauser; *cast* James Cagney, Bette Davis, Alice White, Allen Jenkins; *producer* Robert Lord.

British Agent. Based upon the memoirs of R. H. Bruce Lockhart; *ad* Anton Grot; *c* Orry-Kelly; *e* Thomas Richards; *ph* Ernest Haller; *w* Laird Doyle; *cast* Leslie Howard, Kay Francis, William Gargan, Philip Reed, Walter Byron, Irving Pichel, J. Carroll Naish; *producer* Henry Blanke.

Black Fury. Based upon Judge M. A. Mussmano's book and Harry R. Irving's play *Bohunk*; *ad* John J. Hughes; *e* Thomas Richards; *ph* Byron Haskin; *w* Abem Finkel, Carl Erickson; *cast* Paul Muni, Karen Morley, William Gargan, Barton MacLane, John Qualen, J. Carroll Naish, Tully Marshall, Mae Marsh, Akim Tamiroff, Ward Bond; *producer* Robert Lord. US release: April 1935.

1935

Go Into Your Dance. Directed by Archie Mayo, starring Al Jolson. Curtiz (uncredited) briefly substituted for Mayo when the latter fell ill.

The Case of the Curious Bride. Based upon Erle Stanley Gardner's novel; *ad* Anton Grot, Carl Jules Weyl; *e* Terry Morse; *ph* David Abel; *w* Tom Reed; *cast* Warren William, Margaret Lindsay, Donald Woods, Claire Dodd, Allen Jenkins, Winifred Shaw, Barton MacLane, Warren Hymer, Errol Flynn (briefly); *producer* Harry Joe Brown.

Front Page Woman. Based upon Richard MacAuley's story *Women are Born Newspapermen*; *ad* John J. Hughes; *e* Terry Morse; *ph* Tony Gaudio; *w* Laird Doyle, Lillie Hayward, Roy Chanslor; *cast* George Brent, Bette Davis, Roscoe Karns, Winifred Shaw, J. Carroll Naish; *producer* Samuel Bischoff.

Little Big Shot. Based upon Harrison Jacobs's story; *ad* Hugh Retticher; *e* Jack Killifer; *ph* Tony Gaudio; *w* Jerry Wald, Julius J. Epstein, Robert Andrews; *cast* Sybil Jason, Glenda Farrell, Robert Armstrong, Edward Everett Horton, Jack La Rue, J. Carroll Naish, Edgar Kennedy, Addison Richards, Joe Sawyer, Ward Bond, Marc Lawrence; *producer* Samuel Bischoff.

Captain Blood. Based upon Rafael Sabatini's novel; *ad* Anton Grot; *c* Milo Anderson; *e* George Amy; *montage* Jean Negulesco (uncredited); *m* Erich Wolfgang Korngold; *ph* Hal Mohr, Ernest Haller (the latter uncredited until the film was reissued in 1947); *w* Casey Robinson; *cast* Errol Flynn, Olivia de Havilland, Lionel Atwill, Basil Rathbone, Guy Kibbee, Ross Alexander, Henry Stephenson, Forrester Harvey, Hobart Cavanaugh, Donald Meek; *special effects* Fred Jackman; *fencing master* Fred Cavens (uncredited); *producer* Harry Joe Brown.

The Walking Dead. Based upon a Ewart Adamson/Joseph Fields story; *e* Thomas Pratt; *ph* Hal Mohr; *w* Robert Andrews, Lillie Hayward, Peter Milne; *cast* Boris Karloff, Edmund Gwenn, Marguerite Churchill, Ricardo Cortez, Barton MacLane, Warren Hull, Henry O'Neill; *producer* Louis F. Edelman. US release: February 1936.

1936

Anthony Adverse. Directed by Mervyn LeRoy, starring Frederic March. Curtiz (uncredited) directed the opening location sequences.

The Charge of the Light Brigade. Supposedly based upon Alfred, Lord Tennyson's poem; *ad* John J. Hughes; *c* Milo Anderson; *e* George Amy; *m* Max Steiner; *ph* Sol Polito; *special effects* Fred Jackman; *technical advisers* Major Sam Harris, Captain E. Rochfort-John; *w* Rowland Leigh, Michael Jacoby; *cast* Errol Flynn, Olivia de Havilland, Patric Knowles, Donald Crisp, Henry Stephenson, Nigel Bruce, David Niven, C. Henry Gordon; *director part of charge footage* B. Reeves Eason (uncredited); *producer* Samuel Bischoff.

Stolen Holiday. Based upon a Warren Duff/Virginia Kellogg story; *ad* Anton Grot; *c* Orry-Kelly; *ph* Sid Hickox; *w* Casey Robinson; *cast* Kay Francis, Claude Rains, Ian Hunter, Alison Skipworth, Charles Halton, Alex d'Arcy, Frank Conroy; *producer* Harry Joe Brown. US release: February 1937.

Mountain Justice. *ad* Max Parker; *e* George Amy; *ph* Ernest Haller; *w* Norman Reilly Raine, Luci Ward; *cast* Josephine Hutchinson, George Brent, Robert Barrat, Guy Kibbee, Mona Barrie, Margaret Hamilton, Robert McWade, Fuzzy Knight, Elisabeth Risdon, Marcia Mae Jones; *producer* Louis F. Edelman. US release: May 1937.

1937

Kid Galahad. Based upon a Francis Wallace story; *ad* Carl Jules Weyl; *c* Orry-Kelly; *e* George Amy; *ph* Tony Gaudio, Sol Polito, Arthur Edeson (the last two uncredited); *w* Seton I. Miller; *cast* Edward G. Robinson, Bette Davis, Wayne Morris, Jane Bryan, Humphrey Bogart, Harry Carey; *producer* Samuel Bischoff.

The Perfect Specimen. Based upon a Samuel Hopkins Adams story; *ad* Robert Haas; *c* Howard Shoup; *e* Terry Morse; *ph* Charles Rosher; *w* Norman Reilly Raine, Lawrence Riley, Brewster Morse, Fritz Falkenstein; *cast* Errol Flynn, Joan Blondell, Hugh Herbert, Edward Everett Horton, May Robson, Dick Foran, Beverly Roberts, Allen Jenkins, Dennie Moore, Harry Davenport; *producer* Harry Joe Brown.

Gold is Where You Find It. Based upon a Clements Ripley story; *ad* Ted Smith; *c* Milo Anderson; *e* Clarence Kolster; *m* Max Steiner; *ph* Sol Polito; *special effects* Byron Haskin; *w* Warren Duff, Robert Buckner; *cast* George Brent, Olivia de Havilland, Claude Rains, Margaret Lindsay, John Litel, Marcia Ralston, Barton MacLane, Tim Holt, Sidney Toler, Henry O'Neill; *producer* Samuel Bischoff; technicolor. US release: February 1938.

1938

The Adventures of Robin Hood. *Archery supervisor* Howard Hill (uncredited); *ad* Carl Jules Weyl; *c* Milo Anderson; *e* Ralph Dawson; *fencing master* Fred Cavens (uncredited); *make-up* Perc Westmore; *m* Erich Wolfgang Korngold; *ph* Tony Gaudio, Sol Polito; *technicolor ph* W. Howard Greene; *technicolor director* Natalie Kalmus; *w* Norman Reilly Raine, Seton I. Miller; *cast* Errol Flynn, Olivia de Havilland, Basil Rathbone, Claude Rains, Patric Knowles, Eugene Pallette, Alan Hale, Melville Cooper, Ian Hunter, Una O'Connor, Herbert Mundin, Montagu Love; *co-directed* with William Keighley; *producer* Henry Blanke; technicolor.

Four's a Crowd. Based upon Wallace Sullivan's novel *All Rights Reserved; ad* Max Parker; *e* Clarence Kolster; *ph* Ernest Haller; *w* Sig Herzig, Casey Robinson; *cast* Errol Flynn, Olivia de Havilland, Rosalind Russell, Patric Knowles, Walter Connolly, Hugh Herbert, Melville Cooper, Franklin Pangborn; *producer* David Lewis.

Four Daughters. Based upon the Fanny Hurst novel *Sister Act; ad* John J. Hughes; *c* Orry-Kelly; *e* Ralph Dawson; *m* Max Steiner; *ph* Ernest Haller; *w* Lenore Coffee, Julius J. Epstein; *cast* Claude Rains, Lola, Priscilla and Rosemary Lane, Gale Page, John Garfield, Jeffrey Lynn, May Robson, Frank McHugh, Dick Foran; *producer* Henry Blanke.

Blackwell's Island. Directed by William McGann, starring John Garfield. Curtiz (uncredited) directed additional footage, including the jail break scene and other externals.

Angels With Dirty Faces. Based upon a Rowland Brown story; *ad* Robert Haas; *c* Orry-Kelly; *e* Owen Marks; *make-up* Perc Westmore; *m* Max Steiner; *technical adviser* Father J. J. Devlin; *w* Warren Duff, John Wexley; *cast* James Cagney, Pat O'Brien, Humphrey Bogart, Ann Sheridan, The Dead End Kids (Billy Halop, Bobby Jordan, Leo Gorcey, Bernard Punsley, Gabriel Dell, Huntz Hall), George Bancroft; *producer* Samuel Bischoff.

1939

Sons of Liberty. Based upon the life of Haym Solomon; *w* Abem Finkel, Crane Wilbur; *cast* Claude Rains, Gale Sondergaard; *producer* Bryan Foy; Curtiz's only short film; technicolor.

Dodge City. Based upon the career of Wyatt Earp; *ad* Ted Smith; *c* Milo Anderson; *e* George Amy; *make-up* Perc Westmore; *m* Max Steiner; *ph* Sol Polito, Ray Rennahan; *special effects* Byron Haskin, Rex Wimpy; *technicolor director* Natalie Kalmus; *w* Robert Buckner; *cast* Errol Flynn, Olivia de Havilland, Ann Sheridan, Bruce Cabot, Alan Hale, Frank McHugh, John Litel, Victor Jory, William Lundigan, Henry Travers, Guinn 'Big Boy' Williams, Henry O'Neill; *producer* Robert Lord; technicolor.

Daughters Courageous. Based upon the Dorothy Bennett/Irving White play *Fly Away Home;* *ad* John J. Hughes; *c* Howard Shoup; *e* Ralph Dawson; *make-up* Perc Westmore; *m* Max Steiner; *ph* James Wong Howe; *w* Julius J. and Philip G. Epstein; *cast* Claude Rains, John Garfield, Lola, Priscilla and Rosemary Lane, Gale Page, Jeffrey Lynn, Donald Crisp, Fay Bainter, May Robson, Frank McHugh, Dick Foran; *producer* Henry Blanke.

The Private Lives of Elizabeth and Essex. Based upon Maxwell Anderson's play *Elizabeth the Queen;* *ad* Anton Grot; *c* Orry-Kelly; *e* Owen Marks; *make-up* Perc Westmore; *m* Erich Wolfgang Korngold; *ph* Sol Polito, W. Howard Greene; *special effects* Byron Haskin, H. F. Koenekamp; *technicolor director* Natalie Kalmus; *w* Norman Reilly Raine, Aeneas MacKenzie; *cast* Bette Davis, Errol Flynn, Olivia de Havilland, Donald Crisp, Vincent Price, Alan Hale, Henry Stephenson, Henry Daniell; *producer* Robert Lord; technicolor.

Four Wives. Based upon the Fanny Hurst novel *Sister Act; ad* John J. Hughes; *e* Ralph Dawson; *m* Max Steiner; *ph* Sol Polito; *w* Julius J. and Philip G. Epstein, Maurice Hanline; *cast* Claude Rains, Lola, Priscilla and Rosemary Lane, Gale Page, Jeffrey Lynn, Eddie Albert, May Robson, Frank McHugh, Dick Foran, John Garfield (briefly); *producer* Henry Blanke.

1940

Virginia City. *ad* Ted Smith; *c* Milo Anderson; *e* George Amy; *make-up* Perc Westmore; *m* Max Steiner; *ph* Sol Polito; *special effects* H. F. Koenekamp; *w* Robert Buckner, Norman Reilly Raine, Howard Koch (the last two uncredited); *cast* Errol Flynn, Miriam Hopkins, Randolph Scott, Humphrey Bogart, Frank McHugh, Alan Hale, Guinn 'Big Boy' Williams, John Litel, Douglas Dumbrille, Moroni Olsen; *producer* Robert Fellows (initially Robert Lord).

The Sea Hawk. *ad* Anton Grot; *c* Orry-Kelly; *e* George Amy; *fencing master* Fred Cavens (uncredited); *make-up* Perc Westmore; *m* Erich Wolfgang Korngold; *ph* Sol Polito; *sound recording* Nathan Levinson (uncredited); *special effects* Byron Haskin, H. F. Koenekamp; *w* Howard Koch, Seton I. Miller; *cast* Errol Flynn, Brenda Marshall, Claude Rains, Donald Crisp, Flora Robson, Henry Daniell, Alan Hale, Una O'Connor, James Stephenson, Gilbert Roland, William Lundigan, Julien Mitchell, Montagu Love; *producer* Henry Blanke.

Santa Fe Trail. *ad* John J. Hughes; *c* Milo Anderson; *e* George Amy; *make-up* Perc Westmore; *m* Max Steiner; *ph* Sol Polito; *special effects* Byron Haskin, H. F. Koenekamp; *w* Robert Buckner from his unpublished novel *The Grenadiers*; *cast* Errol Flynn, Olivia de Havilland, Raymond Massey, Ronald Reagan,

Van Heflin, Gene Reynolds, Alan Hale, Guinn 'Big Boy' Williams, Alan Baxter, John Litel; *producer* Robert Fellows.

1941

The Sea Wolf. Based upon Jack London's novel; *ad* Anton Grot; *e* George Amy; *m* Erich Wolfgang Korngold; *ph* Sol Polito; *special effects* Byron Haskin, H. F. Koenekamp; *w* Robert Rossen; *cast* Edward G. Robinson, Ida Lupino, John Garfield, Alexander Knox, Gene Lockhart, Barry Fitzgerald, Stanley Ridges; *producer* Henry Blanke.

Dive Bomber. Based upon a Frank Wead story; *air technical adviser* Commander S. H. Warner; *ad* Robert Haas; *c* Orry-Kelly; *e* George Amy; *make-up* Perc Westmore; *medical technical adviser* Captain J. R. Poppen; *m* Max Steiner; *ph* Bert Glennon, Winton C. Hoch, Elmer Dyer, Charles Marshall (the last two were responsible for the aerial photography); *special effects* Byron Haskin, Rex Wimpy; *technicolor director* Natalie Kalmus; *w* Robert Buckner, Frank Wead; *cast* Errol Flynn, Fred MacMurray, Ralph Bellamy, Alexis Smith, Regis Toomey, Robert Armstrong, Allen Jenkins; *producer* Robert Lord; technicolor.

Captains of the Clouds. *ad* Ted Smith; *c* Howard Shoup; *e* George Amy; *m* Max Steiner; *ph* Bert Glennon, Winton C. Hoch, Elmer Dyer, Charles Marshall (the last two were responsible for the aerial photography); *special effects* Byron Haskin, Rex Wimpy; *technicolor director* Natalie Kalmus; *w* Norman Reilly Raine, Richard MacAuley, Arthur T. Horman; *cast* James Cagney, Brenda Marshall, Dennis Morgan, George Tobias, Alan Hale, Reginald Gardiner, Reginald Denny; *producer* William Cagney; technicolor. US release January 1942.

1942

Yankee Doodle Dandy. Based upon the life of George M. Cohan; *ad* Carl Jules Weyl; *c* Milo Anderson; *e* George Amy; *make-up* Perc Westmore; *montage* Don Siegel; *m* George M. Cohan; *musical arrangements* Ray Heindorf, Heinz Roemheld (uncredited); *md* LeRoy Prinz, Seymour Felix; *ph* James Wong Howe; *w* Robert Buckner, Edmund Joseph; *cast* James Cagney, Joan Leslie, Walter Huston, Rosemary de Camp, Richard Whorf, George Tobias, Jeanne Cagney, Irene Manning, S. Z. Sakall, Frances Langford, Eddie Foy Junior; *producer* William Cagney.

Casablanca. Based upon an unproduced Joan Alison/Murray Burnett play *Everybody Comes to Rick's;* *ad* Carl Jules Weyl; *c* Orry-Kelly; *e* Owen Marks; *montage* Don Siegel, James Leicester; *m* Max Steiner; *narrator* Lou Marcelle (uncredited); *ph* Arthur Edeson; *special effects* Lawrence Butler, Willard Van Enger; *w* Julius J. and Philip G. Epstein, Howard Koch, Casey Robinson (uncredited); *cast* Humphrey Bogart, Ingrid Bergman, Paul Henreid, Claude Rains, Conrad Veidt, Peter Lorre, Sydney Greenstreet, Dooley Wilson, Madeleine LeBeau, Joy Page, S. Z. Sakall, John Qualen, Leonid Kinskey, Curt Bois, Helmut Dantine (uncredited), Marcel Dalio (uncredited), Charles La Torre (uncredited), Ludwig Stossel (uncredited), Ilka Gruning (uncredited), Corinna Mura (uncredited), Dan Seymour (uncredited), Frank Puglia (uncredited); *producer* Wallis.

Mission to Moscow. Based upon the memoirs of Joseph E. Davies; *ad Carl Jules Weyl; c* Orry-Kelly; *e* Owen Marks; *make-up* Gordon Bau; *montage* Don Siegel, James Leicester; *m* Max Steiner; *ph* Bert Glennon; *special effects* Roy Davidson, H. F. Koenekamp; *technical adviser* Jay Leyda; *w* Howard Koch; *cast* Walter Huston, Ann Harding, Oscar Homolka, George Tobias, Gene Lockhart, Eleanor Parker, Richard Travis, Helmut Dantine, Victor Francen, Henry Daniell, Barbara Everest, Dudley Field Malone, Roman Bohnen, Maria Palmer, Moroni Olsen, Minor Watson, Vladimir Sokoloff, Jerome Cowan (uncredited), Manart Kippen (as Stalin, uncredited), Frieda Inescourt (uncredited); *producers* Jack L. Warner, Robert Buckner.

This is the Army. Based upon Irving Berlin's musical revue; *ad* John J. Hughes; *e* George Amy; *musical arrangement* Ray Heindorf; *md* LeRoy Prinz; *ph* Bert Glennon, Sol Polito; *songs* Irving Berlin; *w* Claude Binyon, Casey Robinson; *cast* George Murphy, Joan Leslie, George Tobias, Alan Hale, Ronald Reagan, Charles Butterworth, Dolores Costello, Rosemary de Camp, Una Merkel, Stanley Ridges, Ruth Donnelly, Kate Smith, Frances Langford, Joe Louis, Irving Berlin; *producer* Jack Warner; technicolor.

Passage to Marseille. Based upon the Charles Nordhoff/James Norman Hall story *Men Without a Country; ad* Carl Jules Weyl; *c* Leah Rhodes;; *e* Owen Marks; *montage* James Leicester; *m* Max Steiner; *ph* James Wong Howe; *special effects* Jack Cosgrove, Edwin Du Par; *w* Jack Moffitt, Casey Robinson; *cast* Humphrey Bogart, Claude Rains, Michele Morgan, Philip Dorn, Sydney Greenstreet, Peter Lorre, Helmut Dantine, George Tobias, John Loder, Victor Francen, Vladimir Sokoloff, Eduardo Ciannelli; *producer* Wallis. US release: February 1944.

1944

Janie. Based upon the Josephine Bentham/Herschel V. Williams play; *ad* Robert Haas; *e* Owen Marks; *ph* Carl Guthrie; *w* Agnes Christine Johnson, Charles Hoffman; *cast* Joyce Reynolds, Edward Arnold, Ann Harding, Robert Hutton, Robert Benchley, Alan Hale, Clare Foley, Hattie McDaniel; *producer* Alex Gottlieb.

Roughly Speaking. Based upon a Louise Randall Pierson book; *ad* Robert Haas; *c* Milo Anderson; *e* David Weisbart; *m* Max Steiner; *ph* Sol Polito, Ernest Haller (both uncredited), Joseph Walker; *w* Louise Randall Pierson, Catherine Turney (uncredited); *cast* Rosalind Russell, Jack Carson, Robert Hutton, Alan Hale, Jean Sullivan, Donald Woods, Andrea King, Ray Collins, Jo Ann Marlowe; *producer* Henry Blanke.

1945

Mildred Pierce. Based upon the James M. Cain novel; *ad* Anton Grot; *c* Milo Anderson; *e* David Weisbart; *make-up* Perc Westmore; *montage* James Leicester; *m* Max Steiner; *ph* Ernest Haller; *special effects* Willard Van Enger; *w* Ranald MacDougall, Catherine Turney (uncredited); *cast* Joan Crawford, Jack Carson, Zachary Scott, Ann Blyth, Eve Arden, Bruce Bennett, George Tobias, Lee Patrick, Moroni Olsen, Veda Ann Borg, Jo Ann Marlowe; *producer* Jerry Wald.

Night and Day. Based upon the life of Cole Porter; *ad* John J. Hughes;

choreography LeRoy Prinz; *c* Milo Anderson; *e* David Weisbart; *montage* James Leicester; *m* Max Steiner; *md* Ray Heindorf; *ph* Ernest Haller (uncredited), Peverell Marley, William V. Skall; *songs* Cole Porter; *special effects* Robert Burks; *technicolor director* Natalie Kalmus; *w* Charles Hoffman, Leo Townsend, William Bowers, Jack Moffitt; *cast* Cary Grant, Alexis Smith, Monty Woolley, Jane Wyman, Alan Hale, Eve Arden, Victor Francen, Ginny Simms, Mary Martin, Dorothy Malone, Donald Woods, Selena Royle, Henry Stephenson, Paul Cavanagh, Sig Ruman; *producer* Arthur Schwartz; technicolor. US release: July 1946.

1946

Life With Father. Based upon the Russel Crouse/Howard Lindsay play; *ad* Robert Haas; *c* Milo Anderson; *e* George Amy; *make-up* Perc Westmore; *montage* James Leicester; *m* Max Steiner; *ph* Peverell Marley, William V. Skall; *special effects* Ray Foster, William McGann; *technical adviser* Mrs Clarence Day Junior; *technicolor director* Natalie Kalmus; *w* Donald Ogden Stewart; *cast* William Powell, Irene Dunne, Jimmy Lydon, Edmund Gwenn, Elizabeth Taylor, Zasu Pitts, Emma Dunn, Moroni Olsen; *producer* Robert Buckner; technicolor. US release: August 1947.

1947

The Unsuspected. Based upon Charlotte Armstong's short story; *ad* Anton Grot; *c* Milo Anderson; *e* Frederick Richards; *make-up* Perc Westmore; *m* Franz Waxman; *ph* Elwood Bredell; *special effects ph* Robert Burks, *special effects directors* Harry Barndollar, David C. Kertes (David Curtiz); *w* Ranald MacDougall, Bess Meredyth; *cast* Claude Rains, Joan Caulfield, Audrey Totter, Constance Bennett, Hurd Hatfield, Michael North, Fred Clark, Jack Lambert; *producer* Charles Hoffman for Michael Curtiz Productions.

Romance on the High Seas (aka *It's Magic*). Based upon a Carlos Olivari/S. Pondal Rios story; *ad* Anton Grot; *choreography* Busby Berkeley; *c* Milo Anderson; *e* Rudi Fehr; *make-up* Perc Westmore; *md* Ray Heindorf; *ph* Elwood Bredell; *songs* Jule Styne (music), Sammy Cahn (lyrics); *special effects ph* Wilfred M. Cline, Robert Burks; *special effects director* David Curtiz; *technicolor director* Natalie Kalmus; *w* Julius J. and Philip G. Epstein, I. A. L. Diamond; *cast* Jack Carson, Janis Paige, Don De Fore, Doris Day, Oscar Levant, S. Z. Sakall; *producer* Alex Gottlieb for Michael Curtiz Productions; technicolor. US release: July 1948.

1948

My Dream is Yours. Based upon a Jerry Wald story; *ad* Robert Haas; *choreography* LeRoy Prinz; *e* Folmar Blangsted; *md* Ray Heindorf; *ph* Ernest Haller; *songs* Harry Warren; *w* Harry Kurnitz, Dane Lussier; *cast* Doris Day, Jack Carson, Lee Bowman, Adolphe Menjou, Eve Arden, S. Z. Sakall, Selena Royle, Edgar Kennedy; *producer* Curtiz himself for Michael Curtiz Productions; technicolor. US release: March 1949.

Flamingo Road. Based upon Robert Wilder's novel; *ad* Leo K. Kuter; *e* Folmar Blangsted; *m* Max Steiner; *ph* Ted McCord; *w* Robert and Sally Wilder, Edmund H. North, Ranald MacDougall (uncredited); *cast* Joan Crawford,

Zachary Scott, Sydney Greenstreet, David Brian, Gladys George; *producer* Jerry Wald for Michael Curtiz Productions. US release: May 1949.

It's a Great Feeling. Directed by David Butler, starring Jack Carson and Doris Day. Curtiz made a cameo appearance as himself; technicolor.

1949

The Lady Takes a Sailor. Based upon a Jerry Gruskin story; *ad* Edward Carrere; *e* David Weisbart; *m* Max Steiner; *ph* Ted McCord; *w* Everett Freeman; *cast* Jane Wyman, Dennis Morgan, Eve Arden, Robert Douglas, Allyn Joslyn, Tom Tully, Fred Clark; *producer* Harry Kurnitz.

Young Man With a Horn (aka *Young Man of Music*). Based upon a Dorothy Baker novel; *ad* Edward Carrere; *c* Milo Anderson; *e* Alan Crosland Junior; *make-up* Perc Westmore; *montage* David C. Gardner (probably David Curtiz, for Kertesz is Hungarian for gardener); *md* Ray Heindorf; *ph* Ted McCord; *trumpet music* played by Harry James, technically the musical adviser; *w* Carl Foreman, Edmund H. North; *cast* Kirk Douglas, Lauren Bacall, Doris Day, Hoagy Carmichael, Juano Hernandez, Jerome Cowan, Mary Beth Hughes; *producer* Jerry Wald. US release: February 1950.

1950

Bright Leaf. Based upon a Foster Fitzsimmons story; *ad* Stanley Fleischer; *c* Leah Rhodes; *e* Owen Marks; *ph* Karl Freund; *w* Ranald MacDougall; *cast* Gary Cooper, Lauren Bacall, Patricia Neal, Jack Carson, Donald Crisp, Gladys George; *producer* Henry Blanke.

The Breaking Point. Based upon the Ernest Hemingway novel *To Have and Have Not*; *ad* Edward Carrere; *e* Alan Crosland Junior; *m* Ray Heindorf; *ph* Ted McCord; *w* Ranald MacDougall; *cast* John Garfield, Phyllis Thaxter, Patricia Neal, Juano Hernandez, Wallace Ford, Victor Sen Yung; *producer* Jerry Wald.

Jim Thorpe – All American (aka *Man of Bronze*). Based upon the life of Jim Thorpe and Russell Birdwell's biography; *ad* Edward Carrere; *e* Folmar Blangsted; *m* Max Steiner; *ph* Ernest Haller; *w* Douglas Morrow, Everett Freeman, Vincent X. Flaherty; *cast* Burt Lancaster, Charles Bickford, Phyllis Thaxter, Steve Cochran, Dick Wesson; *producer* Everett Freeman. US release: June 1951.

1951

Force of Arms. Based upon the Ernest Hemingway novel *A Farewell to Arms* (unacknowledged); *ad* Edward Carrere; *e* Owen Marks; *m* Max Steiner; *ph* Ted McCord; *w* Orin Jennings, Richard Tregaskis; *cast* William Holden, Nancy Olson, Frank Lovejoy, Gene Evans, Dick Wesson, Slats Taylor, Paul Picerni; *producer* Anthony Veiller (initially Jerry Wald).

I'll See You in My Dreams. Based upon the life of Gus Kahn; *ad* Douglas Bacon; *choreography* LeRoy Prinz; *c* Leah Rhodes, Marjorie Best; *e* Owen Marks; *make-up* Gordon Bau; *md* Ray Heindorf; *ph* Ted McCord; *w* Melville Shavelson, Jack Rose; *cast* Doris Day, Danny Thomas, Frank Lovejoy, Patrice Wymore, James Gleason, Mary Wickes; *producer* Louis F. Edelman. US release: January 1952.

1952

The Story of Will Rogers. Based upon the life of Will Rogers; *ad* Edward
Carrere; *e* Folmar Blangsted; *m* Victor Young; *ph* Wilfred M. Cline; *w* Frank
Davis, Stanley Roberts; *cast* Will Rogers Junior, Jane Wyman, James Gleason,
Carl Benton Reid, Eddie Cantor (as himself); *producer* Robert Arthur; techni-
color.

The Jazz Singer. *ad* Leo K. Kuter; *c* Howard Shoup; *e* Alan Crosland Junior;
md Ray Heindorf; *ph* Carl Guthrie; *w* Frank Davis, Leonard Stern, Lewis
Meltzer; *cast* Danny Thomas, Peggy Lee, Mildred Dunnock, Eduard Franz;
producer Louis F. Edelman; technicolor. US release: January 1953.

Trouble Along the Way. Based upon a Douglas Morrow/Robert Hardy Andrews
story; *ad* Leo K. Kuter; *e* Owen Marks; *m* Max Steiner; *ph* Archie Stout; *w*
Melville Shavelson, Jack Rose; *cast* John Wayne, Charles Coburn, Donna
Reed, Tom Tully, Marie Windsor, Sherry Jackson; *producer* Melville
Shavelson. US release: May 1953.

1953

The Boy from Oklahoma. Based upon a Michael Fessier story; *ad* Leo K. Kuter;
e James Moore; *m* Max Steiner; *ph* Robert Burks; *w* Frank Davis, Winston
Miller; *cast* Will Rogers Junior, Nancy Olson, Lon Chaney Junior, Anthony
Caruso, Wallace Ford; *producer* David Weisbart; Warnercolor. US release:
January 1954.

White Christmas. *ad* Hal Pereira, Roland Anderson; *choreography* Robert Alton;
c Edith Head; *e* Frank Bracht; *make-up* Wally Westmore; *md* Joseph J. Lilley;
ph Loyal Griggs; *songs* Irving Berlin; *special effects* John P. Fulton; *technicolor
consultant* Richard Mueller; *w* Norman Krasna, Norman Panama, Melvin
Frank; *cast* Bing Crosby, Danny Kaye, Rosemary Clooney, Vera Ellen, Dean
Jagger, Mary Wickes; *producer* Robert Emmett Dolan for Paramount; technicolor; Vistavision. US release: August 1954.

1954

The Egyptian. Based upon a Mika Waltari novel; *ad* Lyle R. Wheeler, George
W. Davis; *e* Barbara MacLean; *m* Bernard Herrmann, Alfred Newman; *ph*
Leon Shamroy; *w* Philip Dunne, Casey Robinson; *cast* Edmund Purdom,
Victor Mature, Bella Darvi, Peter Ustinov, Gene Tierney, Michael Wilding,
Jean Simmons, Judith Evelyn, Henry Daniell, John Carradine, Carl Benton
Reid; *producer* Darryl F. Zanuck for Twentieth Century-Fox; De Luxe color;
Cinemascope.

1955

We're No Angels. Based upon the Albert Husson play *La Cuisine des Anges*; *ad*
Hal Pereira, Roland Anderson; *c* Mary Grant; *e* Arthur Schmidt; *make-up*
Wally Westmore; *m* Frederick Hollander; *ph* Loyal Griggs; *special effects* John
P. Fulton; *technicolor director* Richard Mueller; *w* Ranald MacDougall; *cast*
Humphrey Bogart, Aldo Ray, Peter Ustinov, Joan Bennett, Basil Rathbone,
Leo G. Carroll; *producer* Pat Duggan for Paramount; technicolor; Vistavision.

The Vagabond King. Based upon the Rudolf Friml operetta; *ad* Hal Pereira,
Henry Bumstead; *choreography* Hanya Holm; *c* Mary Grant; *e* Arthur

Schmidt; *fencing adviser* Fred Cavens; *make-up* Wally Westmore; *m* Victor Young; *ph* Robert Burks; *special effects* John P. Fulton, *technicolor consultant* Richard Mueller; *w* Ken Englund, Noel Langley; *cast* Oreste, Kathryn Grayson, Walter Hampden, Rita Moreno, Sir Cedric Hardwicke, Leslie Nielsen, Jack Lord; *producer* Pat Duggan for Paramount; technicolor; Vistavision. US release: September 1956.

1956

The Scarlet Hour. *ad* Hal Pereira, Tambi Larsen; *e* Everett Douglas; *m* Leith Stevens; *ph* Lionel Lindon; *w* Rip Van Ronkel, Frank Tashlin, John Meredyth Lucas; *cast* Carol Ohmart, Tom Tryon, James Gregory, Jody Lawrance, E. G. Marshall, Elaine Stritch; *producer* Curtiz himself for Paramount; Vistavision.
The Best Things in Life are Free. Based upon the careers of Lew Brown, Buddy de Sylva, and Ray Henderson; *ad* Lyle R. Wheeler, Maurice Ransford; *c* Charles LeMaire; *e* Dorothy Spencer; *make-up* Ben Nye; *md* Lionel Newman; *ph* Leon Shamroy; *songs* Lew Brown, Buddy de Sylva, Ray Henderson; *special effects* Ray Kellogg; *technicolor consultant* Leonard Doss; *w* William Bowers, Phoebe Ephron, John O'Hara; *cast* Gordon MacRae, Ernest Borgnine, Dan Dailey, Sheree North, Tommy Noonan, Murvyn Vye, Phyllis Avery, Larry Keating, Tony Galento, Norman Brooks; *producer* Henry Ephron (initially Zanuck) for Twentieth Century-Fox; De Luxe color; Cinemascope.

1957

The Helen Morgan Story (aka *Both Ends of the Candle*). Based upon the life of Helen Morgan; *ad* John Beckman; *choreography* LeRoy Prinz; *e* Frank Bracht; *md* Ray Heindorf; *ph* Ted McCord; *w* Oscar Saul, Dean Riesner, Stephen Longstreet, Nelson Gidding; *cast* Ann Blyth, Paul Newman, Richard Carlson, Gene Evans, Alan King, Cara Williams, Walter Woolf King, Rudy Vallee; *producer* Martin Rackin (initially Richard Whorf) for Warners; Cinemascope.
The Proud Rebel. *ad* McClure Capps; *e* Aaron Stell; *m* Jerome Moross; *ph* Ted McCord; *w* Joseph Petracca, Lillie Hayward, James Edward Grant; *cast* Alan Ladd, Olivia de Havilland, David Ladd, Dean Jagger, Cecil Kellaway, Dean Stanton, Henry Hull, John Carradine; *producer* Sam Goldwyn Junior for Buena Vista; technicolor. US release: April 1958.

1958

King Creole. Based upon the Harold Robbins novel *A Stone for Danny Fisher*; *ad* Hal Pereira, J. Macmillan Johnson; *c* Edith Head; *e* Warren Low; *make-up* Wally Westmore; *m* Walter Scharf; *ph* Russell Harlan; *special effects* John P. Fulton; *w* Herbert Baker, Michael Vincent Gazzo; *cast* Elvis Presley, Carolyn Jones, Walter Matthau, Dean Jagger, Dolores Hart, Paul Stewart, Vic Morrow; *producer* Paul Nathan for Hal Wallis/Paramount; Vistavision.

1959

The Hangman. Based upon a Luke Short story; *ad* Hal Pereira, Henry Bumstead; *c* Edith Head; *e* Terry Morse; *m* Harry Sukman; *ph* Loyal Griggs; *w* Dudley

Nichols; *cast* Robert Taylor, Tina Louise, Fess Parker, Jack Lord; *producer* Frank Freeman Junior for Paramount.

The Man in the Net. Based upon a Patrick Quentin novel; *ad* Hilyard Brown; *e* Richard Heermance; *m* Hans J. Salter; *ph* John Seitz; *w* Reginald Rose; *cast* Alan Ladd, Carolyn Jones, Diane Brewster, Charles McGraw; *producer* Walter Mirisch for United Artists/Mirisch Brothers-Jaguar.

1960

The Adventures of Huckleberry Finn (aka *Huckleberry Finn*). Based upon the Mark Twain novel; *ad* George W. Davis, McClure Capps; *e* Frederic Steinkamp; *m* Jerome Moross; *ph* Ted McCord; *w* James Lee; *cast* Eddie Hodges, Tony Randall, Mickey Shaughnessy, Archie Moore, Neville Brand, Judy Canova, Andy Devine, Buster Keaton, John Carradine, Finlay Currie, Josephine Hutchinson; *producer* Samuel Goldwyn Junior for Metro-Goldwyn-Mayer; Metrocolor; Cinemascope.

A Breath of Scandal. Based upon the Ferenc Molnar play *Olympia*; *ad* Gene Allen; *e* Howard Smith; *m* Alessandro Cicognini; *ph* Mario Montuori; *w* Walter Bernstein, Sidney Howard; *cast* Sophia Loren, John Gavin, Maurice Chevalier, Isabel Jeans, Angela Lansbury; *producer* Carlo Ponti for Paramount; technicolor; Vistavision.

1961

Francis of Assisi. Based upon the Louis de Wohl book *Joyful Beggar*; *ad* Edward Carrere; *c* Vittorio Nino Novarese; *e* Louis Loeffler; *m* Mario Nascimbene; *ph* Pietro Portalupi; *w* Eugene Vale, James Forsythe, Jack Thomas; *cast* Bradford Dillman, Dolores Hart, Stuart Whitman, Eduard Franz, Pedro Armendariz, Cecil Kellaway, Finlay Currie, Mervyn Johns, Athene Seyler; *producer* Plato A. Skouras for Twentieth Century-Fox; De Luxe color; Cinemascope.

The Comancheros. Based upon the Paul I. Wellman novel; *action sequences director* Cliff Lyons; *ad* Jack Martin Smith, Alfred Ybarra; *c* Marjorie Best; *e* Louis Loeffler; *make-up* Ben Nye; *m* Elmer Bernstein; *ph* William Clothier; *w* James Edward Grant, Clair Huffaker; *cast* John Wayne, Stuart Whitman, Ina Balin, Nehemiah Persoff, Lee Marvin, Pat Wayne, Jack Elam, Bruce Cabot, Edgar Kennedy, Henry Daniell, Guinn 'Big Boy' Williams (uncredited); *producer* George Sherman for Twentieth Century-Fox; De Luxe color; Cinemascope.

INDEX OF PERSONALITIES

INDEX OF FILM TITLES